A Public Relations Primer

In this age, and this country, public sentiment is every thing. *With* it, nothing can fail; *against* it, nothing can succeed. Whoever moulds public sentiment, goes deeper than he who enacts statutes or pronounces judicial decisions. He makes possible the inforcement[sic] of these, else impossible.

—Abraham Lincoln

A Public Relations Primer
Thinking and Writing in Context

PAULA MARANTZ COHEN
Drexel University

Prentice-Hall, Inc., Englewood Cliffs, New Jersey 07632

Library of Congress Cataloging-in-Publication Data

Cohen, Paula Marantz, date.
  A public relations primer.

  Includes bibliographies and index.
  1. Public relations. I. Title.
HD59.C544   1987   659.2   86-12296
ISBN 0-13-738709-1

Editorial/production supervision and
  interior design: Madelaine Cooke
Cover design: George Cornell
Manufacturing buyer: Ed O'Dougherty

© 1987 by Prentice-Hall, Inc.
A division of Simon & Schuster
Englewood Cliffs, NJ 07632

All rights reserved. No part of this book may be
reproduced, in any form or by any means,
without permission in writing from the publisher.

Printed in the United States of America

10 9 8 7 6 5 4 3 2 1

ISBN 0-13-738709-1 01

Prentice-Hall International (UK) Limited, *London*
Prentice-Hall of Australia Pty. Limited, *Sydney*
Prentice-Hall Canada Inc., *Toronto*
Prentice-Hall Hispanoamericana, S.A., *Mexico*
Prentice-Hall of India Private Limited, *New Delhi*
Prentice-Hall of Japan, Inc., *Tokyo*
Prentice-Hall of Southeast Asia Pte. Ltd., *Singapore*
Editora Prentice-Hall do Brasil, Ltda., *Rio de Janeiro*

Contents

FOREWORD   xi

PREFACE   xiii

1 **WHAT IS PUBLIC RELATIONS?**   1

   Historical Overview   6

   Public Relations Today   10
      Agency Public Relations, 10   *In-House Public Relations*, 12
      Public Relations Trends, 14   *Public Relations
      Education*, 17   *Issues in Public Relations Practice*, 18

   Exercises   24

2 **ACQUIRING THE BASIC BUSINESS COMMUNICATION SKILLS: COMMUNICATING INTERNALLY**   28

   Oral Communication   29
      One-on-One Meetings, 29   *Group Meetings*, 30
      The Telephone, 31

   Written Communication   32
      The Inter-Office Memo, 32

Model Case Studies
Defining a Public Relations Function In-House   35
Developing an Internal Communication Program   36
Gathering and Organizing Background Information for Client Use   39
Getting Creative Input from Colleagues   41
Communicating with a Client   43

Exercises   45

3   DOING RESEARCH AND EVALUATION FOR A PR PROGRAM   49

Research as the Groundwork for a Public Relations Program   49
Informal Surveys and In-Depth Interviews, 51
Public Relations Opinion Audits, 53
Additional Research, 57

Research for Publication: Visibility Studies   58

Evaluation of a Public Relations Program   59
Level of Exposure, 61   Level of Reaction to Exposure, 62

Model Case Studies
Performing Informal Survey Research for a Small Organization   62
Initiating a Communications Audit   67
Employing a Visibility Study as the Centerpiece of a Public Relations Program   69
Preparing a Routine Evaluative Report   72

Exercises   75

4   FORMULATING A PR PROGRAM   79

The Foundation for the Program: Audience, Objectives, Message   79

The Program Format   82

Model Case Studies
Developing a Program to Clarify and Refine a Client's Identity   85
Developing a Public Information Program for a Nonprofit Organization   95

Developing a PR Program for Both an Internal
and an External Audience   101

Exercises   106

5   DEVELOPING VISIBILITY I: ENGAGING MEDIA INTEREST   112

Publicity Content   113
What Is News? 114   What Is Newsworthy? 114

Publicity Context   115
Publicity Outlets, 115

Methods of Publicity Implementation   116
*The Telephone Pitch, 116   The Press Release, 119
Photos and Captions, 124   The Broadcast Release, 125
The Pitch Letter, 126*

Model Case Studies
Publicizing a Routine Development   127
Finding a Newsworthy Angle for a Story   130
Dealing with the Media in a Crisis   135
Handling a Non-Event   141

Exercises   143

6   DEVELOPING VISIBILITY II: PLANNING A PR EVENT   151

The News Conference   157
*Deciding Whether to Hold a News Conference, 158
Pitching a News Conference, 159   Question and Answer
(Q & A) Sessions, 160   The Press Party, 160*

The Special Event   161
*Pitching a Special Event, 163   Setting Up a Newsroom
for a Special Event, 164   Variations on the Special
Event, 164*

Model Case Studies
Developing a Format for a News Conference   165
Tasks Involved in Developing a News Conference   171
*Media Lists, 171   Invitations, 171   Calls, Mailings,
Confirmations, 172   Physical Set-up, 172
Presentation, 173   Media Kit Materials, 174
Follow-up, 174*

Selecting the Right Special Event for a Client   175
Developing Tie-ins and Spin-offs to a Special Event   177

Exercises   179

7 DEVELOPING VISIBILITY III: CONTROLLING THE MESSAGE   182

Controlled Messages in Print   183
*Flyers and Posters, 183   Brochures, 185
Annual Reports, 188*

Controlled Messages in the Electronic Media   190
*Films and Tapes, 191   Public Service
Announcements (PSAs), 192   Slide Presentations, 195
Alternatives to Slides, 196*

Model Case Studies
Preparing an Annual Report   197
Preparing a Public Service Announcement   203
Preparing a Mini-Doc   205

Exercises   209

8 DEALING WITH ISSUES   213

Identifying Issues   215

Depth Tools   216
Impersonal Depth Tools, 217   Personal Depth Tools, 218

Model Case Studies
Presenting an Issue Through a Fact Sheet
  and Backgrounder   227
Presenting an Issue Through an Op-Ed Article   231
Presenting an Issue Through a Speech   235

Exercises   242

9 DEVELOPING NEW BUSINESS   249

Methods of Developing New Business   251

Pre-proposal Research   252

The Proposal Letter   252

Follow-up   253

The Proposal Meeting   254

Model Case Studies
    Developing a Rifle Shot Prospect   255
    Developing a Shotgun Prospect   259

Exercises   261

10 ENTERING THE PUBLIC RELATIONS FIELD   264

Coursework   264

The Job Hunt   265
    Focusing a Search, 265   *Research,* 266
    Letters and Résumés, 268   *The Interview,* 270

Internships   271

On the Job   272

Exercises   273

PR GLOSSARY   279

INDEX   283

Foreword

Although a veritable library of books on public relations has been produced over the last several decades, there has long been a need for a well-thought-out and comprehensive presentation of the many components of public relations practice that can give the beginner a clear idea of what the field is all about. Paula Marantz Cohen has done a brilliant job of filling that need with *A Public Relations Primer: Thinking and Writing in Context*.

Anyone who spends time studying the material in this book will have a thorough knowledge of the field and will be in a strong position to pursue a career in public relations.

What is most impressive about the book is its excellent combination of theory and practice. Readers can learn not only how to take the steps necessary to accomplish a public relations goal but also why these steps make sense. The author is clearly someone who is an experienced public relations professional; she is also an accomplished teacher who knows how to present her subject effectively. It would be a significant contribution to the improved practice of public relations if all those who decided to enter the field had the benefit of a careful study of the material covered in this textbook.

The true test of a practitioner in public relations, as in other fields of endeavor, is how he or she performs on the job. There probably is something like an intuitive sense of public relations that is possessed by those who are cut out to be successful in the field. This intuition is not something that can be taught, and people have to find out for themselves whether they have it or not. The practical exercises in Paula Marantz Cohen's book can be helpful in this respect; for as one completes the exercises dealing with the various facets of public relations activity, one can judge whether one's instinctive responses seem to be on target.

For all these reasons, *A Public Relations Primer* is a valuable addition to the educational literature. Coming at a time when an increasing number of people are considering a career in public relations, it will undoubtedly help raise the level of knowledge and performance for a generation of practitioners.

David Finn
Chairman and Chief Executive Officer
Ruder Finn & Rotman, Inc.
New York City

Preface

This book was written in response to a personal need. After working in the public relations field and then returning to university teaching, I found myself looking for an appropriate textbook for my undergraduate introductory public relations course. My own experience at a large, independent New York public relations agency had given me a vivid sense of how public relations is practiced in the "real world." I knew that to be true to the field, a course in public relations—especially on the introductory level—had to be stimulating and not oppressively academic. But the available texts either were too long and advanced for my purposes or did not deal realistically with the kinds of skills and knowledge that were necessary for success in the field. What I needed was a textbook that would teach basic public relations activities, illustrate these activities with easy-to-follow case studies built around the principal PR writing forms, and offer creative exercises that students could do both on their own and as a class. Because no such book existed, I decided to write one.

With *A Public Relations Primer: Thinking and Writing in Context*, I have sought to write a new kind of public relations textbook. I have consciously avoided an academic presentation and have kept to an absolute minimum the graphs, charts, and statistical information that encumber so many PR textbooks. Footnotes have been included only when they direct students to sources that are both practical and compatible with their level of understanding of the field: hence, most references are to the *Public Relations Journal*, a publication that deals with the principles of day-to-day practice, and to the *New York Times* and *Wall Street Journal*, newspapers that seem to express the attitude of an educated general public toward public relations topics.

In short, I have tried to strip explanations and examples down to their simplest and most vital forms in order to reflect the real priorities of PR practice and reveal the basic thinking process which underlies all effective PR work.

This approach is the rationale for the textbook's title. To be successful in public relations, one must learn to engage in public relations *thinking;* that is, to think about one's environment holistically and to understand the nature of the key public relations functions: informing, persuading, and integrating. By mastering this thinking process, it becomes possible to accommodate oneself to the various and changing demands of modern PR practice.

To think effectively, one must also *write* effectively. The two activities are not separate functions; they are interconnected ones. Writing helps to structure and direct thought, and writing in a new form or style can often generate new ways of thinking. Writing also teaches the *process* aspect of all PR work. While a particular writing form must comply with certain conventions of length and style, there is no end to the number and kind of potential documents that can be generated on behalf of a client as part of a PR program. And the program itself need end only when the client chooses to terminate it. In the Model Case Studies at the end of each chapter, I have tried to introduce public relations writing forms in context. This way students learn that writing a press release, a speech, or a brochure is not an end in itself but is one part of the larger process that is public relations.

Finally, along with the practical and concrete details of PR thinking and writing, I have tried to avoid reducing anything to formula so as to maintain a sense of the *art* of public relations—of the variety and creative potential inherent in a field that is still in the process of shaping itself.

ACKNOWLEDGMENTS

This book owes its existence to my students at Drexel. They inspired me to write it, and their response to earlier drafts helped me revise it to its present form. Special thanks also to Amos Landman, Gertrude Penziner, and Professor Gerald Powers.

Parts of this book were written under a Drexel University Mini-Grant.

1

What Is Public Relations?

Unlike doctors, lawyers, accountants, and other professionals, public relations people often have a hard time defining what they do. This is because their work takes many different forms and occupies many different arenas. It is also because public relations is a relatively new field. Although we can identify activities which reflect public relations motives and strategies reaching back to the earliest days of civilization, it was not until after World War II that the profession began to perceive itself formally *as* a profession—to classify its activities, develop standards for practice, and initiate the apparatus of meetings and conventions, professional literature, and educational programs which we now associate with the field.

Edward Bernays, one of the founders of public relations, was among the first to define PR as a bona fide profession. His 1952 definition (revised from a less comprehensive 1923 definition) still stands as one of the simplest and yet most accurate definitions of the field. Public relations, says Bernays, is

1 information given to the public;
2 persuasion directed at the public to modify attitudes and actions; and
3 efforts to integrate attitudes and actions of an institution with its publics and of publics with those of that institution.[1]

Inform, persuade, integrate—these are the principal verbs that govern public relations practice. These verbs imply the linking of one entity with another: an organization (the client) with a public or publics. Bernays' definition also makes clear that this linkage is not one-way. Objective information as well as subjective impressions about an organization are relayed, but the public's needs and perceptions are also taken into account in determining what gets disseminated. Thus, public relations is both *active* and *receptive* (see Figure 1-1).

In its official statement, the Public Relations Society of America (PRSA), which is the professional association for the field, specifically enumerates the active and receptive aspects of PR practice (see Exhibit 1-1). Steps 2, 4, and 5 are *active*—attempts to influence opinion and initiate change. They are informed by the *receptive* activities of steps 1 and 3, which involve monitoring, researching, and evaluating trends and information.

Another way to look at the public relations function is to visualize its position at the crossroads of two sets of messages. From one side, it receives messages from a *client organization* which generates ongoing information about its operations, policies, officers, employees, and so forth. From the other side, it receives messages from at least one, and usually more, *target publics* (the segmented audience that the organization wishes to reach and whose opinions are crucial to the organization's success). These two sides have obviously different interests. The organization may want to increase sales, build its membership, attract stockholders, or improve the productivity of its employees. Its target audience may want high-quality, inexpensive products, good service, high dividends, or good employee benefits and working conditions. In some cases, the interests of the two sides may be in actual conflict. If, for example, an organization wants to streamline its management structure and thus lay off a certain percentage of its work force, its employee public is sure to oppose the idea. Sometimes conflict arises when various target publics have interests in opposition to one another—as can often happen among members of an association, a club, or a religious organization.

People who work in public relations (called *public relations practitioners*) must deal with the messages which arise out of these different and opposing interests. Of course, PR practitioners are not disinterested parties; they are *advocates* on behalf of their clients. But since effective advocacy involves diplomacy and creative problem-solving, public relations people try to mediate among the various interests involved to come up with compromises or solutions which will satisfy or at least minimize conflicts among all concerned.[2]

Some public relations theorists have suggested that the mediating function

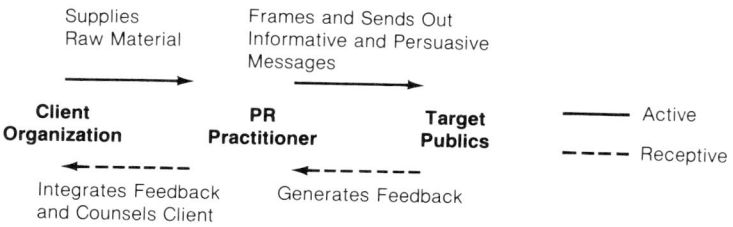

FIGURE 1-1 Active and Receptive Phases of Public Relations

EXHIBIT 1-1 Official Statement on Public Relations. Formally adopted by PRSA Assembly, November 6, 1982. (Reprinted by permission of PRSA.)

Public relations helps our complex, pluralistic society to reach decisions and function more effectively by contributing to mutual understanding among groups and institutions. It serves to bring private and public policies into harmony.

Public relations serves a wide variety of institutions in society such as businesses, trade unions, government agencies, voluntary associations, foundations, hospitals and educational and religious institutions. To achieve their goals, these institutions must develop effective relationships with many different audiences or publics such as employees, members, customers, local communities, shareholders and other institutions, and with society at large.

The managements of institutions need to understand the attitudes and values of their publics in order to achieve institutional goals. The goals themselves are shaped by the external environment. The public relations practitioner acts as a counselor to management, and as a mediator, helping to translate private aims into reasonable, publicly acceptable policy and action.

As a management function, public relations encompasses the following:

1. Anticipating, analyzing and interpreting public opinion, attitudes and issues which might impact, for good or ill, the operations and plans of the organization.
2. Counseling management at all levels in the organization with regard to policy decisions, courses of action and communication, taking into account their public ramifications and the organization's social or citizenship responsibilities.
3. Researching, conducting and evaluating, on a continuing basis, programs of action and communication to achieve informed public understanding necessary to the success of an organization's aims. These may include marketing, financial, fund raising, employee, community or government relations and other programs.
4. Planning and implementing the organization's efforts to influence or change public policy.
5. Setting objectives, planning, budgeting, recruiting and training staff, developing facilities—in short, managing the resources needed to perform all of the above.

Examples of the knowledge that may be required in the professional practice of public relations include communication arts, psychology, social psychology, sociology, political science, economics and the principles of management and ethics. Technical knowledge and skills are required for opinion research, public issues analysis, media relations, direct mail, institutional advertising, publications, film/video productions, special events, speeches and presentations.

In helping to define and implement policy, the public relations practitioner utilizes a variety of professional communication skills and plays an integrative role both within the organization and between the organization and the external environment.

of public relations as it is practiced today reflects our modern ecological-minded society in which interdependence is important for survival.[3] In such a society, they say, PR cannot attempt to impose the client's message unreflectively, but must consider the well-being of the client and its audience together. Indeed, more and more public relations practitioners are coming to realize that operating within a larger "we" perspective is more creative, more ethical, and ultimately more profitable for their clients. At the Public Relations World Congress held in Mexico City in 1978, this perspective was spelled out in the formal definition of public relations adopted by the international gathering of professionals in the field:

> Public Relations Practice is the art and social science of analysing trends, predicting their consequences, counselling organisation leaders, and implementing planned programmes of action *which will serve both the organization's and the public interest*.[4] (emphasis added)

It should now be clearer why some popular assumptions about public relations are really misperceptions. Public relations is not press agentry. A press agent seeks *publicity* (getting a client mentioned in the media at all costs), while a public relations practitioner seeks publicity only as it fits into a larger program which takes into account organizational goals and public opinion.

Another common mistake is to confuse public relations with advertising. In advertising, an organization pays for space in newspapers, magazines, TV, radio, or another medium, and then inserts its message in the space allotted. This means that the message is under the complete control of its sponsor. Unlike advertising, most public relations messages are *uncontrolled messages*—that is, when they are relayed to the media, they are subject to interpretation and change by reporters and editors. In this sense, the media acts as an intermediary target public which may revise, or even radically change, the message before passing it on to an organization's ultimate target publics (see Figure 1–2). Even when PR practitioners send *controlled messages* directly to the target audience as in the case of brochures, films, and public service announcements, these materials are generally more objective in presentation and informative in content than their counterparts in advertising campaigns (see Chapter 7).

Publicity and advertising are generally *one-way* forms of communication; public relations is, ideally, *two way* (see Exhibit 1–2). And although both

FIGURE 1–2 Controlled (———) and Uncontrolled (———) Messages

EXHIBIT 1-2 Models of Communication

> PR educators James E. Grunig and Todd Hunt have developed four models which loosely describe the kinds of communication operations within which public relations practice tends to define itself.[5] The foundation for the models is the distinction between one-way and two-way communication. But Grunig and Hunt take this distinction a step further by differentiating between one-way communication which relays a clearly biased or self-serving message to its target audience (what they call the *one-way asymmetric model*) and one-way communication which relays objective information to its target audience (the *one-way symmetric model*). Likewise, they divide two-way communication into communication which uses feedback from public opinion polls and other forms of audience research in order to better manipulate its target publics (the *two-way asymmetric model*), and communication which uses audience research in order to adjust policy to better serve the needs of its publics (the *two-way symmetric model*).
>
> All four models can be said to play a role in the practice of public relations. The one-way asymmetric model which we associate with early public relations (and which may have earned the profession a dubious reputation in the past) still flourishes in the publicity component of present-day practice. The one-way symmetric model is commonly employed by nonprofit organizations which wish to inform the public about issues relating to health, safety, consumer rights, and so on. The two-way asymmetric model is inherent in most advertising and other kinds of controlled messages put out by profit-making organizations. These messages are usually based on elaborate market research and are designed to appeal to audience preferences and tap into societal fads.
>
> Clearly, the two-way symmetric model is the most socially responsible and enlightened of the four and we will associate it with the public relations function at its most modern and comprehensive. Nonetheless, the other models are not to be dismissed as wrong or irrelevant—only as incomplete. As we shall see, they are still very much a part of PR practice today and are often employed under the larger umbrella of the two-way symmetric model.

publicity and advertising can be tools in a PR program, they are not ends in themselves; public relations, when defined comprehensively, is broader in vision and scope than either. At the same time, despite its breadth and the variety of responsibilities it encompasses, public relations is generally not a policy-making function. The public relations practitioner implements programs which clarify and promote existing organizational policy and may counsel management to alter or adjust policy where this seems necessary. But a PR person rarely if ever dictates policy. This is the job of an organization's chairperson, director, or other policy-making official.

HISTORICAL OVERVIEW

Public relations, some practitioners like to say, is the formal application of common sense. Although the field is certainly more complex than this statement would suggest, there is truth to the fact that PR is based on the rational, common-sensical understanding of the way people perceive and react to things around them. This understanding is part of what makes us human beings, and those clever enough to apply this understanding in promoting themselves or others have been engaged in some variety of public relations activity since time began.

In his classic book on public relations, *Crystallizing Public Opinion*, Edward Bernays explains that PR-related ideas have tended to flourish during periods of democracy—when individuals were permitted to express themselves freely and engage freely in economic competition. In all great democratic periods, from the Roman Republic to our present system, pamphlets, articles, speeches, and other forms of public address have been used to sway public opinion. Nondemocratic nations and institutions have, of course, also employed these tools, but where the possibility for debate and critique does not exist, they cannot give rise to the dialogue which we associate with the public relations function in its most socially responsible and comprehensive form. Admittedly, public relations activities are not always two-way (or two-way symmetric in Grunig and Hunt's terms), but in a democratic society, individuals at least are free to interpret and debate the messages they receive, and can respond, if they so choose, with opposing messages.

A good example of public relations skills employed to further democratic ends occurred during the American Revolution. Thomas Paine and Samuel Adams were the great publicists of the Revolution—writing, speaking, debating, organizing, even creating events to draw attention to their cause. The Boston Tea Party, for example, was a special event so effectively staged that, even today, no schoolchild is unfamiliar with it. The publicists of the American Revolution also helped coin slogans and frame themes that would dramatize and popularize the struggle for independence. They were helped by the fact that the British, secure in their sense of military superiority, ignored public opinion and made no effort to counter the revolutionists' claims.[6]

Many of the techniques which contributed to our nation's birth and early development were used to further a variety of social causes and reform movements in the nineteenth century. One of the most important of these was the abolitionist movement—a monumental effort to raise funds and mobilize public opinion against slavery. A similar campaign was staged on behalf of women's rights during this period. Although women did not win the ballot until 1920, the numerous conventions, petitions, editorials, and speeches on women's issues did manage to bring about a series of reforms in the area of divorce, child custody, and property rights.

During the nineteenth century political candidates and officeholders were also learning the value of publicity. This period in history saw the birth of the political press agent—today's press secretary—who helped monitor public opinion on political issues as well as organize speaking tours, ghostwrite speeches, and stage campaign events.

As the nineteenth century progressed, the publicist for social reform and the political press agent soon found counterparts in the commercial sphere. The business world offered steadier employment and the opportunity to develop new, more sensational publicity techniques.[7] P. T. Barnum, the famous nineteenth-century circus promoter, epitomized this new commercial orientation. One of the most creative publicists of all time, Barnum was adept at enlisting the media to assist him in promoting his programs. In one celebrated instance, he wrote letters to newspapers arguing for and against the authenticity of one of his performers. (She was featured on the program as George Washington's nurse, a claim which would have made her 161 years old.)[8] Barnum's letters turned the question of the woman's identity into an issue of public controversy which resulted in more publicity for the exhibition and thus larger attendance figures. (Today, the letter to the editor—albeit written to argue one side of an issue, not both—is a standard PR tool for airing a client's opinion on a timely or controversial subject [see the discussion on the letter to the editor in Chapter 8].) Barnum's tactics were purely sensational, yet as a circus promoter he was never pretending to tackle any of the serious issues which now confront PR practitioners. His objective was unabashedly to arouse interest and to entertain, and his success in coming up with new and creative story "angles" was nothing short of brilliant.

While Barnum initiated a trend in publicity which would reach its full flowering in the press agentry of Hollywood in the 1930s, important changes in American life were also beginning to provide a larger economic arena for public relations activity. Shearon Lowery and Melvin L. DeFleur have noted that three major societal trends in the nineteenth century—*industrialization*, *urbanization*, and *modernization*—were intimately connected with the evolution of public relations.[9] With industrialization came the development of the corporate structure and the need to help corporations shape a clear, unified message out of the tangle of bureaucratic decision-making. With urbanization came the concentration of masses of people in cities and the need to communicate with this mass audience in a cost-effective way. Finally, with modernization came product innovation and variety, creating a greater breakdown of the consumer market and the need to frame and deliver messages capable of reaching these specialized consumer publics.

These trends also brought into being the first large-scale capitalists. Railroad tycoons Cornelius Vanderbilt and Jay Gould along with Andrew Carnegie in steel and John D. Rockefeller in oil were now in control of massive industrial empires and were free to engage in practices that often exploited their workers and placed the public in danger. By the turn of the century these *robber barons*, as they were called, had given rise to a counterforce in the form of investigative journalists—*muckrakers* like Upton Sinclair and Ida Tarbell—who were prepared to let people know what was going on and inspire them to demand a change.

The friction created by the confrontation of the robber barons and muckrakers can be said to have ignited the spark that would give rise to modern public relations. The public was made to see that it had the power to protest exploitative business practices and demand reform. Big business was made to see that it had to take the public into account or else find its products and services boycotted and its employees unwilling to work. In 1906 Ivy Ledbetter Lee, who, along with Bernays, is considered a pioneer in the public relations profession, represented the anthracite coal-mine operators in the face of striking workers. In what would be hailed as a revolutionary approach to labor-management relations, Lee counseled the operators to inform the public of their policies rather than evade questioning. Lee would go on to serve as public relations counsel for the Rockefeller family and would continue in this capacity to urge a more open, interactive relationship between management and labor. Lee always insisted that he was serving not only the powerful interests of his clients but also the interests of working people—humanitarian claims that have been questioned by some critics who argue that they never found their way into actual practice. Nonetheless, Lee was the first to articulate the concept of *corporate social responsibility*, which has become an integral part of the public relations concerns of big business today.[10]

As the twentieth century got underway, activities and strategies used to promote everything from social reform to circuses now began to be viewed together as part of a more unified concept called *public relations*. With U.S. involvement in World War I came the creation of the Committee on Public Information, which applied the concept in building national morale and winning support for the war effort through fund-raising drives. George Creel, who headed the Committee, gathered the cream of the newspaper, publishing, and academic world to create a highly versatile cadre of public relations specialists. It is not surprising that the *New York Times* would dub World War I "the first press agent's war."[11]

After the war, general prosperity spurred the development of market research and more sophisticated strategies for teaching the consumer public to distinguish among products. Ivy Lee, Edward Bernays, and others began to formally espouse public relations as a profession and call themselves public relations counselors. The first college course in public relations was offered in the 1920s, taught by Bernays at New York University. Several public relations counseling firms were formed, and some of the major advertising agencies began to develop public relations capabilities.

Then in 1929 the stock market crash and its aftermath gave public relations the impetus it needed to go beyond publicity to develop a truly interactive relationship between business and the public. During the Depression, President Franklin Roosevelt's New Deal helped consolidate public interest into an important social force. Business needed public relations to rebuild its credibility with a skeptical public and to defend itself against the trend of Roosevelt's programs, especially since government had come to utilize PR methods to promote its own policies.

With World War II, a large-scale Office of War Information (OWI) was established, which would become an important training ground for future public relations practitioners. By virtue of its size alone, OWI served to make public relations techniques more widely recognized and helped popularize the concept of public relations with other government agencies and with private industry as well. In 1948 the Public Relations Society of America (PRSA) was created to insure standards of practice, act as a meeting ground for professionals, and serve as caretaker and clearinghouse for research materials in the field. The formation of the PRSA was a significant event in the history of the profession, demonstrating that public relations had finally come of age.

Since the mid-1950s, the PR field has experienced extraordinary growth. In the private sector, this has been spurred by the proliferation of government regulations and the increase in consumer protection groups, pressures which have made business more conscious of the need to be responsive to various publics. In the nonprofit area, PR methods have been increasingly enlisted to help organizations make their services known, assist in fund-raising, and foster desired legislative measures. Public relations has also become an increasingly important tool in the political arena, assisting candidates in the development of their campaigns and helping government officials and legislators "sell" target publics on proposed policies and legislation.

According to one scholar, public relations developed as a profession in "response to problems connected with growth and complexity."[12] In a world of many and mixed messages, someone was needed to sort and interpret these messages and to act as a liaison among groups with different vocabularies and values. As mass media developed, special expertise was also required to understand what communications channels were available and how they could best be capitalized upon. Finally, the evolution of the public relations function has been termed a component of, as well as a contributor to, the shift into "welfare capitalism" in twentieth century. This has been a period when free enterprise geared to private economic gain has been obliged to coexist with government intervention designed to protect the public interest. Within this context, public relations has emerged as a management function uniquely qualified to mediate among the many publics to which our modern society gives a voice.

10 What Is Public Relations?

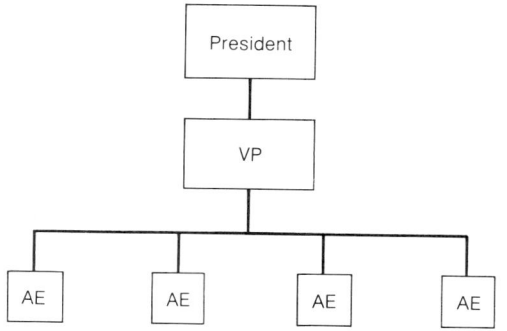

FIGURE 1-3 Organizational Structure of a Small PR Agency

PUBLIC RELATIONS TODAY

Agency Public Relations

A public relations agency is an organization devoted to providing public relations support to other organizations. These organizations are its *clients*—they are the *accounts* which the agency handles.

Public relations practitioners usually enter agencies as *account executives* or, in some agencies, *junior account executives*. As they gain experience and demonstrate ability, they may be promoted to titled positions within the agency's hierarchy, beginning with *account supervisor* and continuing to *vice president* and (in some firms) *senior vice president*.

Each account in an agency is assigned to an *account team*, which usually

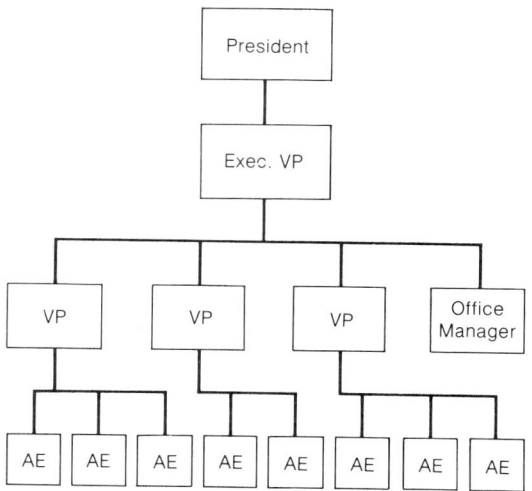

FIGURE 1-4 Organizational Structure of a Middle-Sized PR Agency

consists of at least one titled agency executive who manages the account and one or more account executives who handle the day-to-day planning and implementation. The amount of time an executive spends on any given account depends upon a combination of factors: the money the client is paying the agency, the billing rate of the executive (the hourly rate which the agency charges for the individual's work),* and the judgment of the agency's management concerning the ability of the executive to contribute to the particular account. Account assignments change as projects are completed, old clients leave the agency, and new business is added.

The organization of public relations agencies varies. Figures 1-3, 1-4, and 1-5 provide generalized examples of typical agency structures.

*An agency will often bill a client by calculating the hourly rate that executives spend working on the account (often referred to as "staff time" on the budget); sometimes, however, a flat fee is charged instead, or sometimes a retainer fee *and* an hourly rate are charged.

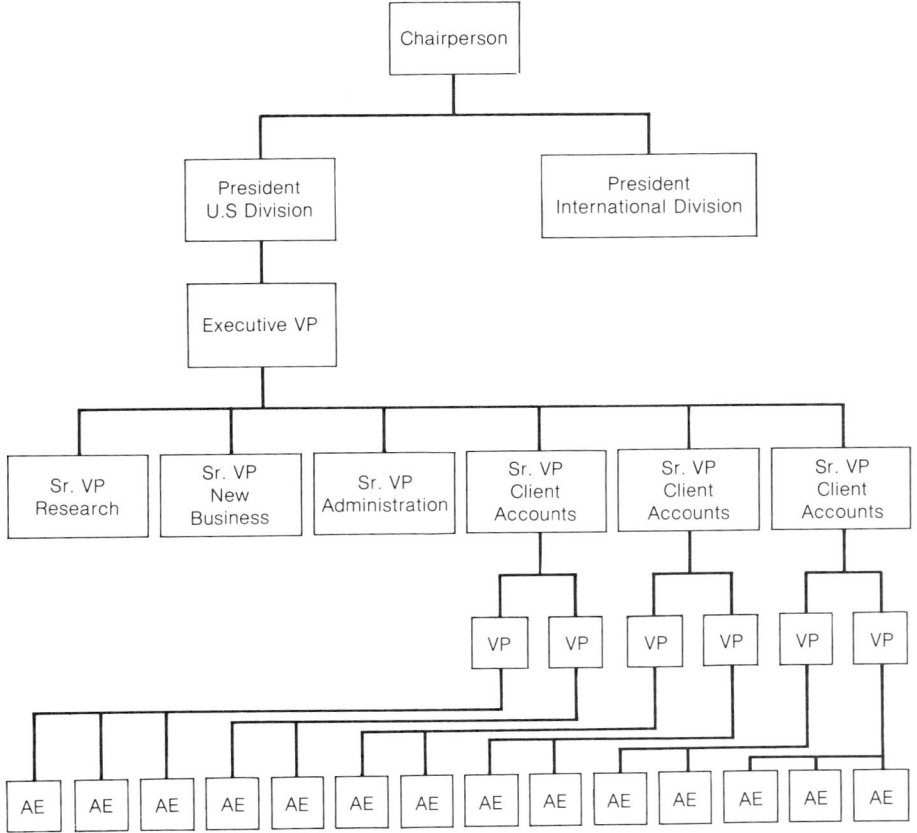

FIGURE 1-5 Organizational Structure of a Large PR Agency

In-House Public Relations

In-house public relations is a PR function inside a larger organization. An in-house PR executive has one client: the organization for which he or she works. When we speak of in-house corporate PR, we are referring to the public relations department or counsel within a profit-making company. When we speak of in-house nonprofit PR, we are referring to the public relations function within a hospital, school, professional association, or other nonprofit institution.

A few decades ago, in-house public relations tended to be a one- or two-person operation, but today many in-house PR departments are extensive, with divisions of their own. Figures 1-6, 1-7, 1-8, and 1-9 provide generalized examples of how some public relations departments may be positioned within an organizational hierarchy. Note that the public relations function may be subdivided into specialized capabilities such as financial relations, employee relations, labor relations, and so forth, and that it may be grouped with marketing, personnel, or advertising. The generalized PR function may also be given a substitute title like *public information* or *public affairs*. In nonprofit organizations, public relations may be merged with fundraising. Some organizations do not try to integrate the public relations department into the general organizational hierarchy at all, designating it instead as a counseling or staff function with direct access to the president or chief executive officer (CEO). The autonomy accorded to the PR function within an organization usually has to do with how well public relations is understood by top management officials and how willing they are to integrate public relations concepts into their long-range planning.

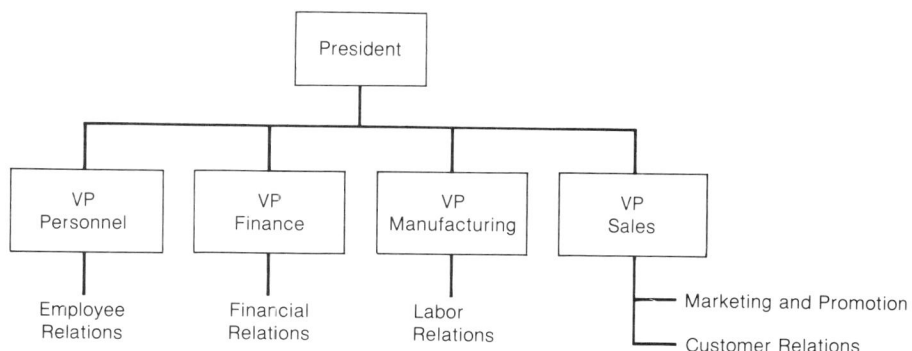

FIGURE 1-6 In-House Corporate PR-Related Functions

What Is Public Relations? **13**

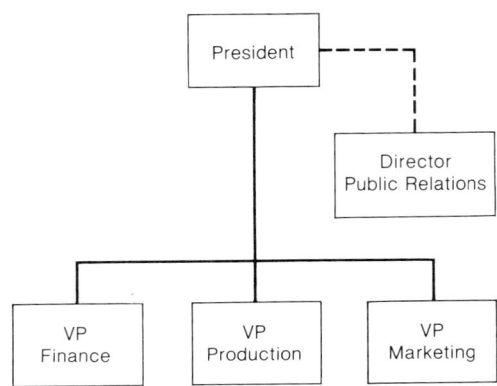

FIGURE 1-7 In-House Corporate PR

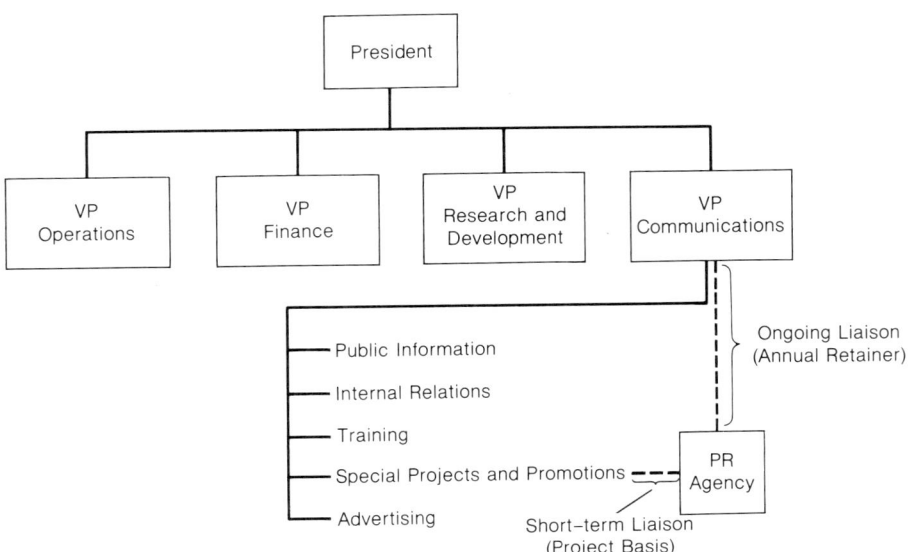

FIGURE 1-8 In-House Corporate PR and PR Agency Liaison

14 What Is Public Relations?

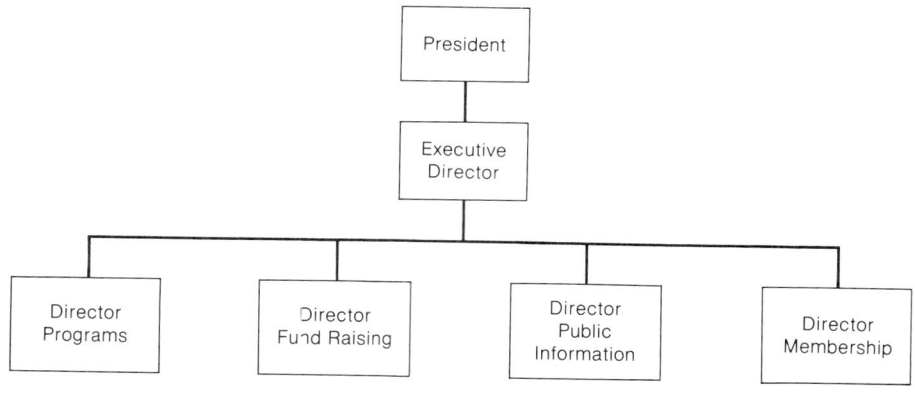

FIGURE 1-9 In-House Nonprofit PR

Public Relations Trends

SPECIALIZATION WITHIN THE FIELD

Even as public relations has grown more coherent and unified as a profession, it has also experienced new kinds of fragmentation and diversification. This is seen most obviously in the variety of names by which the public relations function is presently known. Thus, department titles such as *corporate communication*, *corporate relations*, *public information*, and *public affairs* are now commonly used as pseudonyms for public relations. Allen H. Center, an eminent educator in the field, laments what he calls the "name game" as a divisive tendency in a still maturing profession. "We simply are not ready for the burdens of bureaucratic pluralism," he says.[13] Indeed, the multitude of names used to describe the same function tends to make it even more difficult for people outside the field to understand what public relations is all about.

Yet the pluralism that characterizes public relations today is also a reflection of the profession's health and growth. While many of the names for public relations are merely cosmetic variations on the same idea, others represent genuine attempts to clarify and particularize the PR function.

As our society has become more complex and other professions have grown more specialized, PR has responded accordingly. In planning a PR program, it has now become necessary to understand the various divisions and subdivisions that make up an organization's target audience and to understand precisely how these publics overlap and diverge from each other. To facilitate the process of linking an organization with its appropriate publics, functional specializations within the PR field have developed. Today, there are PR agencies and in-house PR departments with specialized divisions devoted to community relations, employee relations, financial relations, industrial relations, and international relations, among others. There are also PR divisions assigned to handle specialized communications activities: research, broadcast communications, writing, publicity, and so on. Specialization is taken even further by agencies which handle only a particular industry or type of organization such as education, travel, beauty and fashion, health care, or financial/investor relations. This is to name only a few of the specializations listed in the *O'Dwyer Directory of Public Relations Firms*, the major source for PR agency-related information.

Nonetheless, the move to specialize is by no means a pervasive tendency in the field. There are still large and small PR agencies and in-house PR departments which remain generalist in orientation. New firms which are willing to work on everything from supermarket promotions to corporate identity campaigns are opening daily.

Even within the more specialized divisions and firms, the PR practitioner remains, in essence, a generalist, capable of seeing the larger picture where others see only the parts. In this sense, public relations, even at its most specialized, represents a counterforce to the trend toward fragmentation and specialization going on around us. In a speech at the Eighth Public Relations World Congress in London, Arthur Reef, director of public relations and advertising for AMAX, N.Y., invoked the importance of the PR practitioner as an "interpreter of everything from social trends to balance sheets." Public relations, he explained, must be independent of financial and legal specialists, whose focus will necessarily be narrower.[14]

Admittedly, the mandate of public relations—to see the larger picture, synthesize disparate information, and reconcile contradiction—has sometimes had an adverse effect on the image of the field. A familiar criticism leveled against PR people is that they are "quick studies" or dilettantes, that they know a little about a lot. Fortunately, as managers are beginning to recognize the value of a comprehensive vision in a world of specialists, the generalist image of the PR practitioner is gaining more respect. In this context, the definition put forward by some theorists that public relations is "an ecological state of mind and society that balances, over time, the interdependence of people and things"[15] seems especially fitting. This ability to see and understand the patterns and processes which connect institutions to the surrounding society will be the unique task of the PR practitioner in the years ahead.

Allen Center goes so far as to see the public relations function as offering the perspective necessary for leadership. He describes public relations as "a logical stepping stone on the path to the top management position."[16] It still remains to be seen, however, whether PR people will become the chief executive officers of tomorrow.

MERGERS WITH ADVERTISING AGENCIES

In recent years, a number of large independent public relations firms have merged or been bought by advertising agencies, permitting an exchange of resources often profitable to both parties. Clients of these merged firms can now be encouraged to allocate part of their budget to advertising and part to public relations, and the two campaigns, developed together, assure that the same themes and graphic elements will be carried through in both.

Still, some agencies continue to argue the virtues of independence and see mergers of advertising and PR as a step in the wrong direction for the public relations profession. According to Daniel Edelman, chairman of Daniel J. Edelman, Inc., for example, the merger of a public relations agency with an advertising agency "undermines the individuality, the uniqueness, and the special role in our society of the public relations firm."[17]

EVOLUTION OF IN-HOUSE PR DEPARTMENTS

While many public relations agencies may be losing autonomy through mergers with advertising agencies, many in-house public relations departments are gaining autonomy by splitting off from their traditional connection with advertising, marketing, or personnel departments. Such shifts in organizational structure are sometimes precipitated by a crisis which forces an organization to realize the value of an independent public relations function. Managers are also beginning to understand that developing and implementing a PR program not only costs a fraction of what a comparable advertising campaign would cost, but also opens channels of communication with the public and lays the groundwork for future dialogue in a way that advertising does not.

APPLICATIONS OF NEW TECHNOLOGY

As a communications field, public relations has been radically affected by new developments in technology which make the work of PR practitioners easier, more economical, and more effective. The following list includes the most noteworthy applications of new technology in public relations practice:

Word Processing makes possible the personalization of letters and invitations which are part of mass mailings. It also simplifies the labor of compiling and revising lengthy reports and programs and updating press and client lists.

On-line Data Retrieval Systems help facilitate research on topics relating to a client or particular industry. Since many newspaper indexes and general subject indexes are now available on data bases, it is possible to call up bibliographical data on demand. Some journals and newspapers have also put full texts of articles on data bases, an innovation that makes an information search that much easier.

Teleconferencing involves satellite transmission of an event to any location on the globe. An audio hook-up makes it possible to communicate with the transmitting site throughout the broadcast. This technology enables organizations to hold press conferences and employee meetings when the audience is physically scattered.

Computerized Statistical Evaluations facilitate program evaluation.

Evaluating progress is a standard part of public relations activity, yet the success or failure of a program has always been notoriously difficult to quantify. Unlike the evaluation of other kinds of operations where the bottom line becomes the final measure, the variables which make a PR program successful may have no effect on profits for years to come; even then, there is no way of actually tracing the correspondence between the public relations effort and the profit margin. Now, however, a *publicity tracking method* (best known is the Ketchum Publicity Tracking Model, developed by Ketchum Public Relations[18]) tackles the problem of PR measurement by employing computerized computation and data retrieval techniques. The computer is fed the story placements on a given client which have been classified according to the kinds of messages they contain. Then these stories are matched with the demographic features of the media in which they appear. The result is an "index" to the effectiveness of the message and the general visibility of the client in the media.

Although such quantitative measurement techniques represent an important contribution to the field, an element of the unquantitative still remains. Since public relations is concerned with the impressions and subjective opinions of its target audience, the validity of statistical measurement is limited.

Satellite Transmission of Video Releases and Electronic Mail are high-speed forms of communication increasingly valuable in public relations work as it becomes necessary to coordinate activities not only from city to city but also from country to country. Many PR departments of multinational corporations and many PR agencies with offices abroad are supplementing slower and clumsier postal and telex services with this sophisticated technology.

Public Relations Education

When Ivy Lee organized his own public relations agency in the 1920s, his staff consisted of ex-newspaper people like himself. The newsroom was the only training ground available for the PR practitioner then. Even a few decades ago, most public relations professionals still came from the ranks of journalism and had no formal training in public relations before entering the field. But things have changed. Today, practitioners tend to have taken at least one public relations course in college, and many hold undergraduate and graduate degrees in the field (see the discussion of coursework in Chapter 10).*

---

*In addition to taking coursework and earning degrees, practitioners can now gain formal accreditation—if they have worked full-time in the field for five years—by passing an oral and written examination administered through PRSA. Those who pass the accreditation exam are entitled to use the initials APR (Accredited in Public Relations) after their names.

As the demand for public relations education increases, schools throughout the country are upgrading their offerings. The PR curriculum, which in the past was viewed as the step-sister of journalism, is now often housed alongside journalism in a separate but equal division as part of a larger communications department. Public relations offerings are also slowly being incorporated into the curricula of business departments and schools.

As public relations education has become more rigorous and extensive, there has been a corresponding increase in scholarly work in the field. Professional journals like the *Public Relations Journal*, *Public Relations Review*, and *Public Relations Quarterly*, along with a variety of newsletters and tip sheets geared to different aspects of PR practice, are now being published. Articles on public relations have also begun to appear regularly in business and communications journals. This literature, along with a better-informed, better-educated pool of professionals, has helped improve the image of public relations with the media.

In the past, newspeople, trained in the notion of objective reporting, found it hard to understand how a profession based on advocacy could be meaningful and credible. They tended to view their colleagues who went into public relations as "sell-outs" to plusher offices and higher salaries. Now that public relations has evolved into a field with its own educational curriculum and standards for practice, journalists are beginning to understand how PR works and why. Indeed, as it becomes more difficult to recognize and track newsworthy stories in a fast-paced, rapidly changing society, the ability of the PR practitioner to disseminate information and respond quickly to requests for additional information becomes increasingly valuable to the media.

Issues in Public Relations Practice

HOW MUCH TO PROMISE

Since public relations is a service and not a concrete product, its operation is based upon many subjective variables. As a result, it is never entirely possible to predict the outcome of a PR effort. Sometimes timing may be wrong—a good story pitched to a newspaper, for example, may not be publicized because a similar story was printed a few weeks earlier. Or there's always the chance that late-breaking news—a natural disaster, a surprise release from the White House—will eclipse the news conference or special event planned for a client. Suddenly, the prospect of substantial media attendance fades to nothing.

These are the nightmares of the public relations practitioner. Although they rarely happen, there is always the chance that they could, and, therefore, promises to clients should be made with a degree of caution and qualification. While an assumption used to exist among some practitioners that one could promise a client everything and then deliver less, this approach has proven to be unwise. An informed client is likely to distrust a pie-in-the-sky promise over an honest statement. Thus, instead of "We'll have you plastered all over the *New York Times* and the *Wall Street Journal*," the more careful "I think we have a good chance of getting coverage for you in some major New York media" is more advisable.

Promises to clients should also reflect a realistic assessment of what they can expect. Commonly, public relations practitioners are called upon to promote organizations which simply do not generate "big" news. Here it becomes a matter of deciding how much and what kind of coverage can realistically be expected. Remember that not all clients want to appear on network news or in the *New York Times*. Their target publics may be more likely to read trade publications or watch local news. Unfortunately, however, there are always clients who have an unrealistic or inflated sense of their own importance or who may suffer from the delusion that PR people have mysterious access to the highest reaches of the media and can automatically land them front page stories in national publications. It's important in these cases to explain how newspapers, magazines, and TV and radio editors choose their stories and to clarify how PR practitioners work with media representatives. Of course, it's best not to rule out the possibility of a major placement, even if such a placement seems unlikely; one never knows when a newsworthy angle or a reporter eager to fill space might turn up. But it's always better to concentrate on explaining the value of probable placements rather than dwelling on improbable ones.

PROFESSIONAL ETHICS

It is impossible to overestimate the importance of ethics in public relations. As a profession based on advocacy, PR is particularly vulnerable to charges of misrepresentation; thus, practitioners need to take special care to represent information fairly and accurately.

Another reason why honest and straightforward dealings are especially valuable in public relations is because it is a field in which credibility is so important. Even in the infancy of the profession, Edward Bernays could spell out the reasons why truth and accuracy were necessary in PR practice: First, he explained, the media are adept at recognizing when information has been falsified or distorted; and second, once caught in a lie a practitioner can never hope to recover credibility. "Faith and trust," concluded Bernays, "is the most valuable thing he [a PR practitioner] possesses."[19]

To underline the importance of individual ethics in public relations, the PRSA includes a Code of Professional Standards for the Practice of Public Relations on its application form, and aspiring members must sign a statement agreeing to abide by the Code (see Exhibit 1–3). Where an explicit violation of the Code by a PRSA member is indicated, the member can be

EXHIBIT 1-3 Code of Professional Standards for the Practice of Public Relations. (Reprinted by permission of PRSA.)

This Code, adopted by the PRSA Assembly, replaces a Code of Ethics in force since 1950 and revised in 1954. The current Code of Professional Standards including the previous Statement of Principles was approved in 1959 and revised in 1963, 1977 and 1983.

Declaration of Principles

Members of the Public Relations Society of America base their professional principles on the fundamental value and dignity of the individual, holding that the free exercise of human rights, especially freedom of speech, freedom of assembly and freedom of the press, is essential to the practice of public relations.

In serving the interests of clients and employers, we dedicate ourselves to the goals of better communication, understanding and cooperation among the diverse individuals, groups and institutions of society, and of equal opportunity of employment in the public relations profession.

We pledge:

To conduct ourselves professionally, with truth, accuracy, fairness and responsibility to the public;

To improve our individual competence and advance the knowledge and proficiency of the profession through continuing research and education;

And to adhere to the articles of the Code of Professional Standards for the Practice of Public Relations as adopted by the governing Assembly of the Society.

Articles of the Code

These articles have been adopted by the Public Relations Society of America to promote and maintain high standards of public service and ethical conduct among its members.

1 A member shall deal fairly with clients or employers, past and present, or potential, with fellow practitioners and the general public.

2 A member shall conduct his or her professional life in accord with the public interest.

3 A member shall adhere to truth and accuracy and to generally accepted standards of good taste.

4 A member shall not represent conflicting or competing interests without the express consent of those involved, given after a full disclosure of the facts; nor place himself or herself in a position where the member's interest is or may be in conflict with a duty to a client, or others, without a full disclosure of such interests to all involved.

5 A member shall safeguard the confidences of present and former clients, as well as of those persons or entities who have disclosed confidences to a member in the context of communications relating to an antici-

pated professional relationship with such member, and shall not accept retainers or employment that may involve disclosing, using or offering to use such confidences to the disadvantage or prejudice of such present, former or potential clients or employers.

6   A member shall not engage in any practice which tends to corrupt the integrity of channels of communication or the processes of government.

7   A member shall not intentionally communicate false or misleading information and is obligated to use care to avoid communication of false or misleading information.

8   A member shall be prepared to identify publicly the name of the client or employer on whose behalf any public communication is made.

9   A member shall not make use of any individual or organization purporting to serve or represent an announced cause, or purporting to be independent or unbiased, but actually serving an undisclosed special or private interest of a member, client or employer.

10   A member shall not intentionally injure the professional reputation or practice of another practitioner. However, if a member has evidence that another member has been guilty of unethical, illegal or unfair practices, including those in violation of this Code, the member shall present the information promptly to the proper authorities of the Society for action in accordance with the procedure set forth in Article XII of the Bylaws.

11   A member called as a witness in a proceeding for the enforcement of this Code shall be bound to appear, unless excused for sufficient reason by the judicial panel.

12   A member, in performing services for a client or employer, shall not accept fees, commissions or any other valuable consideration from anyone other than the client or employer in connection with those services without the express consent of the client or employer, given after a full disclosure of the facts.

13   A member shall not guarantee the achievement of specified results beyond the member's direct control.

14   A member shall, as soon as possible, sever relations with any organization or individual if such relationship requires conduct contrary to the articles of this Code.

---

brought up before the Society's Grievance Board, which will review the case. (Final review and decision concerning a member's status lies with the PRSA Board of Directors.[20])

Still, in everyday practice, what is or is not ethical cannot always be determined by referring to the PRSA Code. As anyone who has worked in a real-world context knows, questions of right and wrong do not tend to have simple, clear-cut answers. The fact that so much PR work involves situations where disparate judgments and interests are represented can give rise to complex ethical dilemmas as well. For this reason, ethics in the public relations field "must be more situational than theoretical," according to one practitioner.[21] Bringing one's own standards to bear while consulting older, respected colleagues will usually help beginners in the field come to satisfying conclusions. Chester Burger's four lessons relating to ethically responsible behavior (see Exhibit 1-4) provide helpful guidelines.[22]

Also important is the matter of agency ethics. While few agencies will retain a client they suspect to be dishonest, what they *will* tolerate often varies according to the personality and values of the agency's management. Some agencies hold clear-cut political views and will not represent countries or political candidates whose views differ substantially from them. Others are nonpartisan, but will shy away from extremist clients. Still others will represent any client they believe to be honest, even if they disagree with the

EXHIBIT 1-4 Burger's Lessons about Ethically Responsible Behavior. (Reprinted, with permission, from the December 1982 issue of the *Public Relations Journal.* Copyright 1982.)

Lesson 1

Communicators must trust the common sense of their audience. More often than not, the public will justify our trust by seeing accurately the issues and the contenders and the motivations. Communicators should not use clever headlines, gimmicks, distortions, or lies to communicate effectively. Don't underestimate the public's perceptiveness.

Lesson 2

People generally will know or care very little about the issue that concerns you. You've got to inform, to clarify, to simplify issues in a truthful manner, and in ways that will relate to the self-interest of your audience.

Lesson 3

Don't compromise your own ethical standards for anyone. Don't take the easy way out. Don't say what you don't really believe, and don't do for the sake of expediency what you think is wrong. It ain't worth it. Ask yourself how your action would look if it were reported tomorrow on the front page of your local newspaper. Who would absolve you from the responsibility if you said you wrote it or said it or did it because your boss told you to?

Lesson 4

Choices for communicators between right and wrong are rarely black or white, yes or no. Questions of ethics involve degrees, nuances, differing viewpoints. Too many times in my life have I been wrong to feel sure that I know the right answer. A bit of uncertainty and humility sometimes is appropriate in considering ethical questions.

client's stance on an issue. The argument most commonly used by the latter agencies is that public relations should function like the legal profession—every organization should have the right to good public relations representation. Still, agencies realize that the best work is done for a client one believes in. This is why matching the account executive to the account is so important. This is also why some agencies have set up ethics committees or review boards which allow the agency staff at all levels to discuss whether or not a controversial client should be retained.

On the whole, agencies, like individuals, tend to become more certain of their ethical beliefs as they mature.

ROLE OF LEGAL COUNSEL

The practice of public relations involves a host of legal issues. In financial relations, there are the complicated and perpetually changing laws of the Security and Exchange Commission (SEC). In the area of publicity, there are libel and copyright laws as well as Federal Trade Commission (FTC) regulations. Moreover, all commercial dealings involve the drawing up of contracts. In these instances and others which are part of everyday PR work, the assistance of a legal counselor is crucial.

Unfortunately, public relations practitioners rarely work closely with lawyers, and this has tended to enforce misunderstanding between the two functions. It is common, in fact, for the public relations practitioner and the legal counsel of an organization to hold conflicting views. If a company experiences a crisis, for example, a lawyer will often advise that no comment be given until all the implications of the incident have been thoroughly reviewed and a precise statement can be drawn up. But a PR practitioner knows that quick response in the wake of a crisis can win goodwill and help prevent the media from relying on other, perhaps unfriendly sources for information.

To avoid a clash when the stakes are high, it is wise for the PR practitioner to cultivate a good relationship with the legal counsel within the client organization. Getting lawyers to understand the rationale of public relations policies, and learning the rationale for legal policies in turn, can help bring about compromises which can streamline response in the event of a crisis. Such an understanding can also truly benefit both sides. Lawyers, along with providing routine counsel on PR operations, can help practitioners deal with more subtle and long-range issues, such as the legal implications of government legislation affecting clients. PR people, for their part, can help lawyers frame more effective, less jargony statements when there is a need to communicate legal issues to employees or external publics.

SAYING NO

There usually comes a time in every account executive's career when it is necessary to turn down an account assignment for ethical or personal reasons. The factors that cause a given individual to say no are often unique to him or her: An agency executive whose father was an alcoholic may feel he has to refuse work on a liquor company account; a young woman may have to bow out of an account because the client is besieging her with calls at home and asking her to go out on dates. In these cases, the work situation impinges upon the personal life of the executives, and both are impaired. Asking to be taken off a project in such instances becomes a reasonable step.

Many cases, however, are more ambiguous. A client with an abrasive personality, a client who makes unreasonable demands on a practitioner's time, or a client who wants to publicize a not-altogether accurate version of what happened—such cases may involve a lot of soul-searching for those assigned to deal with them. The Code of Professional Standards for the field makes it clear that practitioners are not expected to be partners in questionable actions or personal exploitation. This does not mean that when a client makes a dubious suggestion, it is necessary to beat a hasty retreat. Sometimes it may be possible to effect a change in the client's behavior through rational persuasion. Telling client representatives why a whitewash job would not be a good PR move may help convince them to be more forthright with the public or to adjust policy so that it will indeed coincide with the image they wish to project. In any case, all such dilemmas should be discussed first with a supervisor who will have more experience and perspective, and may offer precedents concerning how individuals have handled similar situations in the past.

EXERCISES

Test Your Judgment

In each case below, decide whether the *active* or *receptive* phase of public relations practice is involved. If the situation is active, state whether it represents *informative* or *persuasive* communication.

1 A drug company holds a press conference to announce that one of its over-the-counter products may produce an allergic skin reaction in some users.

2 A university takes a survey of the current careers and incomes of its alumni before embarking on its annual fund-raising drive.

3 A new restaurant distributes flyers which claim it has the best hamburger in town.

4 A department store chain sponsors a poll to determine which segments of the population engage in the most "impulse shopping."

5 A political candidate delivers a speech explaining the ways in which she plans to improve the economy.

What Is Public Relations? 25

PR Workshop

1 Choose a particular historical event or group of events and exchange ideas in class about the PR-related activities which people may have employeed to promote it. Possibilities might include the Salem witch hunts, the crusade for women's suffrage, the early space program, the Beatles' first American tour, the civil rights movement.

2 Discuss the various target publics which your university would have to address if it were to develop a public relations program. Decide which publics would be most important to reach and why.

3 Thumb through the day's newspaper to find an article that suggests a present or potential public relations problem to you. Make a presentation to the class in which you summarize the problem and suggest some general tactics for dealing with it. After your presentation, have the class discuss the problem and trade ideas concerning its solution.

PR Case Studies

1 For each situation below, write a few sentences explaining how you might deal with the dilemma.
a You are employed by a large PR agency and have been asked to work on the newest and largest account, the Benton Cigarette Company, which wants to begin marketing Benton cigarettes in France. The position would be a challenging one and would involve monthly trips to Paris. The problem is that you are a reformed smoker and like to boast about how proud you are of kicking the habit.
b You are PR director of a small Georgia-based airline. One of the airline's planes recently had a close call when the landing gear jammed. (Luckily, the pilot was able to unjam the gear at zero hour and land the plane safely.) You happen to know that the airline is short-staffed in its ground crew, and you believe that the plane was not properly checked before take-off. You don't know whether the Federal Aviation Administration will order an investigation or whether the press will probe this deeply. Since there were no casualties, it's possible the incident will be ignored.
c You are an account executive at a PR agency and have been assigned to work on an account under a supervisor whom you do not respect. You find this person uninformed and inconsistent in his judgments, and you feel that working for him could damage you psychologically and professionally. Unfortunately, you asked to be taken off another agency account six months ago. This would be your second complaint in less than a year.

2 The following is a list of cliché statements which are often applied to the business world. Consider the ethical implications of each statement.

Choose three clichés from the list and describe concrete situations—from news events or from personal experience—which refute (or modify) the clichés.
a It's OK as long as it's legal.
b Don't make waves.
c The client is always right.
d Let your conscience be your guide.
e Always do what you're told.
f Your job is to make the client look good.
g Never do a favor unless you can count on a return.
h What's the use of playing fair if everyone else cheats?
i A good salesperson can sell anything.
j Always look out for number 1.

NOTES

1. Edward L. Bernays, *Public Relations* (Norman: University of Oklahoma Press, 1952), p. 3.
2. See Paula Marantz Cohen, "The Double Bind Message," *Public Relations Journal*, 40 (August 1984), 12–13.
3. Louis J. Wolter and Stephen B. Miles, "Public Relations Theory," *Public Relations Journal*, 39 (September 1983), 12–16. Also see Andrew B. Gollner, "Public Relations/Public Affairs in the New Managerial Revolution," *Public Relations Review*, X (Winter 1984), 3–10.
4. Sam Black, ed., *Public Relations in the 1980s: Proceedings of the Eighth Public Relations World Congress—London 1979* (New York: Pergamon Press, 1980), p. xi.
5. James E. Grunig and Todd Hunt, *Managing Public Relations* (New York: Holt, Rinehart and Winston, 1984), Also see Grunig, "Organizations, Environments, and Models of Public Relations," *Public Relations Research and Education*, 1 (Winter 1984), 6–29.
6. Philip Davidson, *Propaganda and the American Revolution, 1763–1783* (Chapel Hill: University of North Carolina Press, 1941), p. 3.
7. Alan R. Raucher, *Public Relations and Business: 1900–1929* (Baltimore: The Johns Hopkins University Press, 1968), p. 2.
8. P. T. Barnum, *P. T. Barnum: The Greatest Showman on Earth* (1869; reprinted New York: Chelsea House Publishers, 1983), p. 48.
9. Shearon Lowery and Melvin L. DeFleur, *Milestones in Mass Communication Research: Media Effects* (New York: Longman, 1983), pp. 6–10.
10. Scott M. Cutlip and Allen H. Center, *Effective Public Relations*, 5th edition (Englewood Cliffs, N.J.: Prentice-Hall, 1982), pp. 78–80.
11. Raucher, p. 70. Also see George Creel, *How We Advertised America: The First Telling of the Amazing Story of the Committee on Public Information That Carried the Gospel of America to Every Corner of the Globe* (New York: Harper & Row, 1920).
12. Raucher, pp. 150–153.
13. Allen H. Center, "State of the Art III," *Public Relations Journal*, 39 (October 1983), 20.
14. Arthur Reef, "The Public Relations Professional Must Equip Himself for His New Role," *Public Relations in the 1980s*, ed. Sam Black (New York: Pergamon Press, 1980), pp. 213–15.

15. Wolter and Miles, p. 15.
16. Center, p. 20.
17. Daniel Edelman, "Managing the Public Relations Firm in the Twenty-first Century," *Public Relations Review*, IX (Fall 1983), 7.
18. See Eric Page, "Measuring the Impact of Publicity," *New York Times*, November 30, 1982, sec. D, p. 22.
19. Edward L. Bernays, *Crystallizing Public Opinion* (1923; reprinted New York: Liveright Publishing Company, 1961), p. 198.
20. See Donald B. McCammond, "A Matter of Ethics," *Public Relations Journal*, 39 (November 1983), 46–47.
21. Donald K. Wright, "Ethics in Public Relations," *Public Relations Journal*, 38 (December 1982), 12.
22. Chester Burger, "Ethics in Public Relations," *Public Relations Journal*, 38 (December 1982), 17.

2

Acquiring the Basic Business Communication Skills: Communicating Internally

When you think of public relations, generally you first think of familiar forms of external communication such as news conferences, press releases, speeches, and special events. These, of course, are the more visible manifestations of a public relations effort, but they are far from the whole story. Communication within the public relations field takes place on many levels, and not the least of these is internal: communication with colleagues, supervisors, higher-level management, and others in your organization.

We begin with a treatment of internal communication because we see it as the crucial but often neglected foundation of public relations practice. Public relations ideas are born within an in-house PR department or PR agency, and it is there that they must be nurtured before being sent on their way. If they are not well conceived and well articulated at the outset, it is unlikely they will ever fly beyond the nest. Internal communication is thus the hatching ground and the trial space for any PR effort.

In recent years, internal communication has become a formal public relations specialization, sometimes known as *internal* or *employee relations*. As such, it involves communicating with internal publics using the same kinds of research, planning, implementation, and evaluation techniques used in communicating with other (external) publics. One of the case studies in this chapter deals specifically with an internal communication program of this sort. However, in the following pages we are primarily concerned with more fundamental methods of getting ideas across and profiting by the ideas of others within an organization. In this sense, learning to communicate internally involves acquiring the basic business communication skills necessary for all public relations work.

First of all, understanding how your organization works can help you communicate effectively within it. While every organization has its unspoken rules which can be learned only through some degree of trial and error, there are often external cues available about the way information is relayed internally. For example, in a company where casual dress prevails and executives leave their doors open, there is probably more personal contact and less communication in writing among staff members. Chances are that the organization is less concerned with upholding a communications hierarchy and that junior-level people communicate more freely with higher-level management.

Even architecture can affect internal communication procedures. The *open office plan*—no permanent plaster walls and no doors—became a popular office design in the 1970s. It is said to have brought about a decrease in the use of inter-office memos as executives found it easier to drop in on one another (or merely to shout across the open space). But enter a company where office space is rigidly compartmentalized, where executives hurry briskly through the corridors, where they never answer their own phones—and you are likely to find that all internal communication, even the most minor, is conducted in writing, and that a strict hierarchical structure governs the route this communication must take.

Most organizations, however, include both casual and formal elements and thus rely on a mix of oral communication (*one-on-one meetings, group meetings*, and the *telephone*) and written communication (the *inter-office memo*). Of the two types, the inter-office memo requires the most attention. But before dealing with it, let's first review some of the simple but important rules which govern oral communication.

ORAL COMMUNICATION

One-on-One Meetings

The most obvious advantages attached to a one-on-one meeting are those intangible benefits which come with a smile and a handshake. A personal meeting can be the quickest, most direct approach to obtaining an answer to a question or approval for a course of action. It can help stimulate a rapport with another person or spark new ideas which can help move a project forward more easily. Many PR agencies recognize the advantages of personal contact and schedule regular creative or "brainstorming" sessions in which colleagues meet informally to generate promotional ideas for one another's clients.

Yet, in as many instances as it can help, one-on-one communication can also be inappropriate and actually counter-productive. Dropping by colleagues' offices to chat may be a good way to introduce yourself and warm up a relationship, but chronic visiting to deliver minor or routine messages can be as irritating as it is unwarranted. Where you are merely communicating out of courtesy—to relay a thank you or transmit a personal message—a simple handwritten note would often serve best. And while important messages may necessitate a personal meeting, you should usually prepare an inter-office memo prior to the meeting so that you and the person you're meeting with will have something to refer to as you talk.

Here are some guidelines for one-on-one meetings:

1 Prepare an inter-office memo outlining the major points you wish to cover. This will help you sort out your ideas. A meeting preceded by written communication also tends to be taken more seriously.

2 Make a formal appointment to meet with your supervisor after you've sent the memo. (Don't just drop by the office to get his or her reaction.) In making the appointment, specify the probable length of your meeting so that you are allotted enough time to get your message across gracefully.

If you feel comfortable with your supervisor, you might want to suggest a lunch or breakfast meeting outside the office. Getting out of the work environment and especially out of your supervisor's office can create a more relaxed, democratic atmosphere which facilitates conversation and helps place your ideas in a better light.

3 Practice what you're going to say in advance. In the meeting, try to follow the line of reasoning set forth in your memo. You may want to ask your supervisor to refer to the memo during your discussion. (Bring an extra copy with you in case the copy you sent has been misplaced.)

4 Follow-up with a memo in which you answer any questions which may have been raised in the meeting and thank your supervisor for giving his or her time.

Group Meetings

A surprising amount of work done in organizations is done through group interaction. This is especially true in public relations work, where there are so many parties whose ideas must be taken into account and whose expertise must be tapped in devising a suitable program for a client. *Ad hoc committees* meet regularly within a limited time frame to resolve a given issue, while *standing committees* exist on an ongoing basis to monitor issues or deal with persistent problems.

Formats for meetings may vary depending upon their size, the nature of the constituency, and the nature of the topic being treated. However, for groups to operate effectively they must abide by certain basic rules of oganization and procedure.[1] If you are in the position of initiating and leading a group meeting, you will need to prepare an *agenda*—a brief outline of what you expect to cover. This should be sent to participants in memo form (along with the time and place of the meeting) well in advance. During the meeting you will want to direct the flow of discussion and make appropriate transitions so that all points on the agenda are covered within the allotted time. Finally, effective group leadership will draw on your ability to negotiate, steer opposing viewpoints to a consensus, and assure equal participation of all group members.

While leading a group is certainly the most visible and challenging role, participating as an effective member of a group led by someone else is also a skill. It means contributing to the topic under discussion, but not dominating the discussion or imposing your point of view. When group meetings run well they show a balance of participation in which each member respects and seeks the views of other members.

Where a meeting's results are considered worthy of record, someone must be designated to act as secretary. This is most important when the group needs to prepare a written document as the end product of its proceedings. Committee reports have the reputation of being awkward cut-and-paste jobs in which the original ideas have been diluted or lost. To avoid the pitfalls of writing by committee, the group should agree on an explicit organizing idea and a number of key supporting points for the document. While parts of a final document may be drafted by different people, one person should perform the final rewrite and editing so that the report shows a consistency of style and tone throughout.

The Telephone

Another means of verbal communication—heavily relied upon in the field of public relations—is the telephone. As a tool of internal communication, the phone has the advantage of speed and accessibility. It can cut through the amenities and chitchat—"Got a minute? I've got a quick question"—and get right to the point.

However, since public relations people spend much of their working day on the phone with reporters, editors, and clients, getting through to a colleague may not be so easy. Moreover, even the briefest telephone conversation can be an intrusion when the person on the other end is working on deadline. Telephone etiquette should require that the caller, after identifying him or herself, inquire whether the person being called has "got a minute?"

Phone conversations are not the place for discussions of complex issues. When the subject is complicated or sensitive, write a preliminary memo and set up an appointment to discuss the issue in greater depth in person.

WRITTEN COMMUNICATION

The Inter-Office Memo

Among the most used (and misused) methods of communicating within an organization is the inter-office (or internal) memo.[2] It serves an array of functions. It may outline a conversation before the fact or summarize it later. It may serve to replace conversation altogether. Although organizations vary in their dependence on the internal memo, all organizations use the form some of the time, if only to keep a written record of internal transactions, ideas, and recommendations. Indeed, the old adage that you shouldn't put down on paper anything that you wouldn't want to see on the front page of a newspaper appears paradoxical in respect to the inter-office memo. As a writing form, it presents itself as casual and off-the-record. It is, by definition, an informal mode of communication since it is not intended to be seen by an "external" audience. At the same time, it is written communication that is filed. In the unlikely event of a court case, those files could actually be subpoenaed and your "internal" memo made subject to public scrutiny. Moreover, the tendency to send copies of an internal memo to individuals besides the addressee further qualifies how casually you should view the writing of a memo. (The abbreviation cc stands for "carbon copy" and is used to indicate where else the memo should be routed.) Innocuous as the form appears to be, its potential power to damage or advance the sender may be considerable.

The inter-office memo has as many uses as there are things to say within an organization. For our purposes, however, it is possible to break down the memo into two general types: the *informational* memo and the *idea* memo. Although in practice the two types usually overlap, the following examples demonstrate what each type of memo looks like in its purest and simplest form.

Here is a standard informational memo:

Memorandum

To: Ann Price
From: Linda Rifkin *LR*
Subject: Date of Lord's Fashion Show
Date: March 19, 198_

cc: Joe Evans
Jerry Fallon

In checking our calendar, I find that the date we set for Lord's Fashion Show—April 8—coincides with the date of the Mercury Food Fair. Since the show and the fair attract similar audiences, we may want to consider changing the date of the show.

Alternative dates when the mall area is available to us include
- April 10
- May 1
- June 9

Can we discuss this at our 3 P.M. meeting?

Note that Rifkin has addressed the memo to Price, her supervisor, but has also copied Evans, the vice president in charge of the account, and Fallon, the art director, who will be helping to set up the fashion show. The subject of the memo is succinct—"Date of Lord's Fashion Show"—instead of a more wordy "Whether to change the date of Lord's Fashion Show." Note also how the alternative dates are bulleted and listed vertically so that they stand out. Finally, a specific follow-up proposal is given: discussion at the 3 P.M. meeting.

Now, here is a standard idea memo:

Memorandum

To: Selma Sorrenson
From: Jane Poole *JP*
Subject: Judd Computers—Underwriting Venture
Date: January 16, 198_

We've talked a lot about finding the right kind of underwriting venture for Judd—something with broad appeal and in step with Judd's image as a frontrunner in the microcomputer field. I've got an idea:

A public television series dealing with the subject of "invention"—in the arts, in business, in science and technology. The series could be something on the order of *Cosmos* or *Nova*, but would concentrate on innovative techniques and theories in modern society.

The series would be ideal for Judd sponsorship because
- It would indirectly highlight Judd's leadership in the fast-growing field of microcomputers.
- It would associate the company with innovative business strategies and could be used as part of Judd's employee relations program.
- It could help reinforce and publicize Judd's ongoing sponsorship of community art exhibitions and music festivals.

The supporting materials that could be generated from such a series are enormous: educational books, and tapes, films, museum exhibitions. Each

34 Acquiring the Basic Business Communication Skills: Communicating Internally

> program in the series would have its own target audiences and could be publicized individually.
>
> Judd has never underwritten public television programs before. This would represent a dramatic entry.
>
> What do you think? Perhaps we can discuss this on Friday. I'll check with Judy and confirm a time for us to meet.

Poole's memo is a succinct, clearly written presentation of her idea. In a sense, she has written a kind of mini-proposal to her boss in which she explains the project, lists the reasons why Judd might be interested in underwriting it, and briefly points out some additional advantages. None of her points is treated in depth, but together they offer a good sense of the concept and its rationale, and provide an outline she can follow in her subsequent meeting with Sorrenson. It seems appropriate that the memo has not been copied to others at the agency; it would be presumptuous of Poole to publicize her idea to colleagues or management without first getting the approval of her supervisor. Note again that a clear follow-up proposal is given. Poole doesn't just sit back and wait for her supervisor to come to her to discuss the memo. She takes the initiative and makes it easier on her boss by proposing to arrange a meeting herself.

As you can see from this example, the idea memo is not really distinct from the informational memo; it merely builds on it. Poole bases her recommendation for the TV series on what she knows about Judd. You'll find that the most important memos tend to be hybrid forms: They use information to back up ideas and ideas to interpret information.

Here are some tips for writing effective inter-office memos:

1 Use simple sentences. Avoid bulky subordinate clauses. Use two sentences instead of one long sentence.

2 Use bulleted or numbered lists rather than series. Try for a presentation which is easy on the eye.

3 Don't sound authoritative in a memo to a superior. Use a casual, "suggesting" tone.

4 Always copy your supervisor in a memo to the client. Never copy the client in a memo to your supervisor.

5 In writing to a superior, don't skip steps. Always address the memo to your immediate supervisor. To communicate with someone at a higher level within the organization, copy that individual in a memo addressed to your supervisor. This way, you can get the message across to the right person without seeming to disregard the organizational hierarchy.

6 Try to use brief, concrete examples to back up generalizations.

7 Keep the memo focused on the organizing idea. Don't introduce extra-

neous information. New points should be linked to the general purpose of the memo or made the subject of a separate memo.
8 If you request something, justify it with a reason or reasons.
9 Specify follow-up details. Place the burden on yourself for doing the follow-up.

The following model cases and those in subsequent chapters demonstrate how the skills and concepts described in the chapter can be applied. Although the particulars in these cases have been fictionalized for teaching purposes, the cases are representative of the kinds of situations which confront public relations practitioners daily. With these specially designed cases, we can take you step-by-step through the developmental process involved in a public relations effort and place emphasis on those aspects of PR practice that require the most attention.

Model Case Studies

DEFINING A PUBLIC RELATIONS FUNCTION IN-HOUSE

Many profit and nonprofit organizations handle all or most of their public relations in-house—that is, they do not continuously retain an outside PR consultant or agency to help them promote their product or service. Depending on the quality and scope of the communication activity these organizations require, they have to decide how to incorporate the public relations function into the organizational structure. Many large companies have done this very well, creating public relations (public affairs, or public information) departments which are as organized and efficient as any outside agency. Other organizations have been less ambitious and have created limited public relations departments which periodically have to rely on work done by outside agencies. Still others have neglected the PR function altogether, at best hiring one or two individuals to occupy an undefined communication position.

Where a full-scale public relations department is not in place, how can those structures be forged, decisions reached, and programs implemented? The answer generally lies in effective internal communication.

Jan North has been recently hired by Manning Company, a large leather goods store, to handle customer relations. Upon her arrival, she is told by Joel Freed, the company president, that her job will involve answering customer inquiries and handling related public relations responsibilities. The

PR responsibilities, however, are never specifically defined. After a month of interacting with customers and observing the daily operations of the business, North writes Freed the following memo:

Memorandum

To: Joel Freed
From: Jan North J.N.
Subject: Customer Inquiry Status Report and
         Public Relations Recommendations
Date: February 16, 198_

After a month at Manning, I have responded to 160 inquiries concerning merchandise. Of this total, 20 concerned merchandise which the customer wished to return or exchange. The remaining 140 involved particular requests for items which were out of stock. Of these, 71 specifically requested an item manufactured by Gia, our Italian supplier, and of the 71, 41 were interested in Gia's overnight satchel (which we retail at $40.49). Given the customer response and our unique buying option with Gia, we should perhaps consider the following:
- increasing our stock in Gia products, particularly the overnight satchel.
- conducting a marketing survey of customers who buy Gia products.
- initiating a publicity campaign aimed at potential Gia customers.

I'd like to make an appointment to discuss this with you at your convenience.

North's internal memo deals with what she was hired to do (respond to customer inquiries), then goes on to define the wider range of her responsibilities (marketing and PR). This memo, therefore, serves both as a progress report and as a proposed clarification of her job description. It combines the informational memo with the idea memo since it effectively uses information to back up ideas and ideas to interpret information.

DEVELOPING AN INTERNAL COMMUNICATION PROGRAM

In some sense, internal relations is merely external public relations practiced internally and is therefore dependent upon many of the PR methods discussed in later chapters of this book. However, the rationale behind internal relations programs is the recognition that they bring two levels of benefits to their organizations: They boost the morale of employees and enhance employee understanding of company goals and policies; this, in turn, positively affects overall operations and organizational image among external publics. Thus when the oil company, Chevron U.S.A., shut down part of one of its refineries in 1983, it notified employees first, explaining the rationale for the shut-down. Taking employee reaction seriously helped stem complaints and assured a more positive reception from the media.[3]

Lately internal relations has begun to take on a greater importance within companies concerned with fostering a sense of shared purpose and solidarity among geographically scattered workers. Where a company is large enough to have a fairly diversified product line, the need to assert internal consistency and unity may also be felt. And where acquisitions or mergers have taken place, there is often the need for internal communication programs to help tie the different companies to one corporate identity.

But while many large banks, utilities, and manufacturing companies have initiated sizeable internal or employee relations departments, small companies still tend to assign this function to the personnel department, where the employee relations effort may be limited to a few annual social events.

The need for internal relations is often motivated by a crisis within an organization or industry, or by a change in the nature of the work force. It may then be up to an in-house PR person or an outside PR consultant to recommend that an internal communication program be initiated or expanded.

Several years ago Jeff Donnelli was hired by Dye-Flex, an industrial dye company with a substantial blue collar work force, to handle public relations. Up until now, he has done a good job publicizing the company's products in the appropriate trade publications.

One morning, Fred Stein, the director of operations and the person Donnelli reports to, asks him to attend a meeting that afternoon. Stein wants to discuss the adverse publicity that a competitor has suffered when its workers complained to the press about their exposure to toxic chemicals. Although Dye-Flex has always taken precautions to protect its workers, Stein is worried that the adverse publicity its competitor received might escalate into a chemical company witch-hunt, and that Dye-Flex could suffer as a result. He tells Donnelli that other division directors will be at the meeting and are eager to hear his recommendations about how to handle the situation.

That morning, Donnelli reviews the issues involved and prepares the following memo:

Memorandum

To: Fred Stein
From: Jeff Donnelli
Subject: Analysis and Recommendation Concerning Dye-Flex Public Relations
Date: August 17, 198_

Dye-Flex has always had an excellent record in the area of worker safety and has never, to date, received adverse publicity. To assure that this situation

continues, our first priority lies with our employees. I recommend that we focus our initial public relations effort in the area of employee relations for the following reasons:
- The chemical industry is presently experiencing a negative public image, and this image, if not properly handled, could affect our employees' morale and trust.
- Recent publicity concerning a competitor's possibly hazardous working conditions could lead to fears among our employees and uninformed accusations against us.
- Employee communications is part of our company's social responsibility and will help us to anticipate problems before they occur.
- We have a good record; no one, as far as we know, has ever suffered any job-related health problems at Dye-Flex. We owe it to ourselves to let that fact be known to our employees.

For these reasons, Dye-Flex should consider expanding its employee relations program by developing the following:
- Employee Newsletter
- Regular Management-Staff Meetings
- Worker-Safety Review Teams
- Regular Social Activities (softball games, luncheons, special events)

I look forward to discussing these suggestions with you before this afternoon's meeting.

Donnelli recommends the expansion of Dye-Flex's employee relations program as a public relations measure in response to recent current events. His focus on employee relations reflects his understanding of the priorities of the situation: Adverse publicity of the kind Dye-Flex fears could be either encouraged or discouraged by Dye-Flex employees; a strong employee relations program would therefore be a good defensive measure.

Donnelli will eventually need to meet with the director of personnel, because the employee relations function technically falls within her division (he does not copy her in the memo because he first wants to get his supervisor's approval before informing her of his ideas). Traditionally, however, the company has limited its employee relations to an annual picnic, a Christmas party, and a retirement dinner. Donnelli feels that more social activities would improve company morale. He also feels that employees should be regularly kept informed of company policies and operations, be given the opportunity to ask questions about company procedures, and be encouraged to take an active role in assessing their work environment and making recommendations for improvement. The management-staff meetings and worker-safety review teams would permit this kind of participation.

Donnelli sees the employee newsletter as the backbone of the entire program. The newsletter would be published monthly and would keep workers abreast of all aspects of company life. It would include profiles of new workers or of workers who have performed noteworthy services, would explain new products and processes being developed by the company, and would announce policies and findings (summarizing the results of the management-staff meetings and worker-safety review teams). While he plans to edit the publication and write some of the more general articles himself, Donnelli intends that workers and managers submit articles and collect background material related to their divisions. In time, he hopes to develop a stable of "reporters" from the various divisions to write feature articles and to collect and edit their colleagues' material on a regular basis.*

GATHERING AND ORGANIZING BACKGROUND INFORMATION FOR CLIENT USE

The number of successfully operating public relations agencies has multiplied rapidly in the past several decades. The form these agencies take varies from small consulting agencies to large firms with more than a thousand employees and branch offices throughout the country or the world. Public relations agencies have also followed the trend toward specialization, and many agencies now handle such trade areas as electronics, health care, industrial or financial relations exclusively, or deal solely with issues such as corporate responsibility, crisis management, or cultural underwriting.

Whatever their size or shape, however, all successful agencies have one thing in common—the servicing of clients. And while junior-level people may have little direct contact with clients, their responsibilities involve gathering and organizing information which can serve as the basis for client-related decisions. The effective presentation of such information is, therefore, an important part of internal communication at an agency.

John Brody, a junior account executive in a large public relations firm, has been told by his supervisor, Ellen Norton, to collect background infor-

---

*Donnelli's proposal that the company initiate an employee newsletter is hardly original. *House organs* (the general term for in-house publications) have been around for a long time. In the past, such publications were primarily the tools of management, but in recent years, many companies have begun to utilize house organs as a forum for employee as well management opinions. Workers often write some of the articles themselves and respond to management policy with questions or suggestions. Moreover, many house organs now concern themselves with issues beyond the scope of the company. For example, the company president might write an editorial on foreign policy explaining its bearing on the industry; an employee might comment on economic trends as they have affected spending in her household.

Recently, a number of companies have instituted video newsletters which record on video tape the same kinds of information that would normally appear in a printed newsletter. These taped programs make it possible to capture typical moments in the workday or record important ceremonies, announcements, and personal interviews. The monthly or weekly programs are generally aired on monitors during lunch hours or coffee breaks.[4]

40 Acquiring the Basic Business Communication Skills: Communicating Internally

mation concerning possible locations for a news conference to be held for one of the agency's clients, Key, Inc., a small electronics firm. At the news conference, Key will be introducing a new personal computer with unique features, scheduled to go on the market in six months. Jill Mellinger, another junior account executive, has been asked to begin preparing media materials for the conference.

Brody immediately sits down and draws up the following list of the information he needs before beginning his research of possible conference sites:

Projected date of conference   Expected attendance
Format of conference   Client budget

Brody knows that the more specific information he can get relating to each of these points, the easier it will be for him to narrow the potential options and make a recommendation on a conference site. In speaking with Norton, he learns that the conference will be held sometime in April but that the exact date and the client budget are still up in the air. Meanwhile, Mellinger, who has been preparing the media background materials, informs him that the conference will feature a brief slide presentation followed by a speech delivered by the president of Key. She says that the media list consists of about 100 names but that it is still too early to tell how many will be interested in attending.

With this information in hand, Brody sets out to research available sites. Three days later, he completes the following memo:

Memorandum

To: Ellen Norton   cc: Jill Mellinger
From: John Brody
Subject: Possible locations for Key News Conference
Date: February 18, 198_

For April, two attractive, centrally situated hotels seem to offer appropriate sites for the Key news conference. These are
  • The Grand Hotel   Fourth floor conference rooms can be opened to accommodate anywhere from 30 to 100 people. Audio-visual equipment and special presentation set-ups available. In-house cocktail and catering services available ($2.75 per drink for open bar; cold hors-d'oeuvres at $1.50 per person; hot hors d'oeuvres from $2.50 to $5.00 per person). No room charge. Confirmation needed three weeks in advance of function. Room is attractively decorated, but ceilings are low.
  • The Empire Plaza   First floor conference rooms available. Each holds

approximately 50 people. Audio-visual and special presentation set-ups available. In-house cocktail and catering ($3.50 per drink; elaborate hot and cold hors d'oeuvres [one price] $5.50 per person). No room charge. Booking should be made within the month. Rooms are elegant and spacious.

Summary and Recommendation
The choice between these two options depends upon these three factors:
- How soon we can confirm the date of the conference
- The client budget
- The approximate number of media representatives expected to attend

Since we remain up in the air on these three factors, our best bet seems to be the Grand Hotel, which offers the most leeway in terms of advance confirmation, cost, and space.

Brody's memo is thorough and well-organized. He presents the two best options, enumerates the relevant data attached to each (size and location of rooms, presentation set-ups, cocktail and catering costs, room charge, confirmation deadlines, quality of rooms) and then makes a recommendation in light of the background information available to him. His comprehensive presentation of the two options also gives his supervisor the opportunity to evaluate his recommendation and discuss the determining factors with the client.

GETTING CREATIVE INPUT FROM COLLEAGUES

Part of effective internal communication is knowing how to take advantage of the experience and ideas of your colleagues. This means keeping informed of their interests and talents and being aware of their current projects as well as the projects they've worked on in the past. There are professional ways of getting colleagues to share their expertise with you. You can always invite a fellow worker out to lunch to discuss an idea or ask advice. Or, for more intensive input, you can call a brainstorming (or creative) session—a group meeting governed by special rules (or rather by a prescribed freedom from rules). One authority in the field lists the requirements for brainstorming as follows: (1) criticism is ruled out; (2) freewheeling of ideas is welcomed; (3) quantity of ideas rather than quality is emphasized; and (4) hitchhiking or modification of ideas is encouraged.[5]

Whatever the context in which you're seeking advice or creative input, it makes sense to prepare a memo prior to the meeting containing a background summary and list of the relevant points to be addressed. This will help clarify the subject in your own mind and bring a sharper focus to the subsequent discussion.

Joan Riess, an account executive at a small public relations agency, has been asked by her client, Sprint, Inc., a women's sports equipment and clothing manufacturer, to develop an idea for a sports event which it could sponsor. Two of Riess' colleagues at the agency, Sam Goldstein and Joe Pryor, have worked on sports accounts in the past, and a junior account executive, Gail Page, is a marathon runner and sports enthusiast. Riess decides to ask Goldstein, Pryor, and Page to attend a brainstorming session. She sends them the following memo:

Memorandum

To: Sam Goldstein, Joe Pryor, Gail Page   cc: Herbert Crull
From: Joan Riess JR
Subject: Creative Session for Sprint
Date: May 4, 198_

Sprint, Inc., a manufacturer of women's sports equipment and clothing, is thinking of underwriting a sports event like the L'Eggs mini-marathon or Virginia Slims tennis tournament. Its goal is to associate itself with the latest developments and trends in women's sports.

I'd like your input on the kind of event that would be best for Sprint to sponsor.

In mulling this over, you may want to keep the following in mind:
- Sprint markets its goods only on the East Coast.
- Sprint has a reputation for selling chic sports clothes and equipment (the non-sportsperson's sports apparel?)—a reputation about which it feels ambivalent.
- Sprint's chief executive office is keen on celebrities (TV and popular film stars especially).

Regarding the above points, I raise the following questions:
- What, if any, are the "hot" trends in women's sports on the East Coast?
- What are the "hard" vs. "soft" events in women's sports (for example, "soft" = a three-mile mini-marathon)? Would a "soft" event run counter to Sprint's desire to be in step with the latest trends in sports?
- What are the pros and cons of celebrity affiliation on an underwriting venture? Would a non-sports celebrity destroy the credibility of a sports event?

Can you brainstorm with me at 3:30 P.M. on Friday in the small conference room? Given your various backgrounds, your ideas would be valuable. R.S.V.P. Linda.

Riess' memo is informal but clear in specifying what she'd like to cover in the creative session. It saves time by providing relevant background and highlighting what she considers key questions. The questions are also ones which she feels her colleagues are particularly capable of addressing. After the brainstorming session, Riess will prepare a memo to Herbert Crull, her supervisor, summarizing the principal ideas of her colleagues. She and her supervisor will then discuss these ideas and perhaps come up with others before making a final recommendation to the client.

COMMUNICATIING WITH A CLIENT

A special kind of internal communication takes place between agency and client. We call this internal communication because an agency and a client should ideally act and think as partners. Of course, the relationship is complicated by the fact that not one, but two organizations are involved and that a client can decide at any time (barring contract stipulations) to terminate its relationship with an agency.

When a public relations agency is retained by an organization, someone in the communications division or some other designated official of the organization acts as liaison with the agency and facilitates the flow of information. This individual supplies the background material the agency needs, and grants or obtains approval for the implementation of agency ideas.

Before information leaves an agency and reaches the public on behalf of a client, it passes through a fairly standard developmental process. The client first supplies "raw" data to the agency on a product, a service or an issue; the agency, after consultation with the client, then organizes the information into a tentative form and sends a draft for review to the client; finally, the client sends the draft back to the agency in approved final form or in a form which requires more work and still another review by the client. The achievement of the final form can be quick and painless or long an agonizing, depending upon the nature of the material, the client's temperament and sense of what it wants, and the degree of judgment and care exercised by the agency.

John Bergen is director of communications for the National Society of Civil Engineers (NSCE). The Society has recently hired a public relations agency to help explain its accomplishments to the general public. (Bergen felt that his internal department was too technically oriented to do this well.) The agency assigns Gwendolyn Mason to serve as account executive on NSCE and to work with Bergen in promoting the organization. It is agreed that Bergen will alert Mason to newsworthy events connected with NSCE and supply her with the necessary background information. Mason's job will be to write press releases, backgrounders, and feature articles, and set up interviews and news conferences on behalf of NSCE.

One day, Bergen calls Mason to set up a lunch date. He wants to discuss publicity for NSCE's annual convention to be held in six months in Chicago. The convention is a combination trade fair and technical symposium at which members from all over the country deliver papers on subjects of topical concern to the profession.

To prepare for their meeting, Mason drafts the following memo:

Memorandum

To: John Bergen
From: Gwendolyn Mason *GM*
Subject: NSCE Annual Convention
Date: July 6, 198_

cc: John Paine

There are a number of ways we can go about publicizing NSCE's upcoming annual convention. These include
- developing a general news release on the convention for trade and consumer publications;
- developing feature releases on papers of interest to be delivered at the convention (geared to both trade and consumer publications);
- seeking personal interviews for notable speakers (in trade and consumer publications and on radio and TV talk shows);
- seeking radio and TV coverage of events at the convention that lend themselves to audio and/or visual presentation.

In order to arrange for the above, we need:
- biographies of notable speakers;
- abstracts or advance copies of papers to be delivered;
- a list of noteworthy demonstrations and exhibitions to be featured at the convention;
- photos of speakers, demonstrations, new technology relevant to the presentations, etc.;
- a convention schedule.

Advance copies of the papers are our first order of business, since it will take weeks to review them and develop feature articles and ideas. Let's discuss a timetable for gathering materials at our Friday lunch meeting.

As Mason's memo makes clear, doing a good job depends on Bergen's ability and willingness to supply her with the necessary background materials. First, she will need advance copies of the papers to be delivered at the convention. Once she has these in hand, she will want to sit down with Bergen and discuss which ones might make good feature stories. Next, she will want to call the authors of the papers themselves for clarification and comment. A draft of the feature releases will then be sent to the authors, to Bergen, and (possibly) to other officials at NSCE for review. Mason knows that turning a technical paper into a feature release (a common method by which professional associations gain publicity for themselves) may take several months and may involve numerous drafts before satisfying all the parties concerned (see the discussion of the press release in Chapter 5).

Note that Mason has copied John Paine, her supervisor at the agency. This is standard practice. No document from an account executive should be mailed to the client without also being routed to the account executive's supervisor within the agency. This assures that agency management is kept informed about how an account is being handled. If the correspondence is in any way controversial, it should first be approved by the supervisor before being mailed to the client.

EXERCISES

Test Your Judgment

List the internal communication method or methods you would use in each of the following situations. In the case of a memo, note to whom the memo would be addressed and who would be copied.

1 You want to request a larger budget for a project you're working on.

2 You want to thank a colleague for help on a project.

3 You want to request an explanation for a technical process used in your company.

4 You want to recommend a new promotional idea to your client.

5 You want to get input from your colleagues on a new logo for your client.

6 You want to do a quick check with your sales department on the cost of a company product.

PR Workshop

1 As a warm-up to brainstorming, spend one minute compiling a list of uses for the paper clip. Make the list as long as you can by using your imag-

ination. Then read your list aloud and discuss with classmates how individual responses reflect thinking patterns and creativity.

2   Your instructor will divide the class into four- or five-member groups and will give each group a tea bag to carefully examine. You will then be instructed to spend 20 minutes in a brainstorming session with your group in which you try to come up with an alternative function for the tea bag. At the outset, appoint a group leader to help steer toward a consensus. At the end of the session, this individual should make a formal presentation to the class, announcing the group's final recommendation and the rationale for this recommendation. (Be sure to appoint a secretary to keep a record of the proceedings.)

PR Case Studies

1   You are the assistant director of Mercy Medical Center, a private hospital in an urban area. Although Mercy has one of the best cardiac care units in the region and has just completed a new pediatric facility, it has nonetheless been losing patients over the past several years to nearby suburban hospitals. In addition, the nursing staff at Mercy has been threatening a strike for six months. The nurses want a salary increase which the hospital says it can't afford at the present time.

Write a memo to the hospital director, Harvey White, suggesting that a public relations department be created to help the hospital deal with its problems. Explain why you think such a department is needed and what role you think it should perform.

2   You are an account executive at a public relations agency and have been assigned to handle the Maria Saunders account. Maria Saunders, Inc. is a major cosmetics company which has decided to launch its new perfume, Sultry, by underwriting a television special on the history of fragrance. Your agency has been retained to help promote the special.

Write a memo to your liaison at the company, Jane Ross, outlining the background materials you will need in order to begin planning the promotion. (Your supervisor at the agency is Ellen Riley.)

3   You are an account executive at a public relations firm which handles Secure, Inc., a tampon manufacturer. The firm has recently discovered that the Centers for Disease Control in Atlanta has linked tampon use to a rare disease called Toxic Shock Syndrome (T.S.S.).

Read the following article that appeared in the *New York Times*.[6] Then prepare a memo to your supervisor at the agency (Harold Dillon) outlining what you judge to be relevant information about T.S.S. as it relates to the tampon industry and your client. After presenting the information, give your opinion as to whether or not this is a public relations problem.

EXHIBIT 2-1 Tampons Are Linked to a Rare Disease. (Reprinted by permission of The Associated Press.)

ATLANTA, June 27 (AP)—The use of tampons has been linked to a rare disease called toxic shock syndrome that primarily affects young women, national health officials said today, but preliminary studies show no reason for most women to discontinue tampon use.

The Center [sic] for Disease Control here reported the results of three studies of the syndrome, a sometimes fatal disease characterized by high fever, vomiting, diarrhea, a sunburnlike rash and a rapid drop in blood pressure which frequently results in shock.

Ninety-three women who had the disease were included in the three studies, which were conducted by Federal and state health officials in Wisconsin and Utah. All but one of the women regularly used tampons, officials at the center said in their report.

Since 1978, 128 cases of toxic shock syndrome have been reported, with 10 resulting in death, the report said. Most cases, it said, occur in women under 25, and more than 90 percent began during the menstrual period. But a small number of cases have been identified in men.

Bacterium Is Suspected

Dr. Kathryn Shands, an epidemiologist with the center, said researchers had not determined exactly how tampon use was related to the disease. Earlier studies have indicated that the syndrome may be caused by a toxin associated with Staphylococcus aureus, a common bacterium that causes pus to form in boils and abcesses, the report said.

If such a toxin is the cause, it said, "the use of tampons might favor growth of the bacterium in the vagina or absorption of the toxin from the vagina or uterus—but these possibilities have not been investigated."

Future tests are to be conducted in consultation with the Food and Drug Administration, the report added.

Dr. Shands said about 50 million American women use tampons, but toxic shock syndrome occurs in only about three of 100,000 menstruating women each year.

Discontinuance Not Proposed

"Because we expect only a small number of women to get the disease, we are suggesting that women not discontinue tampon use unless they have had toxic shock syndrome already," she said.

The center's report added, however, that women "who wish to decrease their small risk of T.S.S. may choose to use tampons during only part of their menstrual period or to use napkins or minipads instead."

Women who have had the disease should refrain from using tampons for at least several menstrual cycles after their illness, Dr. Shands said. Antibiotics can be used to reduce the risk of recurrence.

> Dr. Shands said 2 to 15 percent of American women may carry the Staphylococcus aureus bacterium in their bodies, but "we don't know why some of them get sick and some don't."
> Health officials do not recommend testing for the bacterium unless a woman has shown symptoms of toxic shock syndrome, she said. Women who believe they may have the symptoms should consult a physician.
>
> **Industry Helping Studies**
>
> No particular brand of tampon has been associated with the disease, the center said.
> Representatives of the tampon industry noted that toxic shock syndrome is rare and said they were cooperating with the center's studies.
> "We have not encountered the illness at any time during more than 40 years of clinical testing of our product, so we have no direct knowledge of the illness," said Robert L. DeSanti, executive vice president of Tampax Inc. of Lake Success, N.Y., which has a 40 percent to 50 percent share of the market in tampon products.

NOTES

1. See Ernest G. Bormann, *Discussion and Group Methods: Theory and Practice* (New York: Harper & Row, 1969).
2. See William R. Thierfelder, III, "The Misused Memo: Diagnosis and Treatment," *Journal of Technical Writing and Communication*, 14 (1984), 155–62.
3. Dale E. Basye, "Communicating a Cutback," *Public Relations Journal*, 40 (February 1984), 34–36.
4. See Jeffrey M. Goldstein, "Employees in the Picture," *Public Relations Journal*, 39 (March 1983), 26–27.
5. Alex Osborn, *Applied Imagination*, 3rd edition (New York: Charles Scribner's Sons, 1979).
6. *New York Times*, June 28, 1980, sec. 1, p. 17.

3

Doing Research and Evaluation for a PR Program

It has been argued that every field must undergo a developmental process in which instinct and guesswork are replaced by more rigorous, scientific thinking. Edward J. Robinson maintains that public relations is presently experiencing this evolution, moving out of what he calls its "individualistic stage" and into the "scientifically derived knowledge stage."[1] Indeed, we see evidence of this evolution when we examine the status of public relations research. Data retrieval systems now available on computers have made library research on client-related issues much easier and more comprehensive. Sophisticated statistical techniques as well as new theories of individual psychology and group behavior have helped public relations survey research become a more refined and reliable tool. But the most important change has been in the attitude of practitioners themselves who now take PR research more seriously and use it more creatively.[2]

RESEARCH AS THE GROUNDWORK FOR A PUBLIC RELATIONS PROGRAM

For a public relations program to be effective, it must be based on sound objectives, directed at the right audience, and presented in a fashion that appeals to that audience. Identifying and acquiring a thorough understanding of a client's *PR objectives*, *target audience*, and *PR message* are therefore important goals of public relations research as the groundwork for preparing a public relations program. And since these variables are interconnected, clarifying one variable can help clarify the other two* (see Figure 3-1).

PR objectives are objectives relating to the *communication* needs of a client. This is largely misunderstood. Management officials may seem to know what their PR objectives are, but they are not always familiar enough with the rationale of public relations thinking to be able to judge these objectives accurately. In one instance, for example, a company equated its PR objectives with its organizational objectives, which were to increase sales for the next year. But further research revealed that a genuine PR objective resided in the need to create a better rapport between the company and the local community. Although the problem of poor community relations wasn't directly affecting sales, it was serving to weaken the company's image, thereby making it less attractive to customers, distributors, and shareholders. In another case, an owner of a teen clothing boutique thought that her PR objectives should simply involve making her shop better known among teenagers in the area. She failed to take into account the high price of her clothes relative to most clothes for teenagers. More than visibility, her PR objectives should have been to develop and promote a quality image which would help distinguish her product from the competition and make her potential customers feel it was worthwhile paying a little extra for clothes.

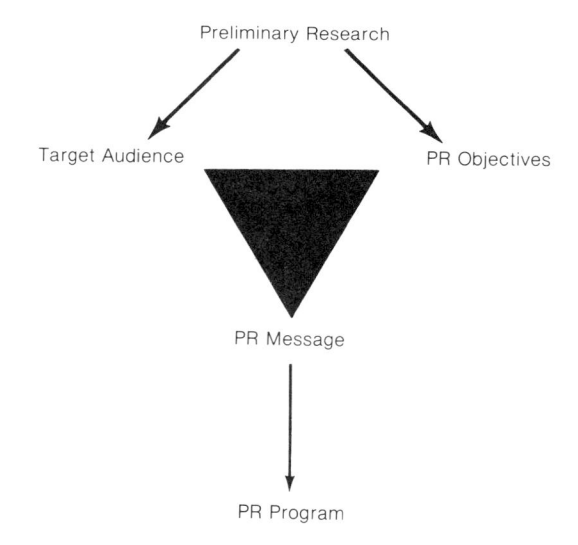

FIGURE 3-1 Groundwork for Preparing a PR Program

*A PR message can generally be deduced from a knowledge of the PR objectives and the target audience, although sometimes research is done to determine which of several potential PR messages would be most effective.

A more dramatic example of how an incorrectly conceived PR objective can have serious repercussions is the well-known case of the Coca-Cola company's launching of a new Coca-Cola taste. The company had directed its campaign around the PR objective of communicating to the public that *new Coke tastes better than old Coke*. However, it failed to realize that people were emotionally attached to the traditional Coca-Cola taste. The PR objective should have been to convince the public that *a change in taste is desirable*. Had the company identified its true PR objective, it may never have introduced the new Coke at all.

Clearly, to develop a public relations campaign around an incorrect or inadequate PR objective is to waste time and money. This is why some form of preliminary research in this area is almost always necessary. By interviewing management and employees, reviewing sales and membership records, and monitoring the economic climate and social trends within which an organization operates, these objectives can be brought into focus. It is also possible to clarify your PR objectives through a better understanding of your target audience.

Since public relations is, by definition, concerned with maintaining an ongoing dialogue between an organization and its target publics, identifying and understanding the target audience is crucial to any public relations effort. This is especially true since the definition of "audience" in public relations has expanded to include not only external publics (customers, media, legislators, and so on), but also internal publics (employees, shareholders, members). Since an organization's internal and external publics affect virtually all aspects of a PR program, they are probably the most important source of information in the research phase of developing the program. Here are some key questions about your audience that you should be able to answer before embarking on the development of a program:

1. Who are the key publics now being reached by my client?
2. Which publics should be reached and aren't currently being reached?
3. What are the interests and needs of these various publics?
4. How do they perceive my client's product, service, organization, or related issue?

Where you lack answers to these questions, a variety of research tools can help you gather the necessary information.

Informal Surveys and In-Depth Interviews

In the case of many small organizations, the scope of operations may be so limited and the budget allotment so small that formal research hardly seems a practical option. Yet, in preparing a program for such organizations, some kind of informal research is nonetheless advisable since management is often too close to the situation to see things clearly and may be operating with false, distorted, or outdated perceptions about who its publics are and what they need.

You can begin research in such cases by reviewing sales or membership records and engaging in discussions with management. To supplement this information, informal surveys can be done on issues which appear to need clarification. This may involve interviewing and/or distributing questionnaires to employees, clientele, general consumers, local opinion leaders, and the media.

Surveying of this kind is not scientific. It is a combination of what Edward Robinson calls "accidental" and "purposive"; that is, it chooses respondents according to subjective criteria and/or as they turn up. Yet, it makes sense if the organization's scope of operations is limited, and if you have a general idea of who its target audience is and simply want to learn more about that audience.

Even in informal surveys, however, you should frame the survey questions so that they can be analyzed quickly and consistently. Good questionnaires generally contain three kinds of questions: *dichotomous* (true/false; yes-no), *multiple-choice*, and *open-ended* (requiring the respondent to explain something or give an opinion). Dichotomous and multiple-choice questions can be easily collated and should make up the bulk of the questionnaire, but several open-ended questions should also be included, preferably toward the end of the questionnaire for easy reference. Although the answers to open-ended questions can't be easily tallied, they can give insight into the personality of your audience and can sometimes provide fresh ideas.

Personal in-depth interviews can also be an important source of data. Unlike informal surveys where there is some attempt at gathering *quantitative* information, in-depth interviews supply essentially *qualitative* information—information which involves a "quality" relationship to the subject matter rather than a statistical, or "quantity," relationship. Interviews can be conducted over the phone or face to face. Though you may want to use a prepared questionnaire as a starting point, you will also want to probe more deeply into the attitudes, opinions, and suggestions of your subject. The most free-form interviews, called *elite* interviews, give the interviewee more or less free reign in defining the interview situation and shaping the direction of the discussion.[3] Elite interviews can be helpful when you aren't precisely sure what you want to find out, or if you are simply interested in getting new ideas and insights about your client. When your objectives are more clear-cut, you may want to maintain more control over the points discussed. (This will assure more economical use of time and will provide you with responses which are easier to evaluate.) The best personal interviewers combine control with flexibility. They are able to set a direction for the interview and yet are willing to pursue a new avenue of questioning should it appear promising.

Although one-on-one interviewing is more widely used, interviewing of *focus groups* is also a popular form of qualitative research. Here the group dynamic can be helpful in gaining insight into how external publics react as groups to issues involving your client. Sometimes focus groups can function like brainstorming sessions, helping organizations come up with new ideas for promotions or themes. In the case of Connecticut General Life Insurance Company, for example, focus groups drawn from the client's target markets selected the theme "innovation" from among a number of proposed themes. On the basis of this recommendation the company went on to use the theme as the foundation for a corporate identity campaign.[4]

In research which involves interviewing (whether of individuals or of groups), it is important to avoid wording questions to reflect an implicit bias. Instead of "Is nuclear power the only energy option for the future?" ask, "What do you think is the major form of energy for the future?" Be aware of more subtle types of manipulation as well. It is possible, for example, to unconsciously indicate that an answer is preferred through your tone of voice or manner. To guard against such interviewing errors which can "pollute" results, practice your interviewing technique with colleagues who can point out inconsistencies and help objectify your style.

Finally, it's a good idea to tape the personal or group interview, since this frees you from note-taking and allows you to interact better with respondents. It also provides an exact record of the transaction, which can be helpful if you wish to incorporate direct quotation into your summary of results. However, always ask the respondent if he or she is willing to have the session taped before you begin.

Public Relations Opinion Audits

In the case of larger organizations which need to gain a more detailed understanding of their target publics, or of organizations which know little or nothing about their target audience, more formal, scientific research may be called for. In his discussion of various research methods, Kenneth R. Hoover offers a valuable distinction between scientific and nonscientific research. A nonscientific study, he explains, is one in which "the author expresses values, develops a general thesis, examines relevant examples, and states the conclusions." On the other hand, in a scientific study, "the author states his or her values, forms hypotheses, lays out a testing procedure, carefully selects and discusses measurements, produces a specific result, and relates this to the hypothesis."[5] While nonscientific research can be carried on by practitioners themselves, scientific research demands the assistance of experts who can at least recommend an appropriate testing procedure and perform the basic statistical analysis.

In some organizations, formal marketing studies have already been done for sales or other operations purposes. These should, of course, be consulted, but remember that this information often has a focus which does not reflect a communications perspective. Where such a perspective is needed, a *public relations opinion audit* (also known as a *communications audit*) can be done. This is a scientific survey done with the concepts of public relations (as opposed to sales or fund raising) in mind. Unlike market research, a communications audit is less interested in the respondents' attitude toward specific products and services and more interested in their response to general questions involving communication. Such questions might include the following:

How well known is the product, service, or organization?
How clear and available is the literature on the product or service?
How quickly does the organization respond to media requests?
How clearly do employees and external publics understand corporate goals?

Surveys designed to answer these questions are called communications audits because (1) they zero in on communications-related issues, and (2) they are intended for internal use; that is, they supply PR practitioners with the information they need to plan programs. The insights gathered from these audits are often summarized in the program itself as a means of justifying the choice of a particular methodology or implementation tool. Public relations opinion audits tend to be used when communications problems or issues are of immediate concern to organizations; however, some practitioners see the value of carrying out these studies on a regular or ongoing basis in order to monitor issues which could potentially affect their organizations in the future[6] (see Chapter 8).

Two variations on the communications audit which have become particularly popular in recent years are the *identity audit* and the *social responsibility audit*. Both audits are generally, though not always, performed for large, profit-making organizations which are concerned about the identities they project to their target publics. The identity audit seeks to understand how a company is misperceived and to clarify the identity which it *should* project. Once this information has been determined, it becomes possible to prepare an *identity program* (or *image campaign*), which promotes an accurate and clearly defined corporate identity. (See the discussion of developing a PR program to clarify a client's identity in the Model Case Study in Chapter 4.) The social responsibility audit seeks information about corporate identity as it specifically relates to the company's social role. It will address such questions as

Is the company seen as a good corporate citizen?
Is the public aware of the corporation's sponsorship of social programs and services?
What other social programs and services would be worth sponsoring?

CONSTRUCTING THE AUDIT

Many large public relations agencies and corporations have their own research departments which are capable of constructing and administering public opinion audits of any size and complexity. But smaller agencies and organizations which operate without an ongoing research budget are not likely to have professional researchers on staff and must bring in independent consultants to do this work when necessary.[7] To cut costs, these organizations will often use research consultants to perform the basic technical tasks of designing and administering the questionnaire, constructing the random sample, and collating responses, while the organizations will handle the printing and mailing of materials and will write the summary and interpretation of statistical findings themselves.

Whether or not you take part in the research process directly, you should know the steps to be followed so you can be sure the job is performed according to proper scientific method and reflects an understanding of public relations concepts. Knowing these basic steps can also give you a better sense of where your input would be helpful or would save your client money. The following is a standard sequence of operations in the professional preparation of a communications audit. (The specific areas where the PR practitioner can contribute have been designated.)

The Identification of Information Needed Before embarking on a communications audit, it is obviously important to decide what you want to know. As a PR practitioner, you should have a clear idea of the data you need to lay the groundwork for your PR program. This information will probably fall under one or more of the three components which serve as the backbone for the program: PR objectives, target audience, and PR message. In discussion with the research consultant, your needs will be matched to an appropriate research format.

The Identification of the Audience from Which a Sample Will Be Taken Though you may not know the specific publics you wish to reach, you can usually describe the general audience (called the *universe*) within which these publics will fall. Professional researchers say that the size of the sample need not be very large. A sample of 500 to 1,000 people can be enough to give a fairly accurate gauge of the opinions of a target audience of 100,000 or more. More important, however, is that the sample be properly chosen, which is why its construction should be left in the hands of a professional researcher. He or she will also determine the kind of sample that is best suited to your audit. An *area sample*, for example, randomly chooses a certain number of people within a given zip code area; a *quota sample* chooses people from a designated group according to the percentage that they are considered to be important to your organization. The professional researcher should, of course, explain the rationale for the sampling method chosen.

The Development of a Questionnaire   While you will want to assist in the construction and review of the questionnaire, the actual wording and arrangement of questions should be done by a professional who has experience in framing questions which are objectively and economically worded and in sequencing them in the most logical fashion. It is common for several versions of the questionnaire to be written, each with a set of questions specifically tailored to a target group being surveyed. Thus, an audit directed at an internal and an external audience might be written in at least two versions. The portion of the audit directed at employees might include a set of questions pertaining to the communications hierarchy within the organization. The portion of the audit directed at the media would likely include questions about how well company representatives respond to requests for information. An area of overlap might be a set of questions relating to the way the company communicated a major change in its corporate policy, since this would be relevant to both internal and external audiences.

The Pretesting of the Questionnaire   The questionnaire should be administered in a preliminary trial to a small sample group. Pretesting can help determine omissions and redundancies in the questionnaire so that these can be corrected before the larger sample is surveyed.

The Administration of the Questionnaire   Surveys may be administered through the mail, over the telephone, or in face-to-face interviews. Often a combination of methods is used with face-to-face, in-depth interviews as open-ended supplements to the close-ended questions administered by mail or phone. Money can be saved by having questionnaires printed and mailed through your client's organization rather than through the research firm.

The Analysis of Data and Preparation of a Final Report   While the statistical analysis of the audit should be left to the professional, you may want to prepare the interpretive report on the findings yourself. This involves writing a summary in which you highlight important statistics and place them in a context which provides insight into what the organization is doing or should do. Whether or not you write the report yourself, you should certainly review the answers to open-ended questions, since these can offer important insights into your target audience.

Additional Research

Communications audits can provide your client organization with valuable information if it wants to initiate a public relations program or improve upon an existing public relations program. But the information gained from such studies is necessarily limited to the target audience reflected by the survey sample. To place this information in context, it is important to gain a larger picture of the industry or field of which your client is a part and to understand the economic climate in general. Indeed, you should try to maintain a sense of this larger picture at all times so that you are not taken off guard should an event occur that either directly or indirectly affects your client or your client's industry (see Chapter 8).

To keep abreast of social and economic trends, begin by reading at least one good newspaper a day. In most New York City public relations agencies, account executives spend an hour or more in the morning thoroughly perusing the *New York Times* and the *Wall Street Journal*. In other cities, the local paper often supplements at least one of these two papers. In addition to newspapers (which tell what happened but don't trace economic and social trends), you should consult the books and periodicals which come out regularly and which attempt to place news events in some kind of context. (John Naisbitt's *Megatrends* and *Megatrends Newsletter* are good examples of trend analysis.) To keep up to date on particular trends in your client's industry, also review the trade and special interest publications relating to that industry. You may be surprised by how many of these there are.* If your organization doesn't subscribe to at least some of these key publications, suggest to your supervisor that it do so. Reading the trade publications regularly, becoming familiar with the kinds of articles that run in them and with the reporters who write for them will also serve you well when it comes time for you to "place" stories about your client (see Chapter 5).

If you are interested in gaining access to information on a specific event, individual, or issue, a library search of the topic may be in order. As more and more organizations become computerized, practitioners have gained access to *on-line data bases* which can greatly facilitate this research. On-line data retrieval systems are computerized card catalogs and periodical indexes which a user can "call up" by means of a modem and appropriate communications software. This way, you can get bibliographical materials and, in some cases, abstracts (summaries of articles) and even full transcripts in a matter of seconds.

The key to using data bases, besides mastering the simple commands of the machine and the vendor, is to draw up a list of "key words" relevant to

---

*To find out what these publications are, check the *Bacon's Publicity Checkers* or *N. W. Ayer's Directories*, as well as any periodical indexes which might contain relevant listings.

the topic you are searching and to feed these to the computer using the appropriate syntax. Thus by typing out on line one (1:)*

1: nuclear adj power adj plants and accidents

you would turn up bibliographical information (author, title of article or book, and/or number of volume, issue, date of publication, and page numbers). Note that line syntax employs *adj* (adjacent) to connect works that make up one term (nuclear power plants) and *and* to connect two independent terms. (Specific syntax can vary, but the concept remains essentially the same for all data base systems.) Here, the computer will provide bibliographical information in that area in which articles dealing with nuclear power plants overlap with articles dealing with accidents. The result: articles about all accidents relating to nuclear power plants. If you wished to limit your search further—for instance, to investigate nuclear power plant accidents in one particular year—you would simply add the year as a new term to the search:

2: nuclear adj power adj plants and accidents and 1979

or, more simply:

2: 1 and 1979

where "1" refers to the information in line one (1:).

Of course, for the data base to be an effective tool, it must contain the kind of information your organization can use. For organizations which need to have access to specialized books and periodicals, it becomes important to carefully review the data bases offered by different vendors before making a commitment to a particular service.

RESEARCH FOR PUBLICATION: VISIBILITY STUDIES

Another kind of research which has become a popular public relations tool in recent years is the *visibility study* (also called the *public issues study*) in which research results are no longer an internal resource but become the centerpiece of the PR program. Organizations sponsor visibility studies in order to generate research which is newsworthy and can be publicized.

According to Peter Finn, chairman of Research & Forecasts, N.Y.C., the best visibility studies are the most ambitious. The key is to choose an issue that is both topical and important which would be of interest to the sponsor's target publics.[9] Thus, a pharmaceutical company concerned with developing its health-care products market might choose to sponsor a visibility study

---

*The syntax given in this example is used by BRS, a popular vendor. Other vendors may use a slightly different syntax, but follow the same general principles. DIALOG and Mead Data Central are two other popular services which are well equipped with data bases for business-related research.[8]

which surveys the public's perception of health care. The statistics derived from the study would be analyzed by professional researchers, and press releases and feature articles would be developed based on the results. If the figures were dramatic enough, the complete survey with supporting interpretive material could be published in book form.

A visibility study can also take the form of an in-depth investigation on an issue of public interest conducted by a panel of experts. These research panels prepare formal reports, or *white papers*, from their findings, which can be made available to the media. Again, a white paper allows a sponsoring organization to have its name linked with the research results and gain publicity for itself.

For visibility studies to have credibility with the media and the public, they must be performed by professionals who have no vested interest in the outcome. Surveys must be conducted according to scientific research methods, and white paper panels must be made up of acknowledged experts in the subjects under investigation.

When organizations cannot afford full-scale visibility studies, *omnibus* (also called *caravan*) questions offer an alternative. These are questions which clients add on to periodic national surveys performed by independent research firms. The results, if interesting enough, can be publicized in conjunction with the sponsor organization in the same way that visibility studies are publicized. (Professional researchers can help you frame questions which are likely to produce newsworthy results.) In some cases, omnibus questions also serve to supplement communications audits by providing information about public response to an issue, a product, or an event, which can be useful for internal planning purposes.

EVALUATION OF A PUBLIC RELATIONS PROGRAM

An activity which is a crucial part of public relations practice is the evaluation of a PR program during its implementation or after its completion. Evaluative reports are usually written for one or more of the following reasons:

1 To tell clients what they're getting for their money.
2 To justify the need to expand a program beyond its present scope.
3 To explain the need to shift the focus or direction of a program.

In the case of the second two reasons above, evaluation of a PR program can actually serve as preliminary research to determine a *revised* target audience and *revised* PR objectives leading to a *revised* PR message, which can in turn serve as the foundation for a *revised* PR program. This process, by which

60 Doing Research and Evaluation for a PR Program

evaluation of an existing program leads to the development of a revised program, can be repeated indefinitely (see Figure 3-2).

There are two kinds of progress which may be subject to evaluation in public relations practice: the *level of exposure* and the *level of reaction to exposure*.

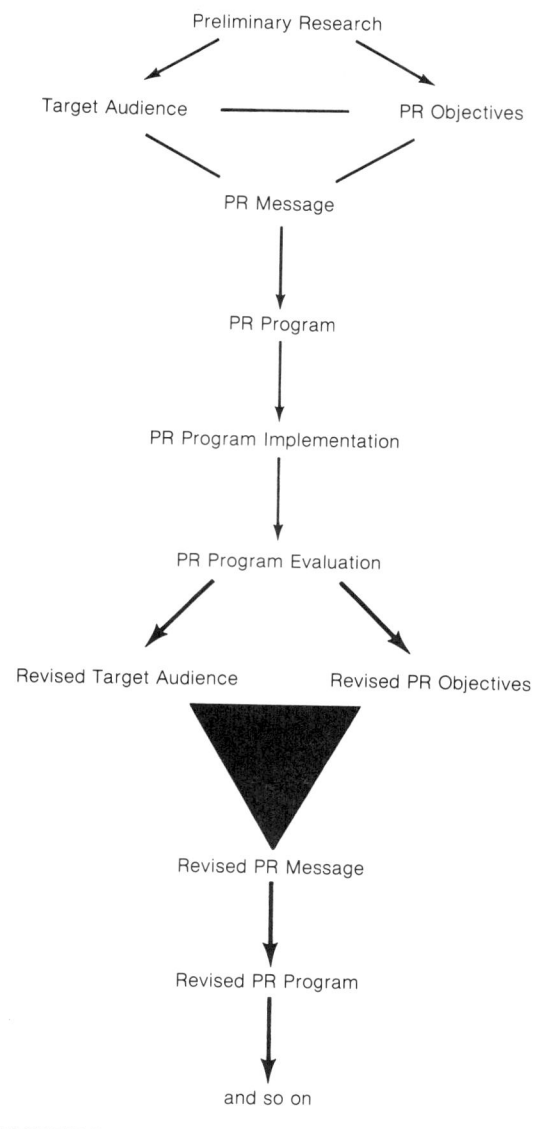

FIGURE 3-2 Development of a Revised PR Program

Level of Exposure

Level of exposure measurement involves the enumeration and evaluation of the various activities performed for a client. Some clients—those who don't really understand public relations objectives—insist on measuring the level of exposure purely in terms of the number of stories which have been generated in the media on their behalf. More sophisticated clients understand that the number of placements alone is no indication of the success or failure of a PR effort. Instead, they will expect that some form of *content analysis* be done—that is, that editorial placements be evaluated for the *kinds* of messages they contain.[10] Criteria for evaluating messages can be any that you decide are important. These might include the amount of positive commentary, the amount of critical commentary, or the number of times the client is mentioned in a particular context.* The ultimate goal of the analysis should always be the same—to determine whether or not the message addresses the correct publics and will assist in the accomplishment of the client's larger PR objectives. Content analysis should also be used to evaluate outgoing messages such as press releases, speeches, and brochures, since if such messages conform to desired content criteria, there is a better chance that media placements will reflect these same criteria.†

Where level of exposure is a high priority, it is a good idea to retain a clipping service to monitor placements. Services are usually retained separately for print and electronic media. In the case of the electronic media, services will send full transcripts of programs or segments of programs which you have asked them to monitor. Print clipping services will supply you with monthly clippings of articles that fall within a predetermined subject area. In retaining a print clipping service you need to specify what word or words should be monitored. (Some practitioners want to receive only stories which contain the client's name; others want all stories dealing with an event, a product, a service, or an industry.) By designating a more general term or subject area, you pay more for the service, but you have the advantage of being able to follow trends in a particular field and keep track of a competitor's activities as well as collect stories on your client.

A relatively recent means of measuring the level of exposure "scientifically" is through computerized publicity tracking. By feeding a computer the kinds of editorial placements made on behalf of a client, an *overall exposure index*

---

*You can perform an informal content analysis of limited scope yourself, but a more comprehensive and statistically sophisticated analysis generally requires the assistance of an outside research firm or academic consultant.

†Along with content analysis, outgoing messages should also be evaluated for *readability*. There are a number of methods for evaluating readability based on formulas for calculating such variables as the average number of syllables per word and words per sentence. (The Flesch Readability Formula is probably the best known.) However, we feel that asking someone representative of your target audience to read over a document and then discuss its content with you is the easiest and most effective way of evaluating readability.

and an *overall value index* are estimated. One figure represents the amount of visibility in the media, the other offers a kind of content analysis in that it represents how often the desired message is present in the placements.

Level of Reaction to Exposure

To evaluate the other area crucial to a PR effort—the level of reaction to exposure—the practitioner must find a way to measure how the target public has perceived and reacted to the activities performed on the client's behalf. For some organizations, an indication of audience reaction can be gathered by simply checking sales or membership figures. If there is an appreciable improvement in such figures that seems to parallel the public relations effort, you can argue that the program has made the difference. When figures are dramatic, this can be a convincing argument. But since public relations doesn't generally affect the bottom line directly or right away, you may not have the luxury of pointing to increased sales or membership.

A more reliable way of measuring audience reaction to a program is by performing an opinion audit for evaluation purposes. This can measure public opinion during or after a program and ascertain whether it is on course or has successfully communicated what was intended. An audit performed at the completion of a program is especially effective when an audit has been done prior to the program's implementation. This makes it possible to compare the results and statistically measure the change in public opinion.

Model Case Studies

PERFORMING INFORMAL SURVEY RESEARCH FOR A SMALL ORGANIZATION

For a small organization that has ready access to its target audience, much can be learned simply by engaging in exploratory interviews with the organization's management, customers, members, employees, and others. Questionnaires can also be distributed through direct mail, at a reception area, counter, nearby shopping mall, or as part of advertisements in local newspapers and magazines. The data derived from such surveys can help reinforce what you already suspect about the organization or bring to light information that you may have dismissed or overlooked. Such informal research can also help you clarify and sort out your client's priorities and get back in touch with the needs of the target audience. At the end of your research you should be able to describe the PR objectives, target audience, and PR message on which a subsequent PR program should be based.

Karen Daly has recently graduated from college and returned to her hometown to look for a job in public relations. Less than a week after her return, she receives a call from Jeff Hanson, the owner of Delight Bakery. Hanson had gone to school with Daly's brother and had heard that she was home looking for work in PR. He offers her a job—to develop a promotional program for his bakery which has been steadily losing business in the past few months, ever since Fair Mart Supermarket opened across the street. Hanson explains that formerly most of the bakery's shoppers had been homemakers, many of whom now seem to be buying their baked goods, along with the rest of the family groceries, in the supermarket. He is afraid that the bakery, which has been in his family for two generations, will not survive if sales continue to decline.

Offering Daly an admittedly low base salary, Hanson promises that he'll provide a substantial bonus if business starts to improve. Daly, who has never turned down a challenging opportunity and who relishes the chance to work on her own, accepts the offer.

Although Hanson has asked Daly to draw up a program immediately, Daly objects. She insists that she would not feel comfortable writing a program for a business with which she is unfamiliar without first engaging in some informal research. She assigns a week to this activity during which time she checks sales records for the past six months and holds a series of informal discussions with Hanson and with the employees in the shop. She asks about the variety of baked goods available, the relative popularity of different items, the store hours and the possibility of changing them, the kinds of clientele and their breakdown, and the kind of publicity or advertisement the store engages in, if any. She also visits other bakeries in the area and inspects the selection of baked goods in the supermarket across the street in order to get a sense of the competition. She then draws up the following short questionnaire:

Delight Bakery Customer Questionnaire

What is your occupation?   homemaker   office worker   construction worker   student   other _____

How often do you shop here?   often   sometimes   rarely

When do you shop here?   morning   noon   afternoon

What do you tend to buy (or what did you purchase today)?
bread and rolls   pastry   cake

How many items do you tend to buy (or how many did you buy today)?   one   several   more than five

Where else do you buy baked goods?   Fair Mart Supermarket
Flavio's Bakery (High Street)   other_____

How did you first hear about Delight Bakery?   word of mouth
local newspaper ad   just happened to drop by

Why do you come to Delight Bakery?

Daly remains in the shop for several days handing the questionnaire to customers as they enter and collecting them as they leave. For the remainder of the week, she goes to the parking lot of the supermarket across the street. There she interviews shoppers who are entering or leaving the market. She introduces herself to random shoppers in the following way:

> Hello, I'm Karen Daly with Delight Bakery across the street. I'm doing an informal survey on where shoppers buy their baked goods and why. Would you mind answering a few questions?

Daly first asks each shopper relevant questions on the prepared questionnaire, marking off the answers herself. Then she proceeds to ask more open-ended questions about the respondents' shopping habits as well as their specific opinions about Delight Bakery and its products. When the respondents are agreeable, she tapes the interviews; otherwise, she simply takes notes.

Daly collects 150 questionnaires from bakery customers and engages in 40 parking lot interviews (for each, she also fills out a questionnaire), thus giving her a total of 190 completed questionnaires. In order to analyze this data, she constructs a chart for checking off the responses:

	H (85)	OW (51)	CW (14)	S (40)
buys one item	0	47	10	33
buys several items	35	4	4	7
buys more than five	50	0	0	0
buys bread and rolls	65	10	3	0
buys pastry	85	49	12	40
buys cake	12	0	0	0

comes often	25	45	8	33
comes sometimes	50	6	3	1
comes rarely	10	0	3	6
morning	75	50	14	0
noon	0	25	0	0
afternoon	10	3	0	40
shops at Fair Mart	80	5	0	0
word of mouth	70	30	4	20
newspaper ad	3	0	0	0
dropped by	12	21	10	20

Key: H = homemaker; OW = office worker; CW = construction worker; S = student

The chart provides a preliminary audience profile. Hanson had been right—homemakers make up the majority of Delight's shoppers. As expected, the major competition for Delight among homemakers is clearly Fair Mart Supermarket across the street. Yet Daly also discovers some surprises: Office workers (though they tended to buy only one item in the morning or at noon) are more frequent buyers than her interviews with Hanson and the shop's employees had indicated. Another substantial audience consists of students who come in the afternoon, when school presumably lets out, and purchase one item. Daly also notes that most customers have learned about the bakery through word of mouth or a chance visit. Obviously, Hanson's newspaper ad isn't very effective.

Reviewing the open-ended responses on the questionnaires, she discovers that a large number of respondents praised Delight's freshly baked danish and donuts and said they were worth a special trip.

Finally, Daly reviews her notes and listens to the tapes from her interviews. The vast majority of those interviewed are homemakers who admit that they now buy more of their baked goods at the supermarket because "it's more convenient." But she also discovers an interesting reason why they feel Delight is inconvenient: These people park in the supermarket lot and say they don't like crossing the busy thoroughfare (with no traffic light) to get to the bakery. Some explain that though they prefer Delight's donuts to the supermarket brand, they don't think they are worth the dangerous crossing, often with small children in tow.

Once Daly has thoroughly reviewed all the data from the questionnaires and interviews, she puts together the following memo summarizing her findings for submission to Hanson the next day.

To: Steve Hanson
From: Karen Daly KD
Subject: Results of informal research on Delight

My survey of 150 customers inside the bakery and 40 respondents in the Fair Mart parking lot during the week of June 8 has provided me with a fairly clear sense of your target publics and their attitudes toward the bakery.

You presently have three important sets of customers:
- homemakers—who tend to buy in bulk in the morning
- office workers—who tend to buy a snack item in the early morning and/or at noon
- students—who tend to buy a snack item in the afternoon when school lets out

All groups were especially fond of your donuts and danish.

As you suspected, Fair Mart is making inroads into your clientele, primarily among homemakers. My interviews show that many of them now buy their baked goods at the supermarket because they find it more convenient.

Yet my findings also suggest that they would be more likely to frequent your store if it were easier to cross the street between the supermarket and the bakery. Many noted that there is no traffic light and that they did not like making the crossing with small children. This seems important since many of these same respondents admitted to preferring Delight's baked goods to those of the supermarket.

My informal research also shows that the ad you've been running in the local paper has had little effect in attracting customers. Clearly, a different kind of promotional strategy seems called for.

Given these findings, here is my assessment of the target audience, PR objectives, and PR message which should serve as the basis for Delight's PR program.

Your target publics
   homemakers
   office workers
   students

-more-

2/Research Findings

Your PR objectives

1 To improve visibility with the target publics of office workers and students (perhaps providing an incentive for them to buy in bulk on their way home from work or school in the afternoon and evening).
2 To improve the convenience of shopping at Delight for homemakers (perhaps by hiring a traffic officer for the crossing at certain hours during the day).
3 To communicate the superior quality of Delight's baked goods, particularly its donuts and danish, to the target publics.

Your PR message
Delight offers superior baked goods which are worth a special trip.

I'd like to meet with you tomorrow at your convenience and discuss the development of a program based on these findings. I'll stop by the store around 10 A.M. to see if you're free.

INITIATING A COMMUNICATIONS AUDIT

The conventional communications (public opinion) audit measures how effectively an organization communicates with its target publics. Recently, however, many communications audits also survey another audience—those individuals whose opinions carry weight with an organization's target publics. Such audits, in other words, supply two levels of information: the level of public perception and the level at which public perception is shaped by the opinion leaders and decision-makers who occupy the most important positions within a particular field, industry, or in society in general. Knowledge of these two levels has become increasingly important as PR practitioners seek to establish a place for their clients in a larger communications picture as well as perform specific communication tasks. In planning a social responsibility or identity campaign, an understanding of an organization's role within a larger economic and social context becomes especially important.

John Flint is public relations director of Jenson Electrical, Inc., a large electronics manufacturing company. He is concerned that his company is never mentioned in general articles dealing with new developments in the industry. Although Jenson is certainly working in the same areas as other electronics companies, the media seem hardly aware of the company's existence. Moreover, while sales continue to be respectable, there have been none of the spurts in profits which other electronics companies have experienced in recent years, nor has the price of Jenson Electrical's stock had much upward movement on the market. Flint isn't even sure how Jenson's own employees perceive the company and its products. What is needed, he concludes after pondering the problem, is a corporate identity program which will give Jenson a higher profile with its target publics. But then he isn't quite sure what this profile should look like.

Fortunately, common sense tells Flint that the first step toward solving the company's image problems should be to research why Jenson is projecting such a nondescript image and what identity it really should be projecting. After consulting informally with ComData, Inc., an independent research firm,* Flint learns that a communications audit would help answer some basic questions about the company's identity and thus lay the proper groundwork for a PR program. Unlike a standard communications audit, the audit which ComData suggests Jenson perform would not only focus on the company's specific publics (consumers, stockholders, and electronics-publication reporters likely to write about the company) but would also survey leaders in the electronics industry and related industries, top government and organizational officials, and important people in the general business media. The rationale, as explained to Flint, is that these people shape the opinions of their subordinates and, by tapping their views, the company can get at the root of how it is perceived (or not perceived). With this information, Jenson can discover what's wrong with the way it presents itself and how to go about remedying it.

Flint decides to retain the research company to develop the communications audit. It recommends that the audit be constructed in two parts. One part will consist of a written questionnaire to be administered to a random sample of internal employees, customers, and reporters. The other part will consist of a series of face-to-face in-depth interviews with designated opinion leaders in the industry and in the media.

Wishing to keep costs down, Flint specifies that the research firm perform only those tasks which he and his staff cannot effectively perform themselves. The breakdown of tasks finally agreed upon is as follows:

To be performed by ComData, Inc.:

1 Construct questionnaires.
2 Identify 15 to 20 external respondents.

---

*Flint chooses the research firm on the basis of the recommendation of an industry colleague whose opinion he trusts. It's a good idea to have a reference when choosing a research firm (or any outside consultant for that matter). You may also want to develop a checklist of questions to ask independent researchers before retaining their services. Questions should include "How are interviewers trained?" "What methods are used for selecting and evaluating samples?" "What is the margin of error that the sample will yield?" and "Have you had experience doing research for other organizations like mine?"[11]

3 Take random sample of respondents for questionnaire.
4 Do all external interviewing and all statistical analysis.

To be performed internally:

1 Do all printing of questionnaires and mailing from company office.
2 Write interpretive report based on the statistical analysis.

Originally, Flint wanted his own employees to do some of the interviewing, but he is convinced after speaking with the professional researchers that their position inside the company is not an objective one and that they might unconsciously phrase their questions in a biased fashion. Moreover, for this particular external audit to be effective, the organization sponsoring the audit must remain anonymous to the respondents.

After the division of tasks has been agreed upon, a timetable (see Chapter 6) is drawn up by the company in conjunction with the research firm to assure that a final report will be available for presentation at the company's board meeting six months hence. Flint hopes at that time to win approval from the board to begin work on a new identity program for the company based on the audit data.

EMPLOYING A VISIBILITY STUDY AS THE CENTERPIECE OF A PUBLIC RELATIONS PROGRAM

Why would an organization choose to underwrite a visibility study? For one thing, the study's sponsor has the benefit of associating its name with an issue of topical concern. For another, the statistical information produced from a visibility study can be presented from a variety of angles and thus generate multiple stories with appeal to a variety of target publics.

Take, for example, a visibility study sponsored by a children's clothing manufacturer to survey attitudes about child-rearing in this country. Some of the information generated by the survey might be developed into a story for popular women's magazines; other data might be of special interest to the education media; still other material might serve as the basis for articles in journals of sociology and psychology. Thus, the study promises to appeal to a spectrum of publics—from a popular mass audience to a specialized academic one.

Another advantage to a well-conceived visibility study is that it often paves the way for follow-up studies. Just as certain movies naturally beg for sequels, certain surveys are so interesting and timely that readers are bound to want updates. The Virginia Slims American Women's Opinion Poll (sponsored by Philip Morris U.S.A.), for example, has been repeated fairly regularly since 1970 so that now the possibility of comparing the changes in women's opinions over a prolonged period is as interesting as the results themselves for any given year. In the case of The Figgie Report, a visibility study on American responses to crime sponsored by A-T-O, Inc., sequels have taken a somewhat different form. First administered in 1980, each new Figgie Report has investigated attitudes toward crime as they relate to different target publics, from the general public to the corporate executive.

Since the visibility study is primarily intended for external use, it is especially important that it be carried out using impeccable research methods. Faulty data or non-objective procedures will negate the value of the study and reflect badly on the sponsor organization.

Stanley Fisher is owner and president of Video Gamesmanship, Inc., a manufacturer of video games whose market consists primarily of teenagers. Fisher believes that the company, which has been involved in an aggressive advertising campaign since its inception six years ago, is now ready for a more serious marketing strategy. However, instead of pouring more money into standard advertising and public relations—thereby relaying messages similar to those being disseminated by a myriad of other video game manufacturers—Fisher feels that the company should associate itself with the concerns of its youth market in a more profound way.

Fisher majored in sociology in college and is naturally curious about the rise and fall of fads and social trends. In particular, he is intrigued by his own success. Why is it, he wonders, that video games have "taken off" in the past ten years? What particular kind of gratification do the games offer the modern adolescent? The idea of researching this question appeals to Fisher, and he decides to consult the research arm of a major public relations agency concerning the kind of study that would be of interest to a wide audience. The PR agency's research director, Dr. Karl Madson, is impressed by Fisher's flexible, creative thinking and suggests a variety of research options of varying size (and expense) which might suit his needs.

Madson believes that Fisher's curiosity about the video game phenomenon would not in itself warrant a visibility study, but he does feel that some of the questions Fisher raises could be used as *caravan* questions on a large national survey. A typical caravan question for a teenage audience might be "Do you play a video game at least once a week?" If the percentage of "yes" answers were impressively high, this might make an effective "hook" for a feature release about new games on the market put out by Fisher's firm.

But Fisher explains that he is interested in sponsoring a survey that would illuminate a trend or an issue in some depth and which would have real sociological value. He is also willing to pay an additional fee for an accompanying PR program (to be developed and carried out by the PR agency associated with the research firm). In short, he wants to sponsor a full-scale visibility study.

In order to plan an appropriate visibility study that would have value to Fisher's business, Madson begins by identifying the target audience which Fisher most wants to reach. Fisher describes his target audience as the 10- to 20-year-old age group. Madson decides to limit the target slightly to include only ages 13 to 19—the formal teenage years.

The original focus on video games had seemed too narrow, but Madson notes that video games fall into the more general category of leisure activity. He suggests that a visibility study dealing with teenagers' attitudes toward and use of leisure time could yield provocative results which would be of interest not only to teenagers themselves but also to their parents and to society at large. He explains that the best sampling method would be a *multistage, stratified probability sample* of interviewing locations. First, after all the counties in the nation had been stratified by population size within each geographic region, counties would be chosen at random proportionate to population. Then, cities and towns within the sample counties would be drawn at random proportionate to population. Finally, high schools within the selected cities and towns—where the actual surveying would take place—would be drawn at random. Within each high school, ten students selected at random proportionate to age would be surveyed (using face-to-face interviews and questionnaires). Since 100 high schools would be selected through this method, 1,000 students would be surveyed in all, providing an accurate gauge of the opinions of more than 100,000 teenagers.

While there certainly could be no predicting what the results of the survey would be, the very nature of the questions asked could guarantee interesting if not startling results. Some typical categories in the survey might be Sports and Games, Partying, Family Outings, Television-Watching, and Illicit/Illegal Activities. Under each, a series of multiple-choice and dichotomous questions would reveal such information as how much time is spent at a particular activity, how much it is preferred over other activities, where and with whom it is performed, and so on.

The statistics gathered from the survey could be compiled into a book which would explain them in the context of larger social trends and issues. In addition, the opportunities for spin-off publicity would be enormous. Particular categories of findings could be highlighted to generate potential stories in special interest publications such as teen magazines, sports magazines, parents' and women's magazines, as well as in the feature sections of newspapers. Fisher, as an amateur sociologist and as the father of three teenagers himself, would be a natural spokesperson for such a survey. Madson hopes to be able to place his client on local and national TV and radio talk shows to discuss the results.

Finally, an advantage to the survey topic is that it lends itself to continual updating, in the form of new surveys on teenage attitudes and surveys on the use of leisure time of other age groups. While such subsequent surveys might have a less direct bearing on Fisher's business, they would help establish Video Gamesmanship in the public mind as a company committed to the exploration of social trends. A reputation for this kind of commitment would strengthen corporate identity and help generate goodwill for the company on a large scale.

PREPARING A ROUTINE EVALUATIVE REPORT

The most common form of evaluation which a public relations practitioner is called upon to do is the informal report of progress, usually written at monthly, bi-monthly, or quarterly intervals and, in more comprehensive form, at year-end. Such a report is a standard requirement in agency public relations, though it is also sometimes prepared by in-house departments as a means of keeping a supervisor outside the department up-to-date on what is being done in the PR area.

Most evaluative reports follow a memo format. They begin with a short introduction explaining the goals set for the particular period in question and a summary statement concerning how well these goals were met. This is followed by a specific enumeration of accomplishments, usually in the form of a list of placements or activities. In a report for the year or following the implementation of an important project, there is generally a concluding section which discusses how the reported progress should affect the future direction of the program. This makes the report the natural prelude to a new or revised program proposal.

In order to be able to prepare thorough and convincing evaluative reports, you should keep careful records of what you've done and when. If possible, for example, you should be able to keep track of which news releases resulted in which stories—a task which can require some careful record-keeping when many releases have been sent out over a short period of time. Press clippings, should be kept and carefully labeled (most agencies send copies of clippings along with the report). Remember that your evaluation should, if possible, anticipate your client's request for it, so that you never have to respond defensively to the client complaint: "What have you done for me lately?"

Joe Kutcher, an account executive for the Stiller Agency, a Florida public relations firm, has recently completed work on a short-term project for the Siesta Hotel, a large resort hotel in Ft. Lauderdale interested in developing its reputation as a pleasant and affordable vacation spot for the Northeast college crowd during the winter vacation weeks. Kutcher's agency had been retained for a six-month period—from August through January—with the objective of increasing student awareness of the hotel and thereby increasing student occupancy during the mid-December through January Christmas break. In developing the program, Kutcher targeted the colleges themselves, though he also directed some publicity to local newspapers in New Jersey, New York, and parts of New England which served areas in the vicinity of the target colleges.

At the end of January—the season over and his work for the client done—Kutcher feels it is a logical time to review the results of his effort and write an evaluative report. Although the client has not specifically requested that this be done, Kutcher and his supervisor at the agency, Steve Schultz, feel such a report would not only help assure renewal of the agency for next year but might also convince the hotel to retain the agency to develop a year-round program aimed at other target publics.

In preparing the memo, Kutcher first draws up the following list of points which he wishes to discuss in the report:

Press clippings
Special promotional materials (brochures and flyers)
Advertising (college papers)
Comparative booking figures (last year/this year)

After considering this list, he then arranges the items in a logical order and expands this into a formal outline which he can use as a guide in writing the evaluative memo to the client. His outline looks like this:

I. Introduction
   A. Need for program
   B. Success of program
      1. General increased visibility of Siesta on college campuses
      2. Comparative occupancy figures

II. Kinds of implementation tools employed to achieve these results
   A. Special materials
      1. Brochures
      2. Flyers
   B. Advertising
   C. Editorial
      1. Local newspaper features (list placements)
      2. College newspaper editors' press trips

III. Conclusion
   A. Value of continuing the program
   B. Value of expanding the program year-round to address other target publics

With this outline as a guide, Kutcher writes the following evaluative memo. Note that his supervisor is properly copied on the report.

To: Dan Friedman
Public Relations Director, Siesta Hotel
From: Joseph Kutcher J.K.
Subject: Review of Six-Month Program
Date: January 29, 198-

cc: Steve Shultz

We are pleased to report the completion of a highly successful six-month public relations program for the Siesta Hotel. As we had intended, Siesta is now known on campuses throughout the Northeast as the place to stay in Ft. Lauderdale during Christmas break. Booking figures at Siesta during the Christmas season this year show a *90 percent occupancy rate* during the entire break period—*an increase of 35 percent over last year*.

The program, which was carefully developed by the Stiller Agency in conjunction with Siesta, owes its success to the following PR tools and placements:

PROMOTIONAL MATERIALS

BROCHURES   In August, we began the preparation of a new Siesta brochure designed to appeal specifically to college students. Work on the brochure was a concentrated and intensive effort, since it was necessary to mail copies by late September-early October, when students begin planning their Christmas vacations. Brochures were mailed to complete student bodies of ten "priority" universities in the Northeast, with additional copies sent to student deans, counselors, and activity organizers at 50 other universities.

FLYERS   A special Siesta flyer featuring an eye-catching color photo of the hotel and beach was sent to 100 universities for posting. Wherever possible, Stiller staff members visited universities and posted flyers themselves.

ADVERTISING

Stiller enlisted Dyson Advertising to design a provocative half-page ad for placement in 50 priority campus newspapers during the last week of September.

EDITORIAL

LOCAL NEWSPAPER FEATURES   Stiller staff wrote a three-part feature series on Florida college vacations which contained quotes from Siesta staff and mention of Siesta facilities. (These were not direct sales pieces and therefore had greater credibility with readers.) We achieved successful placements of the series in the following local newspapers in key geographical areas during the month of October:

The Sentinel   circulation 50,000; serves area near Bennington College
The Morris Times   circulation 35,000; serves area near Dartmouth College
The Evening Gazette   circulation 56,000; serves area near Yale

The Times Daily circulation 35,000; serves area near Amherst, Smith, Mt. Holyoke

These features have been instrumental in alerting the local population as well as students in these key geographical areas to the Siesta name.

COLLEGE NEWSPAPER EDITORS' PRESS TRIPS   As a method of generating feature stories about Siesta in college papers, we invited five college newspaper editors from five priority schools to spend three days at Siesta during the Christmas break—all expenses paid. Although articles resulting from these visits have not yet appeared, we expect them to begin running this month and will forward copies to you as soon as they do. (We are in contact with all five editors who assure us that they are at work on the stories.) These articles will not only serve to encourage students to come to Siesta during the upcoming spring break, but, more importantly, will also have considerable reprint value. As part of next year's promotion, we would want to do an extensive mailing of these reprints to students.

In summary, we are pleased with the results of our promotional effort for Siesta, which has brought the hotel into the consciousness of college students throughout the Northeast. However, we feel strongly that the momentum produced by this program must continue to be fueled by additional and ongoing activity. College students have short memories, and graduating students are replaced every year by a new crop. Brochures and flyers need to be updated each year and mailing lists need to be expanded and revised. We also feel that Siesta's status could be further enhanced by the sponsorship of a number of special activities designed for presentation on college campuses.

Finally, we feel that our work for Siesta this year can serve as the foundation for a more extensive PR program aimed not only at students but also at other target publics on a year-round basis. We would be interested in talking to you about some of these ideas, and we'll be in touch to arrange an appointment at your convenience.

EXERCISES

Test Your Judgment

State the kind of research or evaluation tool called for in each of the following situations:

1   An organization with a limited budget wants to get a more precise sense of how it is perceived by its target audience.

2   An organization wants to know how it is perceived by important people in government, media, and industry.

3   An organization wants to know how effectively it communicates with its employees.

4   An organization wants to associate itself with an important issue.

5   A PR agency wants to convince a client to expand a program.

6   An organization wants to know what kind of publicity its competitor is getting.

7   An organization wants to know how effectively it is communicating with the media.

8   An organization wants to survey the general public on a specific, dichotomous question.

9   An organization wants to learn more about the culture of Brazil in order to prepare background materials for its sponsorship of a Brazilian dance company's tour of the U.S.

10   A PR agency wants to inform a client of what has been accomplished in the past year.

PR Workshop

Discuss the key words you might use in a data base search on each of the following topics:

1   The competitive behavior exhibited by pre-medical college students.

2   U.S. corporate merger trends and their effect on the international economy.

3   Political party infighting and how it influenced the outcome of the 1964 presidential election.

4   The differences in French and American attitudes toward child-rearing.

PR Case Studies

1   You are an executive in the public relations department of Fishman Brothers, Inc., a large home appliance manufacturing company owned and operated by the Fishman family for 60 years. Fishman's products were especially popular during the 1950s when it initiated an aggressive marketing campaign directed at housewives. But despite its attempt to update its marketing and advertising in recent years, the fifties housewife image still clings to the company and, you feel, has inhibited the growth of the business with other important markets, namely working mothers and singles. You believe

that a visibility study on the right issue might be a way to improve the image of the company with these other publics.

Write a memo to the department director, Jay Pinto, giving your rationale for the company's sponsorship of a visibility study and suggesting some possible survey topics.

2   Choose a program or service on campus which is supposed to assist students in some way (for example, a student center, tutoring program, job placement office, campus store). Think of this program or service as a client for whom you are doing preliminary informal research concerning the effectiveness of its communication with its target audience. Begin by interviewing employees and others involved with managing the service. Then develop a survey (seven to ten close-ended questions; one or two open-ended questions) and administer it to 20 to 30 students whom you feel fall within the target audience of your client. In addition, perform a number of in-depth interviews with several students chosen at random and with one or two "key" individuals whose opinions carry special weight in relation to your client (for example, student dean, president of the student body, faculty advisor).

Tally the responses from the questionnaires and review the results of the interviews. Using your results, write a memo to your professor in which you support the identification of the *target audience, PR objectives, and PR message* which would serve as the groundwork for developing a PR program for the client. Attach copies of the questionnaire and a list of the interview questions you used in gathering your data.

3   The following list of information concerns a program recently completed by your agency for the fall line of sports clothes by Japanese designer Suki. Write an outline and then an evaluative report to the Suki Company liaison, Michiko Kito, that logically incorporates each piece of information on the list.

a   Interviews on radio and TV talk shows (N.Y.C.–two; Chicago–four; L.A.–two).
b   Editorial placements (five features in national fashion magazines).
c   Three-city tour (N.Y.C., Chicago, L.A.).
d   Fashion shows in department stores (N.Y.C., Chicago, L.A.).
e   Local newspaper stories (N.Y.C.–three; Chicago–five; L.A.–one).
f   Questionnaires administered to department store and boutique shoppers about their reaction to the fall collection.
g   Comparative sales figures (last fall vs. this fall: 20 percent increase).
h   Promotion of next fall's collection (five-city tour?).

4   You are a public affairs officer with the youth organization, the Young Pioneers. The organization has its national headquarters in Washington,

D.C., with regional headquarters in ten key areas throughout the country. The local chapters, of which there are now more than 150, are supposed to report to the regional headquarters which, in turn, report to national headquarters. In recent years, however, the local chapters have become increasingly independent, and many have instituted programs which are not consistent with the national policies. This has affected the organization's image with the general public, who is no longer sure what the Young Pioneers stand for.

You feel that it is necessary to perform a communications audit which will help expose communications problems both within the organization and with external publics. Write a memo to the executive director, Fran Washington, explaining the rationale for such an audit.

NOTES

1. Edward J. Robinson, *Public Relations and Survey Research: Achieving Organization Goals in a Communication Context* (New York: Meredith Corporation, 1969), p. 12.
2. See Peter Finn, "Demystifying Public Relations," *Public Relations Journal*, 38 (May 1982), 12–17.
3. See Lewis Anthony Dexter, *Elite and Specialized Interviewing* (Evanston, Ill.: Northwestern University Press, 1970).
4. Hy Mariampolski, "Qualitative Research Rebounds," *Public Relations Journal*, 40 (July 1984), 21.
5. Kenneth R. Hoover, *The Elements of Social Scientific Thinking*, 2nd edition (New York: St. Martin's Press, 1980), p. 36.
6. See Harry W. O'Neill, "How Opinion Surveys Can Help Public Relations Strategy," *Public Relations Review*, X (Summer 1984), 3–12.
7. See John Crothers Pollock, "Getting the Most from Your Research," *Public Relations Journal*, 39 (July 1983), 16–20.
8. Veronica Kane, "Technology: Tomorrow's Library May Be in Your Office Today," *Public Relations Journal*, 41 (July 1985), 30–31.
9. Peter Finn, "In-House Research Becomes a Factor," *Public Relations Journal*, 40 (July 1984), 19.
10. See Walter K. Lindenmann, "Content Analysis," *Public Relations Journal*, 39 (July 1983), 24–26.
11. For a more detailed checklist, see Michael Ryan, "Ten Criteria for Getting Good Research," *Public Relations Journal*, 39 (July 1983), 18–19.

4

Formulating a PR Program

The public relations program is the game plan which outlines the various activities you plan to pursue for a client. It places each individual public relations act (the writing of a press release, the preparation of a speech, the development of an evaluative report, and so on) into the larger context of an overall effort.

A PR program can encompass the activities to be performed for a client over a period of years (undergoing only routine annual updating), or it can relate to a specific time-bound special event or project. Whatever the case, the program seeks to establish a logical sequence of operations which, in turn, support a larger goal or "rationale." Thus, a program is a practical map of proposed operations as well as a justification for and clarification of the value of these operations as they relate to the short-term and long-term PR objectives of the client.

THE FOUNDATION FOR THE PROGRAM: AUDIENCE, OBJECTIVES, MESSAGE

As explained in Chapter 3, before writing a public relations program you must have in hand information which can serve as its foundation. Research, whether informal or formal, provides this information by helping you identify your *target audience* and your client's *PR objectives*. With these, it becomes possible to deduce an appropriate *PR message*. These three variables are the triangular base upon which the PR program is built (see Figure 4–1).

In some cases, a program may need to be broad enough in conception to

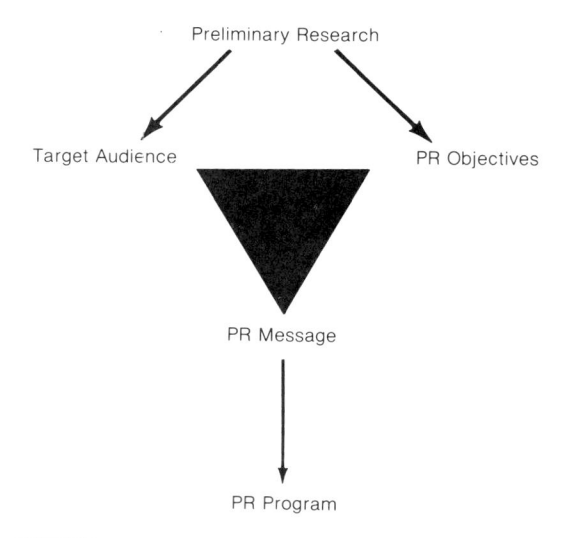

FIGURE 4-1 Groundwork for Preparing a PR Program

encompass many different target publics. In other cases, it may be desirable to select only one or two of the principal target publics so that the program can have a clearer focus and be more limited in scope. (A second or third "phase" to the program can be added later to address other publics.) An understanding of your client's PR objectives can help you decide whether to limit the target audience and, if so, how.

For example, a computer company whose PR objective is to expand its reputation with young professionals might choose to direct a PR program at college students (soon-to-be young professionals), rather than at young professionals already in the work force who would be harder to target. Choosing college students as a target audience would limit the scope of the program and create a greater likelihood that the program's objectives would be achieved. As another example, take the trend, reported in the *Wall Street Journal*, that many department stores are developing public relations campaigns specifically directed at the working woman.[1] By limiting their target audience in this way, the stores are able to develop an array of specialized activities (investment and career seminars, dress-for-success counseling, business courses on the store premises), all of which relate to a well-defined PR objective: to bring more career women into the stores and thus earn their goodwill *and* gain access to their paychecks. By limiting the target audience, special events, promotional activities, and even routine press releases are more likely to hit the target than if an attempt were made to address all the stores' publics with one campaign.

Of course, as explained in Chapter 3, an organization's target publics should be verified through formal or informal research, and professed PR objectives should be evaluated to make sure they are compatible with these publics and with the true nature of the organization. If a company wants to be perceived as a leader in its field, is this a realistic objective or just wishful thinking? Or if an organization claims that it wants to communicate a more youthful, "with it" image to a younger audience, is this a true representation of its character or is the organization really as conservative as ever, better suited to appeal to a more staid, middle-aged public? Convincing a client to present an accurate and honest identity may sometimes involve explaining the limits as well as the potential of a public relations effort; for while a PR program can communicate an organization's strengths and help get a message across more effectively, it cannot change an organization into what it is not, nor hide obvious flaws in its operation. Cover-up campaigns are short-term remedies which almost always backfire in the long-run. Moreover, consumerism has become such a potent force in the marketplace that misrepresentation of products and services is now subject to legal action. We see the effects of this in the product recalls, fines, and disciplinary actions that are reported daily on the business pages of newspapers. The U.S. automotive industry offers perhaps the most striking example of the limitations of public relations when the product doesn't fit the image being projected. Despite enormous promotional expenditures, the industry ultimately lost a large segment of the market to foreign manufacturers. The American public was no longer prepared to accept a lack of quality control and looked for a better product elsewhere.

Depending upon the nature of the program, PR objectives can be very specific or fairly general. Remember, however, that the objectives should be *public relations* objectives and should therefore involve some aspect of communication. For example, your PR objectives might be to communicate the convenience of soft soap over hard soap; to communicate Food World Supermarket chain's interest in the welfare of the consumer; to create greater recognition of the efforts being made by the nuclear power industry to maintain standards of safety and act responsibly toward the public; and so on.

Finally, the information directed at the target public(s) in order to achieve the PR objectives should be carefully conceived. This information is the PR message. The message may be *explicit* in the form of a public-service message or catchy slogan, or *implicit* as an organizing idea for the campaign. Whether explicit or implicit, you should have it in mind before you write the program, since it will help dictate the appropriate strategy and the specific tools for implementation. The PR message should be general enough to encompass all facets of the program, but it should be able to be broken down, if necessary, into a number of secondary messages directed at specific publics or addressing special issues. An auto safety campaign, for example, might be based on the message "Cars Can Be Weapons. Be Auto Safe," while a secondary message like "Wear Seat Belts" could be used to support the general message. In a later

PR program for the same organization, "Wear Seat Belts" might become the general message while a secondary message for this program, directed specifically at children, might be "Get Parents to Wear Seat Belts."

THE PROGRAM FORMAT

Once *target audience*, *PR objectives*, and *PR message* have been established, you are ready to begin writing the program. Keep in mind that, in the course of the writing, you may need to engage in additional research and consultation with the client. A program will generally have to go through a number of drafts before it is ready for final presentation.

Although most programs follow the general format that follows, category headings can be added to permit greater emphasis in a particular area. For example, the description of the target audience is generally covered under the introduction or incorporated under the PR objectives, but a special category describing audience may be included if this seems necessary to justify the thrust of the program. Similarly, the PR message tends to be covered under the program strategy but may sometimes be presented under a separate category, especially if the message takes the explicit form of a slogan or theme. (In the format that follows, an asterisk indicates an optional category.)

Table of Contents

*Executive Summary This one-page synopsis of the major categories addressed in the program tends to be included only in very long programs. Obviously, it should be written last.

Introduction (or Rationale) This is the general background on the client organization and its target audience. The introduction may also contain an overview of the PR problem or issue under consideration.

PR Objectives This is a list of the PR objectives to be addressed by the program. Objectives are usually numbered or bulleted.

*Role of Communications There should be a general explanation of the potential as well as the limits of a public relations effort. This is sometimes included to clarify the function of public relations for the client and to serve as a disclaimer by spelling out what a PR program cannot be expected to do.

Strategy (or Methodology) A general explanation is necessary of how the PR message is to be communicated, whether through an assortment of media events, a combination of editorial and special events, a major underwriting venture, or whatever. Here is where you convince the client that the program implementation which follows has coherence and is achievable.

Program Implementation This is an outline of the communication tools necessary to get the desired message across to the target audience in order to achieve the PR objectives. The tools chosen represent the "meat" of a PR program and draw upon creativity and judgment.

The following are principal PR implementation categories under which we have grouped the major communications tools (to be discussed in more detail in subsequent chapters):

Press Activity These include press releases, news conferences, op-ed pieces, feature articles, and other materials directed at the media.

Speakers Programs These programs involve specialists who are prepared to comment on issues, make public appearances and tours, and be interviewed by the media.

Publications These can be newsletters, brochures, journals, visibility studies, and educational materials.

Electronic Media Presentations These include in-house films, documentaries, mini-docs (radio and TV news clips), slide shows, and public service announcements (PSAs).

Advertising You may wish to recommend that a certain amount of money be allocated to advertising as a tool to assist the larger PR effort. (Describe in general terms what kind of advertising is desirable and in what sorts of media it should be placed.)

Special Events/Promotions Examples are athletic events, fashion shows, art exhibitions, contests, give-aways, and so on.

In explaining each communications tool, be as detailed as possible in justifying its use. Make clear how the tool will carry the PR message and address the target audience.

Some PR practitioners turn the implementation list into a grab-bag, arbitrarily adding activities to fit the size of the budget. This reflects bad public relations judgment. The implementation tools should be chosen carefully to carry through the desired PR message. While standard special events like shopping mall promotions and department store demonstrations are appropriate for some clients, they are certainly not for everyone. Brainstorming with colleagues can be helpful in bringing to light fresh promotional ideas which are uniquely tailored to a client's needs.

The implementation tools must also be compatible with the program budget. Certain types of activities (films, large-scale advertising, and special events) may simply be out of the question on a small budget. Sometimes you will have to exercise judgment as to whether to concentrate expenditure in one area (say, a speaking tour or a news conference) or to spend the money on a greater quantity of less expensive activities (such as telephone pitches and press releases). The tools chosen must also be compatible with the time frame. How long do you have to implement the program and what tools are practical within the alloted time?

Evaluation This is an explanation of how evaluation of the program's effectiveness will be done, how often it will be done, and what results might determine a next phase to the program. The evaluation method is not always included in the formal program; however, it is a good idea to decide in advance upon the kind of evaluative procedure you will be following. Clients often ask for proof of accomplishment later on, even if they never mentioned evaluation when the program was being prepared.

Conclusion This is the wrap-up—a final argument for your approach and its benefits.

*Personnel In the case of a PR agency, general information about the "account team" assigned to the program (relevant credentials on each executive and an explanation of the role he or she will perform) is included.

*Timetable A general time frame within which activities will be planned and implemented is not always formally included in the program, but it is a helpful addition when large-scale activities are being proposed or when timing is crucial to program effectiveness. A formal timetable can emphasize to the client the need to cooperate with you in keeping on schedule. It can also serve as a helpful map for explaining spending oscillations over a period of time. Most programs run a year (or at least six months), and on-going programs are usually subject to annual review and updating.

Budget The budget can be very detailed (breaking down activities into their specific components) or more generalized estimates. This depends upon the client's requirements and the nature of the program. Agency budgets are often organized in two columns, with one column devoted to estimated figures for personnel (staff) time, and the other for out-of-pocket expenses. Staff time is deduced from the billing rate of the executive assigned to work on the program. (This is usually estimated at three times the salary paid to the executive calculated on an hourly basis.) Sometimes a flat fee or retainer fee will be charged instead of (or, in some cases, in addition to) staff time. The amount of time devoted to a program or a specific project should be estimated by referring to past projects of a similar kind or by simply estimating how much time the practitioner can be allowed to spend on the program, with the assumption that the more time spent, the better the results. In-house PR departments will not always include staff time in their budgets since their public relations staff are already on salary with the client organization. Expenses can be calculated by getting quoted estimates from vendors (contacting several for a given service in order to arrive at a competitive price). Costs of services used in similar programs in the past can be used but should be updated to take into account inflation and price fluctuations. Both PR agencies and in-house PR departments may prepare their budgets with high and low estimates where the low estimate represents the minimum that can be done to meet the organization's PR objectives, and the high estimate represents the maximum.

Appendix This contains supporting documents such as research data or articles which clarify or bolster points made in the program. Readers should be instructed wherever relevant in the body of the program to "see Appendix". If several kinds of materials are included, they should be grouped accordingly: Appendix A, Appendix B, and so on.

Model Case Studies

DEVELOPING A PROGRAM TO CLARIFY AND REFINE A CLIENT'S IDENTITY

Some of the most ambitious public relations programs being developed for clients today take the form of identity, or image,* campaigns. Most commonly, these are programs developed on behalf of corporations which feel they are misperceived by their target publics (see Exhibit 4–1). A typical example is

EXHIBIT 4-1 When Is a Corporate Identity Program Valuable?

> According to Stephen M. Downey, a principal at Anspach, Grossman, Portugal, Inc., N.Y.C., a corporate identity program is most likely to be valuable under the following circumstances:[2]
>
> When public perceptions of a company do not reflect reality. Vestiges of past management mistakes, poor earnings, environmental problems, and the like may still be having a negative impact.
>
> When external forces such as a new competitor, a breakthrough product, deregulation, or an existing competitor's new identity require identification countermeasures.
>
> When competitors are slow to form clearly defined and effectively projected corporate and/or product presentation. In this sense, identity is opportunistic and can become a competitive advantage in itself.

*The term *image*, though commonly used to refer to a client's identity, is frowned upon by some members of the profession who feel that it implies a superficial and possibly inaccurate presentation of the client. They argue that the term feeds popular notions about PR that need to be refuted rather than reinforced.

International Business Machines (IBM), which, according to a *New York Times Magazine* profile, has sought to readjust its corporate identity to fit changes in management style and increased product diversification.[3] IBM felt it was perceived as an overly conservative corporation, slow to pursue new ventures and wary of new ideas, even as its "real" identity had evolved—hence, the need to bring the image up-to-date.

Another more sensitive case in which corporate identity was at issue involved the Adolph Coors Company, the beer brewery. In 1983 the company was faced with a mass of lawsuits charging that it engaged in discriminatory hiring and that its chairperson was racist. In 1985 the company felt the need to "clean up its image" by actively proving that these accusations were not, or at least were no longer, true. It launched an identity program to gain visibility and win support among its target audience of young urban professionals. The result, according to the *New York Times*, was a "burst of social and civic programs that may well be unparalleled in the corporate world."[4]

But corporations are not the only ones interested in clarifying and refining an identity. Gary Hart, a contender for the 1984 Democratic Presidential nomination, can be said to have staged a highly effective image campaign. Both the chemical industry and the coal industry have launched identity programs in recent years, in their case to improve industry image in the wake of negative publicity. Many American cities have also initiated identity programs in an effort to stem urban decline or spur continued growth. Here, the focus is often on luring new business to the area by communicating tax, housing, cultural, and other advantages to companies considering relocation or the opening of branch operations.

Ideally, the role of public relations in identity development should be like the role of an editor in preparing a manuscript for publication. Like the editor, the PR practitioner seeks to clarify and emphasize important points, and to reorganize material to enhance meaning. It is *not* the public relations role to apply a quick cosmetic fix or to misrepresent what is there. Experience has shown that such short-term disguises do not profit a company in the long run. Instead, a good corporate identity program is built on and reflects a sound knowledge of the organization's leadership, operations, and general style.

In the past, public relations programs tended to focus on specific products, services, or events, and practitioners were permitted only limited access to top management. Thus, they were expected to carry on without an understanding of the overall organization and its long-range policy goals. With the advent of identity programs, public relations people have been made privy to more comprehensive information. This broader PR perspective has not only helped organizations see themselves and be seen more clearly, but has also helped PR practitioners achieve greater stature as the necessary counselors to top management. At their best, therefore, identity campaigns embody the true goals of public relations practice: to see and articulate a unified vision out of the many and disparate parts that make up the organizational whole.

When Larry Litwin, an account supervisor at a major Los Angeles public relations agency, is assigned responsibility for the Arlaine skin care account, he knows he has his work cut out for him. Arlaine is a 50-year-old Paris-based firm which, for the past decade, has marketed its products in this country. The products are expensive, and Arlaine has never been interested in doing the kind of aggressive advertising which cosmetic companies tend to do. Mademoiselle Marie Arlaine, the company president and granddaughter of the founder, finds advertising "vulgar." Yet, as competition from other skin care and cosmetics companies has escalated in Paris (where the company traditionally did the majority of its business), Mademoiselle Arlaine has recently become interested in expanding her market in the United States. This is why she decides to retain Litwin's agency.

Litwin believes that before Arlaine's products can become popular in the U.S., the company must first establish its identity with its target publics in this country; thus he recommends the development of a corporate identity campaign.

As a first order of business, Litwin decides to administer a communications audit. The audit is directed at the following publics: American consumers with household incomes of $60,000 or more (selected by sampling wealthy neighborhoods in the U.S.); top beauty and fashion editors on national and international magazines; trend setters (fashion models and movie stars) in New York and Paris; existing Arlaine clientele (largely situated in Paris); and Arlaine employees (all operating out of the Arlaine manufacturing complex on the Arlaine family estate in the Perigord region of France).

Litwin discovers from the audit that very few American consumers and fashion experts in the sample have ever heard of Arlaine. Yet his survey of existing clientele reveals that devoted clients are among the wealthiest women in France and that Paris fashion editors and models are familiar with Arlaine as an exclusive but low-profile skin care line. The internal portion of the audit reveals that employees at Arlaine's manufacturing complex view the company as a kind of feudal family with Mademoiselle Arlaine serving as "lady of the manor" and acting as a kind of benevolent dictator. Employees are fiercely loyal, believe their products are unsurpassed, and are themselves perfectionists ("Mademoiselle Arlaine tolerates nothing but the best," one worker explained).

After many discussions with Mademoiselle Arlaine and other top management officials, and after reviewing the research results carefully, Litwin prepares to write the program by first outlining the following basic information.

Target Audience

1 American men* and women who are wealthy, basically conservative (uninterested in fads or gimmicks), and who appreciate quality and tradition.
2 U.S. fashion and beauty editors and fashion trend setters.

PR Objectives

1 To get Arlaine recognized in America as a company dedicated to quality and tradition.
2 To familiarize Americans with the romantic story behind the Arlaine name.

PR Message

Arlaine has a long and impeccable tradition. Both the Arlaine family and the Arlaine product line are "aristocratic." The company, like the family who runs it, will not compromise its standards or deviate from its tradition.

As this preliminary information makes clear, Litwin has concluded that Mademoiselle Arlaine and her company are snobs—but snobs with something to be snobbish about. The company reflects the values of the Arlaine family, which can be traced back to French nobility of the seventeenth century. Litwin believes that this aristocratic identity needs to be articulated to the right audience in order to bring Arlaine the same kind of understated recognition in this country that it has long received in France.

After brainstorming with colleagues, reviewing program ideas and strategy with an agency vice president, and consulting with Mademoiselle Arlaine and the company's financial officers concerning budget constraints, Litwin draws up the following program.

TABLE OF CONTENTS

Introduction	1
Objectives	2
Methodology	3

---

*Although Arlaine products are designed for women, the target audience for the corporate identity campaign includes both men and women. This is because the campaign will concentrate on making the Arlaine name better known rather than selling the product. This approach is in line with most corporate identity programs which are interested in increasing sales only as an indirect result of increased visibility in general.

Implementation
  Editorial Coverage
    Mademoiselle Arlaine Interview Campaign 4
    Press Materials 6
    Ongoing National Publicity 8
  Special Events
    Charity Events 9
    Underwriting Projects 10
      French Antiques Exhibition 10
      Film 11
      Visibility Study 12
Conclusion 13
Budget 14

INTRODUCTION

Arlaine, a company devoted to the manufacture of exclusive skin care products, has a 50-year-old history of quality which has earned it recognition and patronage from among the most elegant and aristocratic families of France. The name Arlaine has been associated not only with a superior product line, but also with a family whose nobility reaches back to the seventeenth century. The Arlaine family estate is one of the most extensive in the Perigord region of France, and the manufacturing complex which occupies a portion of the 300-acre estate has employed meticulous and dedicated workers from the region for half a century.

While the fine families of France are familiar with Arlaine, this familiarity does not yet extend across the Atlantic. Although Arlaine now markets to selective quality retailers throughout the U.S., the company is little known among that exclusive portion of the American population that would be most interested in its products. In order to assist the marketing effort and develop Arlaine's identity in this country, we intend to create recognition for Arlaine with a target audience consisting of the American "aristocracy"—that is, that cream of the American public that wants nothing but the best products and services.

The following program is a blueprint for developing the same kind of respected, exclusive reputation for Arlaine in this country that it has long possessed in its native France.

OBJECTIVES

1 To make the quality and tradition behind Arlaine products familiar to an exclusive American audience.

2 To relay the values and tastes of Mademoiselle Arlaine and the tradition attached to the Arlaine family and family estate to this target audience.
3 To generate feature stories relating to the Arlaine manufacturing complex in Perigord.
4 To attach the Arlaine name to activities of social and cultural value.

METHODOLOGY

This program intends to communicate the Arlaine tradition and its dedication to quality through editorial coverage and exclusive special events. A central feature of the program will be Mademoiselle Arlaine herself. We feel she embodies the company's image, and we would like to use her wherever possible (and wherever convenient for her) in both the editorial and the special events facets of the program.

IMPLEMENTATION

Editorial Coverage

A public relations program for Arlaine must include a major publicity effort, especially since the company does not advertise. We will strive to build and reinforce the Arlaine name by generating publicity in national and local media.

MADEMOISELLE ARLAINE INTERVIEW CAMPAIGN

We know that Mademoiselle Arlaine is an articulate and attractive woman who can serve the company well as a spokesperson. We will therefore capitalize on the news value and availability of an authentic Arlaine family member by arranging media interviews for Mademoiselle Arlaine in selected markets.

1 Interviews for Mademoiselle Arlaine will be arranged by our staff (as her schedule permits) in key cities (L.A., Chicago, New York, Boston, and Philadelphia) with national magazines; society columns; and wide-reaching wire services and syndicated broadcast outlets.
2 Mademoiselle Arlaine's local market exposure will include
   Appearances on TV and radio talk shows.
   Interviews with fashion and beauty editors of major daily newspapers.
3 In her interviews, Mademoiselle Arlaine can discuss such topics as
   The Arlaine tradition of skin care manufacture and the family's commitment to maintaining it.

A personal profile of herself and her family tradition.

Her preferences and tastes on a range of topics relating to beauty and fashion.

4 Any available film footage of the Arlaine factory in Perigord can also be incorporated into Mademoiselle Arlaine's TV presentations to help focus on the Arlaine name and expand the airtime devoted to her.

PRESS MATERIALS

Backgrounder To help communicate the full story of Arlaine to members of the media, we will prepare a general backgrounder recounting the history of the Arlaine family and its dedication to the manufacture of the best creams and soaps.

Press Releases and Feature Stories We will prepare a series of feature stories and press releases highlighting individual aspects of Arlaine such as

The famous Perigord estate of Arlaine.

The romantic history of the Arlaine family and business.

An inside look into the manufacture of Arlaine products.

A profile of Mademoiselle Arlaine.

A by-lined feature ("What is Female Beauty?") by Mademoiselle Arlaine.

Such prepared press material—basic to any public relations campaign—helps focus editors' interests and assists them in writing their stories.

Brochure We recommend that our staff work with you to develop a brochure on the family, the company, and its products. Having a general background brochure for use in conjunction with publicity activities would be helpful to both the media and the consumer public.

The brochure would be elegantly designed to highlight the simple gold-embossed Arlaine family coat of arms. The general design and the coat of arms would be carried through in all Arlaine print materials—press releases, backgrounders, invitations, and so on.

ONGOING NATIONAL PUBLICITY

Through the distribution of press materials and regular personal contact with editors at leading national magazines, we will generate mention and discussion of Arlaine through feature articles on beauty and fashion, as well as through general profile articles on Mademoiselle Arlaine, her family, and her estate.

To help build coverage, we will explore the availability of photos of the Perigord region, the manufacturing complex, and the Arlaine estate for publicity use here in America.

Target media for national publicity would include

Town and Country	*Esquire*	*Vogue*
Gentleman's Quarterly	*Harper's Bazaar*	*Women's Wear Daily*
M	*House & Garden*	*Cosmopolitan*
United Press International	Associated Press	Reuters

Special Events

A variety of special events sponsored by Arlaine will position the company within the proper social and cultural context and help communicate directly with the desired audience.

CHARITY EVENTS

Charity events represent an important means of communicating with some of the country's most respected and important families while also performing a social service. Mademoiselle Arlaine's interest in art and art objects makes her an ideal patroness for cultural benefits organized to assist museums in mounting exhibitions or initiating renovations and capital improvements. A fund-raising event to preserve historical sites or landmark buildings would also be in keeping with Arlaine's traditional image. Our staff will prepare a list of possible cultural and community service projects for your review within the next month.

Whatever project is agreed upon, we feel the fund-raising event should be carried out with care and selectivity. We suggest that Mademoiselle Arlaine serve as hostess, sending out personalized invitations with the gold-embossed letterhead which we will develop for all Arlaine print materials. Guests will be invited from the social register and from specialized mailing lists developed for this purpose by our agency.

UNDERWRITING PROJECTS

The linking of Arlaine's name with events and activities of quality represents an important means of promoting Arlaine's exclusive reputation and values with its target audience.

French Antiques Exhibition   We suggest that the company underwrite a major exhibition of French antiques. Mademoiselle Arlaine's interest in antiques and the fact that she has a superb collection of her own make this the ideal underwriting choice. For maximum visibility, we also suggest that this be a traveling exhibition developed in conjunction with the smaller museums like the Frick and the Morgan Library in N.Y.C. and the Phillips Gallery in Washington, D.C. The exhibition will, of course, contain examples from Mademoiselle Arlaine's collection as well as from public and private collections in this country and abroad. The opening of the exhibition could be marked by a champagne breakfast attended by special guests and selected media representatives.

As a spin-off from this exhibition, we propose that Arlaine develop a series of quality photographs of the antiques for collection into a book. The introduction and supporting text would be in Mademoiselle Arlaine's name (written with the assistance of special consultants in the field).

Film A documentary entitled *Estates of the French Aristocracy* would be a combination travelog and history lesson, which would explore in a half-hour the estates of the great families of France. The film would discuss the architecture, furnishings, and family history of some four or five estates, including that of the Arlaine family in Perigord. The film, if properly produced, could possibly be aired on public television. It could also be subdivided into mini-documentaries for use as feature news clips on selected cable or local TV stations.

Both the full-length film and the shorter clips are sure to be of interest to American viewers, and they would help situate the Arlaine family in the mind of Americans alongside the names of other great French families.

Our broadcast department would produce the film and distribute it for placement.

Visibility Study "The Best-on-the-Best Survey" would survey respondents from among the "best" communities in the U.S. on what they consider to be "the best" in a range of areas (the best restaurant, designer, crystal, investment fund, and so on). The results would be interpreted for release to the press as feature stories and might also be published in book form with illustrations. There would be extensive spin-off possibilities attached to this kind of study.

CONCLUSION

We look forward to the prospect of promoting Arlaine's name and reputation among that portion of the American public which we term the American aristocracy.

Should there be more contained here than you decide to pursue at the present time, we will work with you in making a selection of priority activities and setting a timetable for their implementation.

We regard this program as perhaps a first phase in our service to Arlaine. As our work with you develops, we will want to target more specific audi-

94 Formulating a PR Program

ences and tailor our objectives to accommodate new social and cultural trends and new developments in the skin care industry.

BUDGET

The following estimates have been developed as a general guide to financial requirements.* More detailed budgets will be prepared and submitted for each segment of the program prior to its being launched. It should be noted that estimates have not been included for the charity events, the French antiques exhibition, and the visibility study. These are large-scale independent projects which would require extensive publicity and supporting materials. Should Arlaine agree to undertake them, we would develop independent budgets and time frames for their implementation.

	Staff time	Out-of-pocket
MADEMOISELLE ARLAINE INTERVIEWS Key market and national exposure L.A., Chicago, N.Y.C., Philadelphia, Boston: travel, hotel, meals for Mlle. Arlaine and one agency executive, plus staff time to arrange and supervise interviews	$15,000	$10,000
PRESS MATERIALS Preparation of two backgrounders, three press releases, five photos, including writing, research, printing, photo reproduction, and mailing to national media and newspapers in top 50 markets	$10,000	$2,000
Development, copywriting, and graphic design of Arlaine brochure with printing and mailing of 50,000 copies	$10,000	$25,000
ONGOING NATIONAL PUBLICITY Development of story ideas, continual press contact, research, photography	$15,000	$7,500
FILM Production plus research, travel, lodging, editing of footage, distribution	$150,000	$75,000
Total	$200,000	$119,500

*Figures represent possible agency estimates for these activities in the 1980s.

DEVELOPING A PUBLIC INFORMATION PROGRAM FOR A NONPROFIT ORGANIZATION

Nonprofit organizations which by definition are devoted to public service will often develop public relations programs to educate the public on a particular issue or promote a particular public service message. The local police force, for example, might develop a program to get people to lock their cars, or the local hospital might develop an educational program on high blood pressure. Keep in mind, however, that nonprofit institutions often have to contend with operational problems unique to them.[5] Often they must rely heavily upon volunteers to carry out programs, and they rarely have large budgets to devote to public relations. For this reason, they may welcome the assistance of private companies in underwriting their campaigns. This means that a private company may sponsor all or part of a public information program or may develop "tie-ins" to the program in the form of related or support activities. Many nonprofit organizations also find it practical to combine a public information program with a fund-raising effort.

Dorothy Buchanan is public affairs officer for the local chapter of the National Cancer Association (NCA). A recent survey done by the chapter reveals the startling statistic that teenage smoking has increased by 25 percent in the community within the past five years. This fact, combined with the organization's shortage of funds to assist low-income cancer patients who require long-term hospitalization or nursing care, convinces Buchanan that NCA should launch a new public relations campaign combining a public service message with a fund-raising component.

Buchanan feels that the target audience of the program, at least in its first phase, should be the local teenagers, who seem to have started smoking in such large numbers. Obviously, she wants to convince them to stop smoking, but more than that, she wants to convert this population into active participants in the Association's effort to fight cancer.

With these goals in mind, she fills out the following basic program information:

Target Audience
Local teenagers

PR Objectives

1 To get teenagers who smoke to quit (and convince others not to start).
2 To get teenagers to understand what's being done to fight cancer.
3 To develop a student NCA chapter to carry on this program for us.

PR Message

Smoking can cause cancer. Cancer can kill you. Instead of buying cigarettes, contribute to the NCA and help fight cancer (to be developed into a slogan).

Next, Buchanan prepares a memo elaborating this basic program information and arranges to discuss it in person with the president and vice president of the local chapter. They like the thrust of the program and, with their assistance, she comes up with a series of implementation ideas as well as an appropriate slogan to encapsulate the program message. She then prepares to write the final program to be presented to the NCA regional board of directors, which must approve all new programs for local chapters.

In preparing the program, Buchanan evaluates the implementation ideas against the chapter's present public relations and fund-raising budget. She realizes that the organization can finance most of the new PR campaign itself and will need outside help only to cover the design and printing expenses of brochures. At this point, she makes some calls to local merchants who have contributed to the organization in the past, and is pleased to find that Phil's Pharmacy is willing to underwrite the brochure costs. She also calls local high school administrators to be sure that she can count on their support for NCA-sponsored activities and special projects in the schools. Once assured of their cooperation, she is ready to draw up a full-scale program for review by the NCA regional board of directors. The draft of her program looks like this (the Table of Contents has not been included):

INTRODUCTION

A recent survey has shown that 15 percent of the teenagers in our community smoke cigarettes on a regular or irregular basis, an increase of 25 percent over the past five years. These are dire statistics which we, as the local chapter of the National Cancer Association, need to address.

Teenagers represent a crucial audience for our organization. They are the future: Their values and habits, once developed, will become the norms of tomorrow. Yet they are poised at the turning point between childhood and adulthood and are therefore capable of being easily influenced. If a rational course is clearly and convincingly mapped out for them, it is likely that they will choose that course. If not, they are likely to be seduced into irrational behavior. It is therefore our responsibility to rationally appeal to our teenagers not to smoke by making them understand the cancer risk.

In addition, teenagers represent an important resource to our organization which we have thus far failed to tap. Many teenagers work and can make a financial contribution to our cause now. Others are capable of supplying volunteer service in hospitals and in fund raising. By encouraging student participation in NCA, we guarantee a higher level of participation and contribution later on when our teenagers become wage-earning adults. We also encourage a level of responsibility in our youth which should help to discredit with them the irresponsible habit of smoking.

PR OBJECTIVES

1. To educate teenagers about lung cancer and, in so doing, get them to quit smoking or convince them not to start.
2. To make teenagers aware of what's being done to fight cancer.
3. To encourage teenagers to contribute monetarily to the NCA effort.
4. To establish an NCA student chapter to continue this program for us on an ongoing basis.

PR MESSAGE

The campaign will be built around the slogan

> "Put Your Money Where Your Mouth Is: Stop Smoking and Help Fight Cancer."

The message explicitly links smoking to cancer. It also combines the public service message with the fund-raising message. Although the program is directed exclusively at teenagers, the message has been chosen so that it can be applied to all smokers. We will therefore continue to use it in subsequent programs addressed to other target publics.

STRATEGY

We will attempt to appeal to students at school, at home, and in their places of recreation by disseminating information on the link between smoking and cancer and on the efforts being made to fight and treat cancer. A series of "Smoking Awareness Days," designated by NCA, will help focus media interest and dramatize NCA-sponsored activities and programs in the schools.

We will also urge students to join an NCA student chapter through a variety of media which have access to the youth market in the community.

METHODS OF IMPLEMENTATION

Brochure

An eight-page, four-color brochure will be created containing information on the following topics:

1 Statistics on teenage smoking.
2 The risks attached to smoking.
3 Tips on quitting.
4 Information on cancer research and treatment.
5 A fund-raising pitch.
6 Background on the NCA local chapter.
7 Information on the NCA student chapter and how to join.

The brochure will be developed by professional writers and designers in consultation with NCA chapter officials. All brochure development and printing will be underwritten by Phil's Pharmacy, 60 Main Street (credit will be given to Phil's on the back flap of the brochure).

Brochures will be distributed in local stores and in area high schools. We may also consider doing a direct mail campaign using high school and local youth group mailing lists.

Public Service Announcements

A series of ten public service announcements will be prepared for airing on local radio stations (selected according to the age group of their audience). Each announcement will be written in three versions (20-, 30-, and 60-second spots) announcing the campaign slogan. Each spot will briefly address some relevant topic, such as new statistics on lung cancer deaths, hospitalization costs, or costs for developing cures and treatments. The spots will end urging students to call the NCA local chapter for information about joining the NCA student chapter.

Smoking Awareness Days

NCA will designate five smoking awareness days which will serve as focal points for educational programs, discussion groups, and related activities in the high schools. The five days, spaced throughout the school year, will be publicized with the media in advance, and media representatives will be encouraged to visit the schools and develop appropriate feature stories. Area high school administrators have already agreed to participate in the program. Each awareness day will begin with a special assembly period in which an NCA spokesperson will make an introductory presentation and announce a schedule of the day's events. Events will include speakers presentations from the NCA speakers bureau (see below) as well as informal discussion groups and student-adult panels. NCA's documentary film, *Smokers' Risky Business*, will be shown continuously in the schools' auditoriums throughout the days. NCA officials and volunteers will be on hand to distribute brochures and to recruit members for the student chapter.

Speakers Bureau

NCA will recruit volunteer speakers from among doctors, researchers, psychologists, and other experts who can speak to students about such topics as smoking risks, cancer research, the psychology of addiction, and cancer treatment procedures. We will arrange speaking presentations at local youth groups, religious organizations, and the Community Center. In addition, speakers will take part in the five smoking awareness days at local high schools, where they will present talks and be available for discussion on panels and in smaller group workshops.

Case Studies

Our organization has access to a number of lung cancer patients who have expressed willingness to talk to students about their illness and its link to smoking. We would like to invite the editors of our high schools' student newspapers to interview some of these patients. Case histories, written by students, would have special credibility among students. Such articles could also be reprinted for distribution at other forums later on.

Student Chapter

We hope through the above activities to develop enough interest in a student chapter to compile an initial mailing list of at least 30 students. These students will be invited to attend a first meeting at the chapter office. They will elect their own officers and be directed to draw up a program for carrying on our "Put Your Money Where Your Mouth Is" program. We will also ask the student chapter to develop fund-raising ideas for a teenage audience.

It is hoped that by August of 198- the student chapter will have submitted a program plan and budget request which can be reviewed by the board of the local chapter during their fall session.

CONCLUSION

Through this public relations program we intend to inform young people about the cancer risks associated with smoking and to directly solicit their contribution to the NCA effort. We feel that by making our argument rational and direct and by offering students an actual role in our organization we will be able to convince them to be more responsible—both in terms of their personal health and their social role.

We hope that within a year we will be able to put this program into the hands of a newly formed student chapter. At that time, we will be ready to direct our "Put Your Money Where Your Mouth Is" campaign at a new target audience.

TIME FRAME

We would like to launch this program in early September to coincide with the beginning of the school year. This means that the preparation of materials and the organization of activities must begin in June, prior to the end of this school year, when we can still meet easily with school administrators and gather the resources needed for planning events. We hope to concentrate activities during the fall and winter and have the student chapter in place by late spring.

In order to keep to this schedule, we need to get final approval for the program from the board as soon as possible. We can then begin assigning organizational tasks to chapter staff and recruiting new volunteers where more help is necessary.

NCA Program Budget

Brochure All costs for the professional development, copywriting, editing, graphic design, typesetting, and printing of 5,000 eight-page four-color brochures will be defrayed by Phil's Pharmacy. The following expenses relating to the brochures remain:

Production of 3,000 cover letters and envelopes for direct mail of brochures to target publics	$ 700
Mailing of brochures	$1,000

Public Service Announcements Since we will prepare only print PSAs geared to radio, the cost of production will be minimal.

Smoking Awareness Days

Development of tailored audio-visual materials to be used in presentations (slides, overhead transparencies, flip charts); these will also serve our Speakers Bureau	$2,000

Speakers Bureau

Day-long training seminar for volunteer speakers using outside media training consultants	$1,000

Case Studies

Preparation of reprints of student articles—estimated 3,000 copies of each of three articles (expenses include allotment for envelopes and postage for limited mailing)	$2,200

Student Chapter

Start-up costs for supplies and refreshments for weekly meetings (chapter will submit a subsequent program budget)	$ 250
Contingency (10%)	$ 715
Total	$7,865

DEVELOPING A PR PROGRAM FOR BOTH AN INTERNAL AND AN EXTERNAL AUDIENCE

As explained in Chapter 3, the identification of key publics is part of the backbone of an effective PR program. Traditionally, the concentration has been on external publics, but as public relations has grown more sophisticated and more aware of the complex nature of its social role, internal groups (employees, members, stockholders) have emerged as equally important. Such groups not only determine whether an organization is successful or not, but also set the style and personality of the organization and can serve as its best promoters within the community at large.[6]

An organization may feel the need to initiate an internal PR program if a new management policy is being introduced, if employee morale is low, or if members have stopped paying their dues. But even when there is no specific internal issue or problem to be dealt with, organizations are commonly incorporating internal public relations considerations into their larger PR programs. They realize that internal publics connect up with external publics in many ways and can contribute substantially to the success of an external program.

When Micro Limited, a manufacturer of computer hardware located in New York City, decides to move its plant to Glenson, a small town in southern New Jersey, in order to ease its overhead and tax burden, the company's vice president of operations asks the PR director, Michael Jay, to develop a community relations program to help the company deal effectively with its new neighbors.

When Jay visits Glenson, he discovers that it is a semi-rural community about three hours from New York City and two hours from Philadelphia. He spends some time over lunch with members of the town's chamber of commerce who offer him a hearty welcome; they are pleased to have a successful computer company settle in the area. However, they do let drop that some of Glenson's citizens are not so pleased. "Many of our people are afraid that a high-tech company will dominate this simple little town," explains John Russell, president of the chamber. "People here distrust anything that's too slick and too new."

When Jay returns to New York City that night, he knows that Micro is going to have to convince Glenson's citizens that it is a "friendly" company. But he is also troubled by another aspect of the situation that his boss had not even considered. Jay knows that about 30 of Micro's middle and senior managers will be making the move to Glenson with the company. Having visited the town, he realizes that this will represent a major adjustment for employees and their families who are used to the more cosmopolitan environment of New York City. He himself feels uneasy at the prospect of settling in this semi-rural village. Jay knows that if Micro's employees are unhappy with their new home, this will be communicated to the community and will do nothing to help community relations. Considering the situation carefully, he decides that a strong community relations program must include an employee relations component to ease the adjustment for employees as well as locals. In fact, the more he thinks about it, the more convinced he is that employee relations is as important as community relations in this situation. The two publics are simply two sides of the same coin.

With this orientation in mind, Jay fills in the basic information necessary for the development of a program:

Target Audience

1 Middle and senior management of Micro who are planning to move to Glenson.
2 The local population of Glenson.

PR Objectives

1 To convince employees that Glenson is a good place to live and work
2 To convince Glenson that Micro is a friendly company and will be a positive addition to the community.

PR Message

Micro and Glenson: Each has something to offer the other.

SECONDARY MESSAGES

1 Glenson, though different from N.Y.C., is an excellent place to live and work and offers many advantages over city life. It is an especially good place to raise children.
2 Micro will be a good citizen of Glenson and will help enrich the life of the community.

After discussing his two-pronged plan with the vice president to whom he reports, Jay proceeds to draft the following program for submission to the company president (Table of Contents and Budget have not been included).

RATIONALE

For ten years, Micro has been a New York City company. Its employees have tended to be "big city" types, used to living and working in a fast-paced, cosmopolitan environment. Now that Micro has decided to move to the semi-rural location of Glenson, New Jersey (population 25,000), the senior and middle management employees who have been asked to make this move with the company are bound to experience culture shock.

At the same time, the local population of Glenson will need to adjust to the appearance of a high-tech company like Micro. They must be convinced that the company will "fit in" to the community.

The following public relations plan attempts to address the needs of both employees and community in order to make Micro's relocation as smooth and agreeable as possible for all concerned.

PR OBJECTIVES

1. To help Micro employees adjust to a new working environment.
2. To help Micro employees and their families see the advantages of and adjust to a new lifestyle; that is, make the transition from big city life to semi-rural life.
3. To convince the local community of Glenson that Micro is a good corporate citizen and will enrich the community.
4. To convince the local community that Micro employees are good neighbors.

ROLE OF COMMUNICATIONS

We feel that keeping the channels of communication open to suggestions and complaints from both employees and community members is crucial to the success of this program. Many of the problems which arise from company relocations are the result of misunderstandings when the real needs and desires of the various parties involved are not heard. We therefore feel that openness and flexibility are important.

Needless to say, not everyone can always be reached. Some of our employees may feel that they cannot make the adjustment to a different life style and may choose to leave the company. Some of Glenson's citizens may refuse to see the advantages of a high-tech company in their community. However, we feel these "unreachables" should be a small minority. We trust that the majority will appreciate and respond favorably to our communications effort.

STRATEGY

Our strategy for both the employee and the community facets of this program will be to encourage interaction and cooperation between the two groups wherever possible. This interaction will help each group "sell" the other. The population of Glenson and the employees of Micro are therefore our primary resources. In addition, we will present as much information as possible to Micro employees about Glenson, and to the Glenson population about Micro. Finally, the company will try to make a cultural contribution to the community that will appeal to both Glenson citizens and Micro employees.

IMPLEMENTATION

Employee Relations

MATERIALS

In conjunction with the chamber of commerce, Micro will compile an information kit on Glenson, specifically tailored to its employees' needs. The kit will contain information on schools, real estate, transportation, taxes, cultural events, restaurants, specialty shops, and community services.

EMPLOYEE DISCUSSION GROUPS

The company will sponsor a series of evening discussion groups in which employees and their families can meet for an informal dinner and discussion about the move. These groups will be a forum in which questions and anxieties concerning the relocation can be aired, and responded to by company officials.

INDIVIDUAL PERSONNEL CONFERENCES

Each employee who has been asked to make the move with the company should be scheduled for a one-hour meeting with his or her supervisor to discuss job definition and future prospects with the company. At this time, employees can be given certain limited guarantees concerning salary, benefits, and job security (which should be determined by the Board in the next few months).

Community Relations

OP-ED ARTICLE

Our public relations staff will prepare an opinion piece for the president's by-line for placement on the op-ed page or as an advertorial in Glenson's local weekly paper, the *Glenson Courier*. The article will discuss the contributions which high-tech firms can make to small communities. It will argue that such companies don't have to be cold and anonymous intruders but can be good neighbors, in touch with community needs.

ADVERTISING

A month before the relocation and for several months afterward, Micro will run a series of ads in the local paper and on the local radio station explaining the company's products and philosophy. The ads will emphasize the fact that Micro is a clean industry, labor intensive, highly profitable, and concerned with making a contribution to the community.

PLANT TOUR

Soon after the move the company will sponsor a plant tour for community officials and interested citizens. The tour, followed by a cocktail party and dinner, would be an event where company and community representatives have a chance to get better acquainted.

Combined Employee and Community Relations

THE BUDDY SYSTEM

The Glenson Chamber of Commerce is eager to welcome Micro to Glenson and will work with us in compiling a list of Glenson families who are willing to serve as "buddies" for the 30 Micro employees and their families who are contemplating relocation with the company. This represents an invaluable means of bringing the community and the company together. To get the buddy system off the ground, we will host a day-long series of activities in Glenson prior to the move: a picnic, community tour, cocktail party and formal dinner—giving employees and their families the opportunity to meet their buddies (and other members of the community) and exchange information.

MICRO CHAMBER MUSIC SERIES

In its first contribution to the community's cultural life, Micro will sponsor an annual series of chamber music concerts featuring artists brought in from New York City and Philadelphia. The series will prove that Micro is indeed committed to improving the quality of community life. It will also help assure Micro employees that top-quality cultural events will be available to them in Glenson.

CONCLUSION

In deciding to relocate, Micro has taken a step which will have a major effect on the lives of its employees and on the community which it plans to enter. In dealing responsibly and sensitively with both its internal and external publics, the company should be able not only to make the move smoothly but also to strengthen its relationship with these publics. This program can be only the beginning of an ongoing employee and community relations program. Activities and projects can be added as the needs of our target publics change and make themselves known to us.

EXERCISES

Test Your Judgment

Provide a PR message which is appropriate to the target audience and PR objectives given below. If more than one audience is given, you may break down your general message into secondary messages which address each of the publics directly.

1 TARGET AUDIENCE

Men and women over 65.

PR OBJECTIVES

a To improve understanding among the elderly of how Health Maintenance Organizations (HMOs) operate in making good quality, inexpensive health care available.
b To explain the advantages of HMOs to the elderly.
c To encourage greater use of HMO's by the elderly.

PR MESSAGE

2 TARGET AUDIENCE

a Carlyle University alumni.
b Carlyle University students and faculty.
c Local community.

PR OBJECTIVES

a To develop financial support for a new library planned for construction next year.
b To overcome local opposition to the library, which will replace a town park recently bought by the university for the library site.

PR MESSAGE

3 TARGET AUDIENCE

a Business press.
b Financial analysts.
c Stockholders.

PR OBJECTIVES

a To inform the target audience about Dole Chemical's new president.
b To link the new leadership to a new, more innovative management style and new direction for the company.
c To emphasize an attitude of openness and social responsibility on the part of Dole toward the public.

PR MESSAGE

PR Workshop

1   A charismatic young politician decides to run for Congress, and public opinion polls show that his constituency is strongest among the youngest segment of the voting population (18- to 21-year-olds). Although he terms himself a liberal Democrat, he has not yet developed a clear-cut set of issues for his campaign. This gives him flexibility but makes him vulnerable to his opponents' claim that he is "soft on issues."

His aides tell him that he must develop a program more specifically tailored to his target audience. They show him the following article, then sit down with him to help hammer out an identity program.

Read the article and discuss with the class how you might take it into account if you were working on the candidate's campaign. You might also want to discuss any problems in public relations ethics which this kind of program development might entail.

THE NEW-WAVE MARKET

Just as the values of the '60s rebels did not persist and come to dominate America in the '80s, so the values of New-Wave youth will probably be significant for the remainder of this decade and then fade away or become fundamentally transformed in ways that cannot be anticipated now. New-Wave values, however, will be with us for some time, and companies would be well-advised to understand the implications of that for their products and marketing strategies.

A good example of the difficulties in communicating with New-Wave youth is the jeans and jean-jacket market. Traditional American companies assumed teenagers would reject highly styled jean jackets and jeans, as teenagers had done in the past. But New-Wave youth, who want to look different from their parents, favor highly styled clothes, and one company, Guess Inc., has taken advantage of this attitude. By creating assorted jean colors and using denim in a wider range of styles, Guess is beginning to penetrate the market. Highly styled clothes in general (especially from Japan, England, and Italy) are making significant gains in the New-Wave market.

Manufacturers of computer games misjudged the scope of teenage demand for expensive video-arcade and repetitious home-computer games. As a marketing executive of a major computer company said, "Arcades are growing cobwebs; we goofed by developing only six basic game types and using those to produce endless variations of games they already had." The movement away from arcades to home games enabled teenagers to put their money to other uses since parents typically paid for personal computers and games. Then, the home-game market slumped as teenagers didn't buy the next clone of a game they were already playing.

But the potential attraction of computer games for creating substitute worlds is still very real. New microchip capabilities will result in more realistic and flexible video presentations. We can expect a sales boom of second- and third-generation games that are visually compelling and that require players to move through open-ended, symbolically rich environments rather than simply scoring a "kill" over a rudimentarily sketched enemy.

Anticipating and meeting the needs of New-Wave consumers is not easy. The following are a few basic guidelines:

- Do not assume that young people today think and act like previous generations.
- New-Wave teenagers respond to products and services clearly directed at them (and not immediately suitable for other markets) as an indicator that they are taken seriously. Thus, the market is sharply segmented.
- Style is critical; a clear, identifiable style for a product (especially for movies, clothes, records, computer games, and food) is necessary.

- Advertise the concrete, immediate rewards of a product, not abstract values of health or environmental quality.
- Given an emphasis on substitute worlds, products can be expected to have a relatively short life cycle, and new-product planning should begin even though an existing product is doing well.
- Monitor carefully trends in Europe and Japan, which have been the source of several New-Wave styles.

New-Wave values have recently begun to spread to adult America. We are starting to see advertisements for automobiles and perfume in stark, overdone primary colors, with surrealist scenes and music, and with a close interweaving of fantasy and reality. A better understanding of the New Wave is important for all companies, not just those marketing directly to younger people.[7]

2   Imagine that your class is the public information department of a national health organization. The organization has recently been informed that 65 percent of all Americans are overweight and, as a result, at risk for coronary disease. Among those at highest risk are middle-aged males in high-powered corporate careers.

Discuss how you would go about preparing a national public information program which would address this problem. What kind of additional research might you do? As a class, fill in possible target audience, PR objectives, and PR message.

3   According to a *Wall Street Journal* article, the accounting profession is plagued by a poor public image.[8] Accountants feel that they are perceived as dull and that TV and movies perpetuate this image.

Assume that the profession wishes to do something about this and decides to initiate an identity campaign. Preliminary research indicates that the target audience should consist of media executives and decision-makers, and that the PR objective should be to help inspire a more glamorous rendering of accountants in the media.

Divide into groups of three or four students, with each group working to develop a PR message and an appropriate strategy for an identity program based on the above information. Then brainstorm to come up with two or three implementation tools.

Each group should appoint a leader to steer discussion and a secretary to take notes. At the end of the session, the leader (or an appointed spokesperson) should make a formal presentation of your group's conclusion to the class.

4   As a class, come up with a list of events and programs for your college or university that would serve a public relations function in respect to both internal and external publics. In determining these activities, first discuss the various ways that the institution's internal and external publics relate to each

other. Discuss whether students should be considered as internal or external publics.

PR Case Studies

Since you will need to be familiar with the implementation tools and techniques described in subsequent chapters in order to write effective PR programs, the case study for this chapter should function as an end-of-term project.

1 Develop a PR program for the upcoming academic year based on the research you did in the case study on a student service or program in the Exercises of Chapter 3. In writing the program, try to keep it within a budget range of $5,000 to $10,000 (reasonable for an academic institution). You may charge for your time by determining an hourly rate and estimating hours to be spent on each activity in the program, or you may charge a flat fee for your services; however, be sure to itemize estimates for out-of-pocket expenses. If you feel the budget is too limiting, you may want to organize the program around a core of inexpensive activities and then group more expensive implementation ideas under an optional category.

Don't rule out the possibility that someone may want you to actually implement the program if it appears to answer a real need.

OR

2 Develop a PR program for a client of your own choosing (choose an organization that you have ready access to). Arrange to meet with a client representative to discuss PR needs, and be prepared to do some preliminary informal research to help establish target audience, PR objectives, and PR message. If the client is interested in the possibility of implementing the program, work out a suitable budget in advance; otherwise, establish budget limitations yourself based on the size and nature of the organization.

NOTES

1. *Wall Street Journal*, July 19, 1982, p. 17.
2. *PRSA Newsletter*, II, 4–5 (April-May 1983), 1.
3. David E. Sanger, "The Changing Image of IBM," *New York Times Magazine*, July 7, 1985, p. 12.
4. *New York Times*, July 25, 1985, sec. D, p.1.
5. See the six-part series, *Public Relations Guide for Nonprofit Organizations* (New York: Foundation for Public Relations, 1977).

6. See R. G. Foltz, "Employee Support is the Key to Credibility," *Personnel Administration*, 27 (October 1982), 17–18.

7. From Steve Barnett, "Brave New Wave of the '80s," *Across the Board* (the magazine of the Conference Board), XX, No. 11 (December 1983), 12, by permission of the author and publishers.

8. *Wall Street Journal*, April 26, 1984, p. 1.

5

Developing Visibility I: Engaging Media Interest

The roots of the publicity component of public relations can be traced back to ancient times when monarchs erected monuments, staged spectacles, and waged wars in an effort to build their reputations. To disseminate news of these accomplishments, they relied upon word of mouth. People told other people about what they had seen and these people, in turn, told others, and by this arduous path, legends were born.

But with the development of mass communication, the potential for gaining publicity was enormously facilitated. Instead of the cumbersome transmission of news through rumor and person-to-person storytelling, there was now an intermediary structure that could communicate with masses of people at once. Newspapers and magazines and, later, radio and TV not only were capable of hastening the dissemination of information to a mass audience, but also could target specific groups for the reception of specific messages.

Yet the development of mass communication also complicated the meaning of publicity. While the term *publicity* was first formally used as a synonym for advertising in the nineteenth century, by the beginning of the twentieth century it also began to refer to the disclosure of information brought about by investigative journalism.[1] To some extent, this split definition still persists. Publicity can refer both to the positive exposure of an organization in the media, and to its negative exposure (the revelation by the media of dishonest or otherwise dubious practices on the part of an organization).

In the 1920s and 1930s in Hollywood, press agents—unabashed seekers of publicity—disregarded the distinction. Getting a client's name in the paper was the objective, almost regardless of what was written. It was felt that juicy gossip, even scandal, could help a young starlet rise in the industry by merely making her name known. During this period the adage was born that "good" publicity is a story in which a client's name is spelled correctly; "bad" publicity is one where it's spelled wrong. Hollywood press agent Henry C. Rogers claims that it wasn't until the 1940s, when *he* entered the scene, that actors and actresses began to understand that "getting their names into print was not important in itself. What the item, paragraph, or article said was important. Did it help meet *their objective?*"[2] Whether or not Rogers was responsible, this realization was the beginning of *informed* publicity.

Although the role of publicity in public relations has come a long way since the golden days of Hollywood, publicity continues to play an important part in public relations practice. This is especially true because the number of *publicity outlets* (media channels through which the public can be reached) continue to multiply, making it increasingly possible to reach both a large general audience and targeted special interest groups.

It used to be common for organizations and agencies to hire professional publicity people whose extensive press contacts made them valuable. These people's sole responsibility was to *pitch* a story, often by picking up the telephone and imparting some sensational angle to one of their numerous press contacts. Usually these contacts were built over many years and cemented with periodic lunches and meetings over cocktails. Though this species of publicity-grabber still exists (they are usually ex-newspaper people themselves), it is fast being replaced by a new breed of PR practitioner for whom the publicity function is a less social and more systematized component of the job. One reason for the change is that it is no longer possible to "know," socially or otherwise, all the key people in the media. The number of publicity outlets is too vast, and individuals shift positions too rapidly for the old-style cultivation of contacts to work well, except in a handful of cases.

Another reason why the traditional publicity person is on the wane is because the profession itself has changed. A public relations effort today generally involves much more than a telephone call to an editor or a meeting over drinks with a reporter. Publicity tends to exist now as one part of a larger program, and before a story is pitched, a number of factors are first examined and evaluated in order to determine how the pitch should be made or whether it should be made at all.

PUBLICITY CONTENT

In seeking publicity for a client, it is first important to determine what information is available for you to work with. This information will serve as the *content* of the message which you will ultimately relay to the media.

Content breaks down into two general categories which, for our purposes, we call news and newsworthy information.

What Is News?

News is what's new and important. It implies immediacy, timeliness, urgency. News comes in two varieties: Its newness can represent novelty—a break with what already exists—as in a new product, a new play, a new theory of the universe. Or it can represent a response to a need for new information, as in the response of a company to a survey, an accident, or an accusation.

What Is Newsworthy?

Newsworthy information responds not to a perceived need but to a created need. It engages the curiosity of the public in an area in which it may not have been interested before—or not known it was interested. A newsworthy item may be timeless, or at least not linked to a specific date. It may involve a human interest story, a profile of or interview with an unusual individual, or an assortment of helpful tips in an area with which the reader is concerned.

In journalism, where a similar distinction in content is made between "hard" and "soft" news, preeminence is usually given to hard news. But in public relations, news is not always more important than newsworthy information. In fact, newsworthy information, when effectively exploited, can often generate more and better publicity for a client. One of the most sensational examples of what we mean is a newsworthy story which appeared in the *New York Times* under this headline: "Just a Quiet Dinner for Two in Paris: Thirty-one Dishes, Nine Wines, a $4,000 Check."[3] This extraordinary story—its headline alone makes clear it is not conventional news—nonetheless made the front page of one of the nation's most important papers by the strength of its human interest value alone. The article tells how food critic Craig Claiborne made a winning bid of $300 at a fund-raising auction on behalf of a New York City public television station. The bid bought him a meal at a restaurant anywhere in the world which would be paid for by the meal's donor, the American Express Company. Claiborne and a friend managed to ring up a $4,000 tab at the Parisian restaurant they chose. The cost of the meal may at first seem like an enormous loss to American Express, but when you consider that it won the story front-page placement in the *Times*, the trade-off to the company seems more than worth it. No amount of advertising could have bought such publicity, and few if any news-oriented stories on American Express could have won front page treatment. Here, newsworthiness far exceeded news in its ability to engage media interest.

PUBLICITY CONTEXT

By *context* in publicity we are referring to both the setting or situation in which the content occurred or exists, and the audience to whom the content would be of interest. Take, for example, the case of the space shot in which Sally Ride, the first female astronaut, participated. The context, on the one hand, was the site of the shot, the preparations made, and the scientists, technicians, and other experts available to comment and explain the event. On the other hand, context was also the audience interested in the shot: the general public and the targeted special interest groups—in this case, the scientific audience and women, in particular.

Context supplies the necessary background and determines the angle from which the content should be presented. The publicity outlets through which a message will pass in order to reach its target audience are also determined by the elements of context which make up the story.

Publicity Outlets

In public relations, we tend to regard the media as a collection of publicity outlets—conduits leading to the public or publics we wish to reach. Thus, in the space shot example, the general public was reached through general consumer media, the scientific audience through science and technology media, and women through female-oriented media (these groups, of course, overlapped). In choosing to relay the story through any one of these outlets, a different contextual element had to be stressed. A general consumer story might have included general information about space exploration and simplified explanations of the technology involved. A scientific article might have covered a specific technological procedure or device undergoing tests in the shot. An article geared toward women might have featured an interview with the female astronaut and discussed the role of women in other aspects of the space program.

Access to publicity outlets has become both easier and more difficult in recent years. It is easier because public relations people now have at their disposal a number of reference books, updated frequently, which supply listings and requirements of newspapers and magazines, and radio and TV stations across the country. These publications give information about circulation and editorial policy and provide the names of specialized editors and reporters.* There are also regional directories available for most urban cen-

---

*Among the best known are *Bacon's Publicity Checkers* for newspapers and magazines, and *Radio and TV Reports* for radio and TV listings. *U.S. Publicity Directory* and *Working Press of the Nation* provide listings for radio, TV, and periodicals.

ters, and a variety of newsletters and specialized directories that report on newly created or special interest outlets.*

Where the use of publicity outlets has become more of a problem is in their sheer proliferation. It is now more difficult to know the important editors and reporters in a particular field. And because of increasing specialization, it may not be possible to reach your target audience with one good story but may require a number of stories with different angles to reach the segmented audience within a particular field. With the proliferation of publicity outlets, the context of public relations also demands more rigorous analysis. This is one reason why public opinion audits and other kinds of research have become an important component of PR practice (see Chapter 3). Research supplies the background necessary for establishing PR objectives, identifying target publics and framing PR messages. With this information, it then becomes possible to determine which of the many available outlets should be chosen to relay the established messages in order to reach the desired publics.

METHODS OF PUBLICITY IMPLEMENTATION

In order to obtain publicity for a client, you must begin by *pitching* the client's story to the media. The pitch is where content and context come together in an effective message. In some situations, a telephone call to an editor or a reporter is the best method of pitching a story. In other cases, the pitch works better in writing, either in the form of a press or broadcast release or in the more casual form of a pitch letter. In the following pages, we will consider each of these methods of publicity implementation in detail.†

The Telephone Pitch

The prospect of pitching a story over the telephone can have different effects on different people. Some enjoy the element of surprise and risk which the telephone pitch carries with it: An editor can hang up on you or, then again, can respond enthusiastically with "Hey, that's a great story! Send me all the information you have!" Others shudder at the prospect of calling an editor "cold"—when no previous written material on the subject has been sent.

Most of us fall somewhere between these two extremes. We don't mind the phone on occasion, but we wouldn't relish trying to explain the latest mon-

---

*A fairly comprehensive list of media directories is available through the PRSA Information Center, 845 Third Avenue, 12th Floor, New York, N.Y. 10022. Most good reference libraries have copies of the major directories. Public relations agencies and departments generally order the media directories they need directly from the publisher on an annual basis.

†In Chapter 6, we will discuss the news conference, a public relations event which is the "live" means of pitching a story.

etary actions of the Federal Reserve Governors to a surly editor ten minutes before deadline.

In deciding whether or not it's worth phoning an editor or a reporter or whether it would be preferable to use an alternative method of pitching your story, it's helpful to ask yourself the following questions:

HOW MUCH INFORMATION HAS TO BE RELAYED?

If the content of the message is succinct enough, it may be a good idea to call the editor or reporter before sending out a press release. This will alert him or her to the story and may mean that more attention gets paid to the release when it does arrive. Always identify yourself and your affiliation first; ask if the person you are calling has "got a minute"; then get right to the point. Here's how a typical pitch might go:

Doug Brown: Hello, I'm Doug Brown, student activities chairman at Memorial College. Have you got a minute to hear about our upcoming special event?

Editor: O.K.

Doug Brown: Memorial will be sponsoring a Walkathon for Diabetes in two weeks. We have a lot of community support and are expecting a turnout of more than a thousand people. A release is in the mail. Do you think you'll be able to assign someone to cover the event?

In this case, the information is simple, straightforward, and easy to state briefly over the phone. The editor may ask for the details of date, time, and place on the spot, or wait for the release. Either way, Brown may want to call again once the release has been received to provide additional information and try to confirm coverage.

If the content of the message is more complex than the one quoted above, it generally makes sense to wait until after a press release has been sent before making the first telephone call. In such cases, your call becomes explanatory rather than a cold pitch, as in the following example:

> This is Jim Stahl at Overview Hospital. If you've got a minute, I'm calling to clarify a few points in the release I sent you about our open-heart surgery program. Do you happen to have it handy?

This way, you find out whether the release has been received and read, and you have an opportunity to discuss the story with the editor or reporter in detail.

WHAT IS THE EDITORIAL SCHEDULE OF THE TARGET PUBLICATION?

Since all publications function on some kind of deadline, the telephone gives access to quick information and helps meet that deadline. Keep in mind, of course, that different media have different kinds of deadlines. Assignment editors on live TV news shows, for example, will often tell you to call them an hour before the event. They save their crews for spot news; if there is none, they may be willing to cover your story at, literally, the last minute. For them, changing needs make the telephone the best instrument. For magazines, on the other hand, immediacy has a very different meaning. Many monthly magazines make up their editorial schedules two, three, or even four months in advance; if you call with a story idea three weeks before an issue appears, you'll simply be too late for that issue, no matter how great your story is. Moreover, because of their long lead times, magazines should generally be pitched in writing first, with follow-up by phone.*

Getting to know the pace of various media and the way individual media people work can also help you decide whether to try making a pitch by phone or not. If, for example, the energy editor of a local paper puts out a column on an irregular basis—whenever interesting news comes her way—she may be eager to chat with you on the phone about the new insulation material your client has developed. But if she has a column due every day, she will probably be less willing.

If a story is not specifically time-linked, it's never a good idea to call a morning daily in the late afternoon as deadline approaches. On the other hand, because daily newspapers work on short deadlines, reporters will often appreciate a phone call to alert them to potential news or newsworthy information as quickly as possible.

IS SUFFICIENT BACKGROUND INFORMATION READILY ACCESSIBLE?

Ideally, whenever you decide to pitch a story, whether by phone or in writing, you should have researched and understood it thoroughly. But knowledge is sometimes a relative thing, and what is adequate knowledge in one context may be inadequate in another. In writing a press release or pitch letter, you have the advantage of selecting what you want to include and omit. You can even camouflage gaps in your knowledge by the angle from which you choose to present the material. On the phone, you are more vulnerable; you can never predict what questions you may be asked. While this doesn't mean that you have to be an expert on every subject you pitch over the phone, it does mean that you should have ready access to someone who

---

*It's good practice to keep a list of the deadlines for magazines you might be interested in pitching, making special note of issues devoted to a particular subject or theme. This way, you can improve your chances of placement by planning story ideas to conform with special issue subjects. Many special interest publications will, on request, send you calendars or schedules which give deadlines and guidelines for editorial submissions.

is. It's best to be able to put a reporter in direct contact with your source if there's something you can't answer, by stating:

> I can't answer that, but I can put you in touch with someone who can. Shall I have him call you or would you rather call him?

Barring this approach (if the source isn't or doesn't want to be available to the media), the next best thing is to act as intermediary:

> I'll get that information for you and call you back. By what time must you have it?

Of course, if you make such a promise, be prepared to keep it.

HOW SPECIFIC IS THE TARGET AUDIENCE?

A telephone pitch is most effective when it involves a message with appeal to a specific audience, making it possible for you to pitch a specific editor or reporter. A senior editor of a publication will rarely have the time or patience to listen to anything that isn't a significant story. But while your pitch concerning a new device which helps joggers regulate their breathing probably wouldn't interest the managing editor of a local newspaper, it might interest the science editor, and would be more likely still to interest the sports, health, or leisure editor.

The Press Release

The press release* is probably the best known and most used form of public relations communication. Many newspaper and magazine editors, who receive mountains of press releases daily, complain that it is used indiscriminately. Sometimes they have a point—knowing when not to send a press release can be as important as knowing when to send one. There are many times when a telephone pitch, a pitch letter, or a simple handwritten note would be more effective in relaying the desired message.

The content of your message should determine whether or not a press release is called for. Is the content clear-cut and focused, yet substantial enough to warrant a one- or two-page announcement? A press release always contains a single, coherent message and enough background information to substantiate that message. This is no place for creative writing, vague conclusions, or personal opinion.

The standard press release usually adopts the rules for spelling, punctua-

---

*In this chapter, a distinction is made between a *press release* (a release directed at print media) and a *broadcast release* (a release directed at electronic media). However, *press release* is otherwise used generically in this textbook to refer to both kinds of releases.

tion, and capitalization used by the wire services, Associated Press (AP) or United Press International (UPI). Some publications prefer the *New York Times* or the *Washington Post* style books. If you are sending a release to only one publication, try to use the style it prefers. If you are sending out many, choose one style and be consistent. You can find copies of stylebooks in college bookstores, or you can order directly from a news organization.

Although there may be minor variations in presentation, the typical press release looks like this:

CONTACT: Susan Smithers
Jerome Franklin International
130 Park Avenue
New York, NY 10022
(212) 555-1222   <u>FOR IMMEDIATE RELEASE</u>

JEROME FRANKLIN MAKES WORLD'S LARGEST PURCHASE OF STAMPS; COLLECTION BOUGHT FOR $20 MILLION, TWICE PREVIOUS RECORD

NEW YORK, August 14.—Jerome Franklin International, one of the world's largest international stamp dealers, today announced the purchase of the Jay Hall collection of early U.S. postal covers for a record price of $20 million. The previous record was $10 million.

Sidney Keller, chairman of the board of the company, described the largest purchase in philatelic history at a press conference today at the "21" Club.

The collection of 5,000 items, amassed over a period of 30 years by Jay Hall, a New York manufacturer, is probably the most complete assemblage of early U.S. covers and postal history materials. It encompasses the pre-stamp period through 1869 and includes items signed personally by George Washington, Thomas Jefferson, Andrew Jackson, Abraham Lincoln, and Robert E. Lee, all of whom had franking privileges.

# # #

PRESS RELEASE FORM AND STYLE

Here are some general guidelines on the form and style of press releases (some organizations may use a slightly different format but will generally include the same basic components):

The Contact At the top right- or left-hand corner of the release, the organization's contact is given. Usually this consists of one or two names of people who can be reached easily for more information. Under the name or names is the affiliation (company, association, agency), and the address and the telephone numbers of the contacts. Where the contacts' address and telephone are different from those of the organization being represented, the distinction should be made clear (as in the Model Case Study on finding a newsworthy angle for a story). All contact information should be single-spaced.

The Release Date Toward the right of the page, slightly below the contact information, give the release date—when the event described in the release is happening or when the news may be used. If the event has taken place or is in the process of taking place, use "FOR IMMEDIATE RELEASE." If your piece is timeless, make it "RELEASE AT WILL."

The Headline This should appear in capital letters (underlined if you wish) about one-third of the way down the first page. The purpose of the headline in a release is to catch the eye of the busy editor who is going through a stack of them. A shortened form of the headline, called the *slugline*, should be used for identification along with the page number in the top left-hand corner of succeeding pages.

The Dateline This is the *where* and *when* of the event being described. Indent and capitalize the city (and state, if necessary for identification), follow with the month and day. In releases which are not tied to a specific time, the date on the dateline can be omitted, though a date specifying when the release was written should be included at the end of the copy.

The Body The body of the release should be double-spaced (quadruple spacing between paragraphs if you wish). Paragraphs should be short, in journalistic style. Direct quotes should alternate with indirect quotes and with factual, non-quoted information to ease readability. When a release runs more than one page, type "-more-" at the bottom of each page, except the last. Indicate the end of the release with "-x-," "###," or "-30-."

In writing press releases, you will also want to be aware of the following elements:

The Hook The hook in a release is the first or first few sentences (also called the *lead*), which grab the reader's attention. A good hook either tells immediately why the story is important or arouses curiosity and a desire for more information. If your hook doesn't work, chances are an editor won't read beyond it, and your release will end up in the trash.

References All references in a release should be clearly explained and situated. In referring to people, you should give the relevant affiliations alongside the name. Be especially sure that the relationship to your client is made clear, as in: "Jane Kroll, executive director of Simonds Eastern Division, said . . . "; or "According to Ralph Most, a chemical engineer with the Feld Company and a member of the American Society of Chemical Engineers (ASCE) . . . ." In the first case, Simonds Company is the client; in the second ASCE is the client. In using acronyms, be sure to spell out the full name, giving the acronym in parentheses in the first reference; after this, you are free to use the acronym alone. In referring to companies, or groups not commonly known, designate the nature and location of the organization in your first reference, such as, "Larson and Larson, Inc., a law firm in Hackensack, N.J. . . . " If the location of the reference corresponds to the dateline, use "here": "Larson and Larson, Inc., a law firm here, . . . " Check and double-check the accuracy of all references, and be especially sure proper names are spelled correctly.

Quotations As you know from reading newspapers, most good stories contain quotations. These come either from experts who have specialized knowledge about the subject at hand or from people who are directly involved in the story. In releases, quoting can lend credibility to your subject and give it a greater human interest value. Be careful, however, to quote judiciously. If you need an expert opinion to back up a point, be sure to find the right expert and check his or her credentials. In a release for a company, it's usually the policy to quote the top management official who's most closely related to the subject and/or the senior official in the organization. Though a well-placed quote is an asset, don't clutter your release with quotes that obscure the clear flow of information. It's best to use statements which get across the point in a colorful but succinct fashion. Remember that unlike a newspaper reporter whose job it is to quote sources exactly, you can sit down with your client and discuss what he or she would like to say, then prepare a draft of the remarks and ask for final approval on the finished copy. This gives you leeway to prune or amplify the client's language as may seem appropriate. However, if the source of a quote is not your client and will not be available to approve an edited statement, you are obliged, like any reporter, to quote exactly what was said.

As these guidelines indicate, the press release should look and read like finished copy, ready for insertion into a newspaper or magazine if the editor so chooses. This is not to say that this is the destination of most or even many press releases. Sometimes they are only the springboard from which a reporter goes on to pursue a story; sometimes they are rewritten by an editor to fit the style of the publication or to provide a different angle; many times they simply aren't used at all. Nonetheless, a press release is a convenient means of presenting certain kinds of information to the media.

Although all press releases should follow the general guidelines outlined above, not all press releases contain the same type of information or present it in the same way. There are in fact two general kinds of press releases, each of which deserves to be considered in more detail: news releases (which are based on news), and feature releases (which are based on newsworthy information).

TYPES OF PRESS RELEASES

The News Release In a news release the announcement of news is made as economically as possible with the enumeration of the five journalistic W's (Who, What, When, Where, and Why) in the first paragraph, or occasionally, in the first two paragraphs. The hook of a news release usually resides in the information itself, and you rarely need to dream up a creative angle as you do in a feature release.

The Feature Release In a feature release, newsworthy information takes precedence over hard news. Where the news release is objective (What happened?), the feature release is subjective (What's interesting or out of the ordinary?). Where the news release presents the facts (the five W's), the feature release presents a perspective on the facts (the five W's may be presented later rather than sooner). Because the element of interest is a matter of judgment (what is interesting to you may not be interesting to me), it generally requires more thought to write a good feature release than a good news release. The first step may involve deciding *not* to write a news release. It may mean finding a newsworthy angle on what would otherwise be everyday, run-of-the-mill material, or researching and combining pieces of information which would ordinarily not be viewed together, to produce an original story. Because a good feature release is based on newsworthy information, it probably won't have to run on a specific date. It can be held by an editor and slipped in when there is space—when hard news is in short supply. Sometimes it can be hooked onto current news events and assume special value for readers as a result. After a neighborhood fire, for example, a feature release from a local engineering organization on fire prevention tips for the home becomes a topical story.

The differences between news and feature releases can be seen by examining the following excerpts from two releases, both written for the same client (Census, Inc.) and based on the same material:

NEW SURVEY TAKEN OF U.S. HOUSEHOLDS

NEW YORK, April 5.—A new survey comparing the life styles and habits of Americans in different parts of the country has been conducted by Census Inc., an independent research company in Westchester. During 1982 the firm studied more than 100 urban centers and gathered statistics on family size, income, living accommodations, and use of leisure time.

SURVEY SAYS MORE NEW YORKERS LIVE ALONE

NEW YORK, April 5.—Twice as many people live alone in New York City as in other major cities throughout the country, according to a recent survey by Census Inc., an independent research company in Westchester. The survey also indicates that the number of New Yorkers living alone has doubled in the last decade.

Of the two examples, the feature release (the second one) is clearly more effective, considering the facts which the writer has to work with. That a life style survey has been conducted throughout the country is simply not interesting enough or big enough news to serve as the basis for a news release (the first one). Instead, what makes an effective story (since the release is being distributed to New York City publications) is the newsworthy data concerning New Yorkers' life styles as compared with those of the rest of the country. If the release were to be distributed to publications in other geographical areas, a number of different hooks could be constructed geared to the cities in question (for Chicago papers, for example, a comparison of some unusual statistic relating Chicago life to the rest of the country). In writing a series of targeted feature releases to publications aimed at different geographical regions or with different readerships, only the headline and first paragraph would need to be altered, since general information concerning the survey (who conducted it, how it was conducted, and so forth), appearing after the lead, would be standard material appropriate for all audiences.

Photos and Captions

Many publications are on the lookout for good photographs to enliven their pages and will even, sometimes, print the photo and caption and ignore the release. Also, bear in mind that the caption writer on a publication is frequently not a reporter and may not have easy access to all the background material relating to the story. That's why it's important that your photo caption be clear and complete (see Exhibit 5-1). Full contact information should also appear on the photo caption as well as the release.

EXHIBIT 5-1 *The Associated Press Stylebook and Libel Manual's* Ten Tests of a Good Caption. (Reprinted by permission of The Associated Press.)

> 1. Is it complete?
> 2. Does it identify, fully and clearly?
> 3. Does it tell when?
> 4. Does it tell where?
> 5. Does it tell what's in the picture?
> 6. Does it have the names spelled correctly, with the proper name on the right person?
> 7. Is it specific?
> 8. Is it easy to read?
> 9. Have as many adjectives as possible been removed?
> 10. Does it suggest another picture?
>
> And rule 11, the Cardinal Rule, never, never to be violated: NEVER WRITE A CAPTION WITHOUT SEEING THE PICTURE.[4]

According to recent studies on the use of photos in public relations, the most effective photos (and those most likely to be used by editors) are spontaneous, not posed, shots, and they contain a limited number of items (preferably people, not things) which are centered or positioned to the upper left.[5] The studies say in general that photos, when they appear in print, tend to get readers' attention and reinforce the message better than news or feature stories do.

Unless otherwise indicated, photos should be black and white, 8-inch by 10-inch glossy prints. Specify that color photos are available upon request, if this is the case. A photo caption should be securely pasted to the print to assure that it does not get lost or become associated with the wrong photo.

Of course, not all publications print photos or accept photos not taken by staff photographers. Because prints are expensive, it's worth checking in advance before sending a photo with your release.

The Broadcast Release

Brevity is the key to an effective broadcast release. Follow the same general format and rationale you would for release for the print media, but reduce the copy to one page or less. However, since the release may have to be rewritten (added to or changed) by the broadcaster to fit into the news format, it is also a good idea to include background material (a brochure, a fact sheet, and/or a copy of the longer release you sent to the print media).

Contact information is especially important in a release directed at the broadcast media because an editor may find that he or she needs something clarified right before going on the air. Provide whatever telephone numbers are needed to get hold of you (or another reliable contact) around the clock.

While most broadcast releases contain information intended for incorporation into radio or TV news announcements, the broadcast release can also serve to alert radio and TV people to an event they might want to cover with their own crews (in this case, the release may be accompanied by an invitation). Radio will be primarily interested in a meaty interview. But if you're seeking TV coverage, be sure that what you're pitching has a visual angle too, that there's something to shoot that's interesting to look at. Rarely will a TV crew be sent out to film "talking heads"—people giving speeches or talking to each other. If you're after TV coverage, your release should also be accompanied by a memo that provides relevant information for the crew (on lighting and sound problems, order of events and speakers, and so on). The contact person whose name is on the release should be present at the event and should identify him or herself as soon as possible. The contact should be ready to assist in arranging shots and supplying whatever background information is needed.

If you're interested in obtaining TV news coverage, you should call to find out the assignment editor (the editor in charge of assigning crews and keeping track of story assignments for a given day or night) who will be on duty on the day (or night) of your event. Mail the release and other supporting information to this person. On the day of your event, you can call the assignment editor to see whether coverage has been scheduled.

The Pitch Letter

A pitch letter is a letter to an editor or a reporter suggesting a story idea, providing background on the idea, and offering possible angles from which the story could be approached. It is a more flexible tool than the press release because it is not bound by the conventions of release writing and because it is based on a potentially intimate two-way relationship: the "I" and "you" of a correspondence. The pitch letter also tends to be concerned with newsworthy information rather than news, but unlike the feature release, the context in the letter can shift with each new paragraph.

Use a pitch letter for a multifaceted story idea or a story idea which isn't clear-cut. You might write a pitch letter if you want to see a profile written on a notable individual or "place" someone on a talk show, or if you want to propose that a feature story be written on a company or a city. A pitch letter is meant to arouse the interest of the media and inspire an editor or a reporter to shape a story around an angle you've suggested. The letter should be as brief as possible (ideally, no more than one or two pages)—but tantalizing!

Model Case Studies

PUBLICIZING A ROUTINE DEVELOPMENT

Most public relations people spend a good deal of time publicizing routine developments within their organizations. These events can include

1. The appointment, promotion, or retirement of noteworthy organizational officials.
2. The publication of quarterly or annual financial reports.
3. Public service information.
4. Routine changes or improvements in products, processes, or company literature.

This information isn't world-shaking, but it must be publicized because certain people will always be interested in knowing about it, and because disseminating it serves to maintain the visibility of your organization with the media. Clarity and efficiency tend to be key considerations in relaying this information effectively. In general, it's best to treat these routine events as news items and to present them using the standard news-release form.

Peter Loeb is a public relations official at a newly formed satellite broadcasting company named Satellite, Inc., in New York City. On March 23rd Loeb receives a memo from Satellite's president, Delmore Troy, informing him that two new senior vice presidents have been appointed in the company. Troy attaches the résumés and photos of the new company officers to the memo and instructs Loeb to publicize the appointments. Loeb studies the two résumés, consults the company brochure, and writes the following news release:

CONTACT: Peter Loeb
Satellite Inc.
100 East 59 Street
New York, NY 10022
(212) 555-1111   FOR IMMEDIATE RELEASE

SATELLITE INC. NAMES TWO SENIOR VICE PRESIDENTS

NEW YORK, March 23.—The appointment of John Reardon as senior vice president, Operations, and Philip Gray as senior vice president, Marketing and Sales, was announced today by Delmore Troy, president and chief executive officer of Satellite Inc.

John Reardon came to Satellite from United Telegraph Co., where he was president and general manager of the Field Services Division. Prior to that, he was a Monarch Records vice-president. Reardon is regarded as an expert in installation, sales, service, and technical operations, including data processing. He holds a Ph.D. in economics from Harvard University.

Philip Gray joined Satellite Inc. from Elm Communications' ELM-TV, where he was vice president and general manager and built a highly successful Chicago subscription television operation. Previously, he was the marketing director of Dew Shampoo. He combines classic package goods experience with a hands-on pay-TV operations background. Gray holds an M.B.A. from Columbia University.

Beginning in the fall of 1983, Satellite plans to broadcast five channels of movies, sports, news, and pay-per-view programming to single- and multiple-family dwellings, hotels, hospitals, cable TV systems, multi-point distribution systems, low-power television stations, and satellite master antenna systems.

-more-

> Satellite Senior Vice Presidents/2
>
> The Satellite Inc. service will operate through transponders on the Canadian ANIK-C2 satellite, which is expected to be launched by the U.S. Space Shuttle next summer. Satellite has also contracted for transponders on UCO Satellite Corporation's USTAR satellite, scheduled for launching next year. When the USTAR satellite becomes operational, Satellite's service will be transferred from ANIK-C2 to USTAR.
>
> # # #

Loeb's release is a standard personnel news release. It gives the appointments and the name of the company in the headline and provides the names of the two senior vice presidents and the source of the announcement of their appointments (Satellite's president) in the first paragraph. It also offers some additional information on the background of the appointees in the succeeding two paragraphs (highlights from their previous work experience and noteworthy awards or degrees).

The remaining two paragraphs of the release are about Satellite—its range and capabilities as a satellite broadcast company. This is an important part of the release because it provides an opportunity for a little-known company to gain additional publicity for itself. In fact, the two paragraphs which end this release are standard elements of all releases which Loeb writes for Satellite.

Loeb does a fairly extensive mailing of the release. No doubt some of the general business, TV, and video publications will ignore the announcement as too trivial and specialized; some, however, may devote a line or two to the appointments. Loeb's best opportunities for placement are with the special-interest trade publications in the satellite broadcast field, and with the home town newspapers and college alumni magazines of the appointees. For these, Loeb attaches an additional page with the caption: "FOR HOME TOWN AND TRADE PUBLICATIONS." This addendum gives addresses, marital status, names of children, and additional educational and personal details concerning the new officials. Loeb also includes a captioned photo of one or both of the new officials (Reardon's home town paper will not be interested in running Gray's photo, but a trade publication may run both photos). One of the photo captions sent to a New Jersey paper (which serves the area where Reardon lives) reads as follows:

130   Developing Visibility I: Engaging Media Interest

(PHOTO)

CONTACT: Peter Loeb
Satellite Inc.
100 East 59 Street
New York, NY 10022
(212) 555-1111   FOR IMMEDIATE RELEASE

OAK RIDGE EXECUTIVE NAMED SENIOR VICE PRESIDENT

NEW YORK, March 23.—John Reardon of 50 Spruce Way, Oak Ridge, N.J., has just been appointed senior vice president of Satellite Inc., New York City, a satellite broadcasting company scheduled to broadcast five channels of movies, sports, news, and pay-per-view programming beginning this fall. Reardon is former president and general manager of the Field Services Division, United Telegraph Co., and holds a Ph.D. in economics from Harvard University.

# # #

Finally, since Satellite has manufacturing facilities in Boise, Idaho, and Golden, Colorado, Loeb sends the release to local papers in those communities and in Denver (closest big city to Golden) with a cover note calling attention to the local angle.

FINDING A NEWSWORTHY ANGLE FOR A STORY

While writing press releases on routine news events is a standard public relations activity, another standard part of the job is coming up with newsworthy angles on seemingly conventional material to serve as the basis for feature releases. To do this sucessfully often involves researching the everyday operations of your client and being alert to new ways of dealing with old information. It may also mean keeping your eye on current events and topics that relate to your client's product, service, or industry, and monitoring misperceptions that your client might be able to clarify for the public. If your client is a professional group or association, a steady stream of newsworthy information can be generated by taking advantage of the accomplishments of organization members. Almost any noteworthy activity performed by a member can be publicized to the advantage of the association to which that member belongs. Moreover, if a member is an expert on a topic of special relevance to the association, he or she can be asked to supply evidence and quoted material which can serve as the basis for a feature release on the topic.

Patricia Fine is an account executive with John Meeker Associates, a public relations firm which handles the National Association of Energy Engineers (NAEE), with headquarters in Rochester, New York. The nonprofit association consists of a nationwide membership of engineers and other experts who work in the energy field. In the past several years, NAEE has taken a particular interest in the subject of energy-efficient home construction and maintenance. Though Fine has prepared a number of specialized news and feature releases for NAEE on energy-efficient construction which she has successfully placed in engineering trade publications, she feels it's time for a story that will bring NAEE's energy concerns to the attention of the general public. Such a story is especially desirable now because of a recent article in a popular magazine that has angered many NAEE members. The article claimed that energy-efficient homes could be hazardous to people's health by trapping dangerous pollutants inside. Fine knows that such claims represent a misperception concerning what energy efficiency is all about: With good ventilation, an energy-efficient home is a perfectly healthy environment; only when ventilation systems are faulty or inadequate can indoor air quality be impaired. But how can she get this information across to the general public without seeming defensive and drawing more attention to the controversy than she'd like?

Fine decides that the best way to deal with the issue is to develop a feature release that will address the benefits of energy-efficient homes and clarify the indoor air quality problem in the process. She begins by calling a noted member of NAEE, Dr. James Filimar, and asking him what the public should know about energy saving and how people can make their homes more energy tight. In discussing the subject with him, she is able to collect a number of "tips" which homeowners can follow if they want to check the energy efficiency of their homes. This do-it-yourself approach becomes the hook for her release.

During her conversation, Fine also asks Filimar to explain the relationship between building tightness and indoor air quality. She then edits his explanation so that it fits into the format of the release.

Once a draft of the release is completed, she sends a copy to her liaison at NAEE and to Filimar for review. The final approved feature release looks like this:

CONTACT: Patricia Fine
John Meeker, Assoc.
15 Main Street
Rochester, NY 14706
(716) 555-3212
FOR: The National Association of Energy Engineers (NAEE)

<u>FOR RELEASE AT WILL</u>

SOME DO-IT-YOURSELF METHODS FOR TESTING THE ENERGY EFFICIENCY OF YOUR HOME

ROCHESTER.—Anyone can test for air infiltration in the home, according to Dr. James Filimar, a staff scientist at Peters Laboratory, Berkeley, Calif., and a member of the National Association of Energy Engineers (NAEE), whose headquarters are here. Infiltration is the seeping of cold air into a structure in the winter and the escape of cooled air in the summer. In either season, it is expensive.

There are a number of easy, do-it-yourself methods which a homeowner can use to detect air leakage, said Dr. Filimar. He suggested the simple tactic of walking around inside the house on a windy day and holding a hand an inch or so from the wall to detect the passage of coolness or heat, according to the season. "Often people have a pretty good idea where the problem is if they've lived in a house for a while. Leaky areas tend to be drafty and uncomfortable," Dr. Filimar explained.

Another method of home-testing suggested by Dr. Filimar is to place a fan in a window of the house, carefully taping the window's edges so no air will seep through. Then walk around the area with a source of smoke—even so simple a source as a lit cigarette or cigar. With the fan blowing air into the house, air is forced through any leakage sites. Where leakage is present, the

-more-

Do-It-Yourself/2

smoke will be seen vanishing into any holes or cracks, around the windows and doors, for example. It may then appear on the outside of the building, said Dr. Filimar.

Do-it-yourself testing methods are a good beginning for the energy-conscious homeowner, according to Dr. Filimar. But for a more precise determination of building tightness, he noted, more sophisticated methods are available, such as tracer gas, pressurization, and, most recently, infrared scanners. Infrared scanning or sensing is especially helpful when used in conjunction with fan pressurization to identify major problem areas.

"Many people believe that energy conservation in a house simply means adding insulation," explained Dr. Filimar. "But air infiltration problems may reduce or cancel the benefits of added insulation. Adding insulation before filling holes or cracks in the building envelope can even intensify the problem."

The association of building tightness with poor indoor air quality is another misconception, added Dr. Filimar. "So long as ventilation needs are considered as part of the overall design, air tightness need not get in the way of air quality. Today it is economical and more convenient to provide a tight residence with some form of mechanical ventilation. Tight homes use less energy, are more comfortable, and are quieter, explained Dr. Filimar.

NAEE is a voluntary organization of 50,000 members who are professionally concerned with energy use. It sponsors a program of fundamental research in its field.

# # #

Sept. 1, 198_

134 Developing Visibility I: Engaging Media Interest

Note that Fine has mentioned Filimar's affiliation with NAEE in the first paragraph (in conjunction with the first mention of his name) and has ended the release with the requisite paragraph describing the organization. She also includes the date at the end since it does not appear in the dateline. (As a feature release which can run at any time there is no need to put the date at the beginning.)

Fine sends the release to a variety of local and national publications. She skips the energy and engineering trade publications because she feels the article is a consumer story and not specialized or technical enough for readership within the industry. But she does send it to specialized consumer publications dealing with the home, and to women's publications which feature consumer tips. In some cases, she sends the release twice to the same publication (to the energy and the living editors of the local Rochester newspaper, for example), but in these cases she attaches a note telling who else at the paper has been mailed a copy.

Since the information in the release is too long and complicated to make a good broadcast release, Fine decides to write a pitch letter based on the material for local radio and TV talk shows and for public information programs which concentrate on consumer-oriented topics. Her letter to the contact person at a local TV talk show reads as follows:

John Meeker, Assoc.
15 Main Street
Rochester, NY 14706
September 3, 198_

Mr. Ralph Schaeffer
The Peter Krist Show
NJY
10 North Avenue
Lakeland, NY 14601

Dear Mr. Schaeffer:

Dr. James Filimar, a member of the National Association of Energy Engineers (NAEE), can tell your viewers how to save money by learning some do-it-yourself methods for testing energy efficiency in their homes. He could actually go into someone's home with your crew and demonstrate how tests are performed. At a time when energy costs are a major household expense, Dr. Filimar's tips can make a difference in a family's budget.

> There's also been some confusion lately about what is meant by a "tight" indoor environment. Some people believe, mistakenly, that keeping an energy-efficient home could have adverse effects on the quality of air in the home. This simply isn't true and needs to be clarified by an expert.
>
> Dr. Filimar would make an articulate and lively guest. I've included a press release, a bio of Filimar, and a backgrounder on NAEE, my client, for your reference. I'll give you a call in a few days to find out whether you'd be interested in meeting with Dr. Filimar.
>
> Please don't hesitate to call me at 555-3212 if you'd like to discuss this sooner.
>
> Sincerely,
>
> *Pat Fine*
>
> Patricia Fine
>
> PF/ns
> enclosure

Note that the letter asserts that Fine will call Schaeffer for his reaction unless he chooses to call her first. A follow-up call will give Fine the opportunity to discuss the two topics touched on in her letter and to propose other topics which Filimar could address that might be of interest to the show's audience.

DEALING WITH THE MEDIA IN A CRISIS

In the event of a crisis, the first rule of public relations is to tell the truth about what happened. Lying is not only unethical, it's stupid. Once caught in a lie, you and your client will cease to have credibility. In the political arena where the misdemeanors of candidates seem to be everyday news, it's said that it matters less what was done than how it was disclosed; an open, balanced explanation can keep the situation in perspective and earn respect from the media and the public. Corporations too are now following this lead. In dealing with consumer advocates, government investigators, and investigative journalists, many business executives have decided to embrace a more "open door" policy. As one writer for *Fortune* magazine puts it: "A new willingness to defend the [corporation's] turf and a new desire to make the explorers serve corporate purposes point toward a policy of intelligent candor."[6] While such a policy does not entail an arbitrary airing of dirty linen, it *does* involve the dissemination of accurate, consistent information through the coordination of all participants—hence, the title *crisis management*, in many ways a more focused and intensive form of *issue management* (see Chapter 8).

Crisis management has also been adopted by organizations which realize that no matter how honest or scrupulous they are, there is always the possibility that a natural disaster or an event beyond their control may negatively affect their product or service. The most dramatic example of this kind of crisis in recent years was the discovery that poison had been inserted into some Tylenol capsules after they had been manufactured, packaged, and sent to retailers. After two unrelated incidents which resulted in deaths, Johnson & Johnson, the manufacturer of Tylenol, removed the capsule product from the market. In its assessment of the company's management of this volatile situation, the *New York Times* concluded that Johnson & Johnson appeared "to have struck a balance between what is good for consumers and what is good for Johnson & Johnson,"[7] citing a consumer poll in which the company is credited with acting correctly in the wake of the crisis. Removing the product from the market cost the company a substantial share of its earnings for the year, yet the gain in reputation and public trust that this action inspired made the tradeoff more than worthwhile from a public relations standpoint. The case was a landmark one not only because it dramatized public relations decision making at its most responsible but also because it made other companies realize their own vulnerability: They too could be the victim of crises not of their own making. As a result of the Tylenol poisonings, many companies came to see that to develop crisis plans for the future was not to be premature or overly pessimistic.

As part of any crisis management process, a news release (or at least a written statement) should be issued as soon as possible when a potentially negative event occurs. The value of a written release as opposed to a verbal one is that it cannot be misquoted, thereby assuring some degree of control and consistency at a time when information tends to be easily distorted. As written copy, a release also provides a record of what your organization had to say, which may be useful if a formal investigation should follow. The release should tell all the facts as far as you know them but should attempt to place these facts in a context that will put a lid on panic. Statistics or comparative statements can often serve this purpose. When a keeper at the Bronx Zoo was killed by two Siberian tigers in July of 1985—certainly a public relations crisis of the first order—the zoo's director made sure to include in his statement the fact that this was "the first employee killed at the Bronx Zoo in its 86 years of operation."[8]

Admittedly, a common problem in preparing a crisis release is that you may not have all the facts at your disposal and you risk making inaccurate statements. The instinct of most organizations' lawyers—who will certainly be involved if there is a disaster—is to deliver a "no comment" statement until all the facts are in hand and have been carefully evaluated for their legal ramifications. But from a PR standpoint, almost anything is better than offering no response when the public is clamoring for information. If the media can't obtain an explanation from your client, chances are they'll pump other (perhaps hostile) sources. It's best, therefore, to provide the information you have, making clear in your release that this information is partial and will be subject to revision and updating as soon as more is known. If you demonstrate that you're making a genuine effort to level with the media, you'll win more goodwill and cooperation in the long-run.

Finally, in order to turn out a release quickly, you need to have a support system in place to perform spot research, type copy, address envelopes, and messenger materials to company officials and to the media. You should also know whom to speak to within your organization for formal statements, and what route to follow for speedy approval of the release copy.

Roscoe Stevens is public information officer at the General Chemical Company headquartered in Denver, Colorado. Stevens has worked for the company for ten years, during which time his responsibilities have largely involved publicizing company developments in the chemical trade publications. But at 3 P.M. on June 21 his routine is shattered—an explosion occurs in the company's petrochemical plant in Rockville, 25 miles west of Denver.

Stevens, informed of the explosion by the assistant general manager at the plant, immediately mobilizes the special task force which he had organized to deal with accidents. He then gets on the phone with the director of technology for a comment concerning the possible after-effects of the explosion. He instructs others to call the police, fire department, and local hospitals for details on casualties.

Once Stevens receives a full report from his task force, he calls the president of the company, telling him what has been learned and discussing possible company strategies to deal with the unexplained nature of the accident. At Stevens' suggestion, the president agrees to establish a nonpartisan committee to investigate the cause of the explosion. Finally, after checking casualty figures again with the local hospital and police, Stevens drafts a release and sends it for review to the president, the director of technology, and the company lawyer. As he emphasizes the need for a speedy review, the release is returned within the hour. The approved release reads as follows:

CONTACT: Roscoe Stevens
General Chemical Company
50 North Boulevard
Denver, CO 80203
(303) 555-5000

FOR IMMEDIATE RELEASE

THREE HURT IN CHEMICAL BLAST

ROCKVILLE, June 21.—General Chemical Company said today that an unexplained explosion ripped through its petrochemical plant here at 3 P.M., injuring three employees. Ten additional employees who were in the plant were not hurt. The injured employees, whose names have not yet been released, are reported in stable condition at Rockville Hospital.

George Shulman, president of the company, said that the cause of the blast, the first in the company's history, is still unknown. Shulman announced that the company is establishing a nonpartisan committee to investigate the cause of the explosion and has asked Dr. James Wright, president of All Saints University, to serve as committee chairman.

"We want to establish the cause of the accident so that we can take steps to prevent future accidents. Our deepest concern now is with the well-being of our employees and their families," said Shulman.

Shulman said that a preliminary estimate of damage totaled $20 million.

Dr. Gerald Wilson, General Chemical's director of technology, flew by helicopter to the scene to observe the after-effects of the accident.

-more-

> Explosion/2
>
> "The area appears safe and there is no evidence that there will be further explosions," Wilson said. He nonetheless urged Rockville residents to stay away from the plant site until a full investigation had been completed.
>
> # # #

This release does several things:

It comes right out and acknowledges the accident and the extent of injuries and damages.

It reassures the public as to the contained and limited nature of the disaster without covering anything up.

It makes clear that the company is deeply concerned and is acting responsibly.

It announces that the company will take action to establish the cause of the accident and prevent its recurrence. (The creation of a nonpartisan committee assures the public that this will be a fair investigation.)

Stevens gives the approved release to the messengers in his task force for delivery to local newspapers and wire service bureaus. He also gives copies of the release to his telephone squad so that they can refer to it when responding to calls to the company's headquarters. The squad has been instructed to refer to the statements in the release in answering all questions.

Stevens also prepares a short form of the release and sends it to the broadcast media (see p. 140).

Note that the broadcast release is short and written in a style which is easy to read aloud. TV and radio editors may want to edit the material to fit their news formats, or they may simply read the release on the air as is. Stevens encloses the longer print release with the broadcast release in case more information is needed. He also sends along a company brochure in case background on General Chemical is needed.

In his memo to broadcasters, Stevens demonstrates that he is willing to be cooperative. This way, he can hopefully concentrate coverage of the accident into one or two days and avoid having it drag on over a longer period.

CONTACT: Roscoe Stevens
General Chemical Company
50 North Boulevard
Denver, CO 80203
W: (303) 555-5000 from 9 A.M. to 6 P.M.
H: (303) 555-4321

FOR IMMEDIATE RELEASE

THREE HURT IN CHEMICAL COMPANY BLAST

General Chemical Company has just announced that an unexplained explosion occurred in its petrochemical plant in Rockville at 3 P.M. today. The explosion injured three employees who are reported in stable condition at Rockville Hospital.

Company President George Shulman said he plans to establish a nonpartisan committee to investigate the cause of the explosion. He urged the public to stay away from the plant until the investigation is completed.

# # #

MEMO TO BROADCASTERS

1. An audio statement by Mr. Shulman is available.
2. He is also willing to be interviewed in his Denver office or by phone.
3. The wrecked plant in Rockville can be photographed from a distance of 50 yards. The general manager, Roy Billings, will be available at the outskirts of the site to assist you.
4. The results of the investigation will be issued by Dr. James Wright, president of All Saints University, in a formal press conference as soon as they are available.

Once he has messengered the releases to the appropriate stations, Stevens sets to work collecting updated information and preparing a second release for distribution at a news conference he plans to hold the next day.

HANDLING A NON-EVENT

As early as 1923, Edward Bernays could observe that "the public relations counsel must not only supply news—he must create news. This function as the creator of news is even more important than his others."[9] There are indeed times when the material a public relations practitioner must work with is painfully thin—when there is no news or newsworthy information available. In such cases, it may be necessary to create something out of nothing.

One of the most effective tools in the creation of news is the pitch letter. With a pitch letter, you can "create" a story as much through the style of your presentation as through your content. For while the news release must always remain tightly corseted within a conventional form, the pitch letter is a free spirit—here you can indulge in wit, personal opinion, odd combinations of ideas, and flights of fancy. Writing a good pitch letter is an art. It takes imagination, fluency, and a willingness to take risks on paper.

Archibald Flagler, an account supervisor at a major Madison Avenue PR agency, must do something to promote his client, Otis Flamb, the owner of two New York restaurants. Flagler has already succeeded in getting Flamb's restaurants reviewed by several local food critics, but Flamb wants more original publicity than this. What else can Flagler do?

What he does do is nose around among the restaurateur's employees and friends for some unusual if trivial bit of information which could be developed into one or more story angles. Eventually, he finds such a tidbit: Flamb, in addition to being a restaurant owner, is also a breeder of Black Angus cattle. Flagler believes that his client's unusual dual occupation could make an interesting story in a feature-oriented magazine. The trick is to excite the imagination of the editor by writing a top-notch pitch letter.

Flagler proceeds to compose the following letter:

Janson Public Relations
150 Madison Avenue
New York, NY 10022
May 5, 198_

Janet Ford
Features Editor
Manhattan Today
845 Third Ave.
New York, NY 10017

Dear Ms. Ford,

In the heart of New York City lives a man who owns and breeds some of the finest Black Angus cattle in the nation. His name is Otis Flamb. He also owns two excellent New York restaurants, The Flambé East (on the East Side) and The Flambé West (on the West Side).

Although we tend to associate cattle breeders with Texas ranchers, Otis Flamb is an aberration—a cosmopolitan restaurateur who is considered one of this country's top breeders. He lives on the East Side of Manhattan, though his cattle reside in Texas.

This week, one of his Black Angus cattle, a nine-month old cow named "Gourmet Delight," is on her way for a Parisian holiday. She is about to be flown across the Atlantic for exhibition at the Paris International Agricultural Exposition.

This is no run-of-the-farm cow. She was named Female Calf Champion in Denver three months ago and Supreme Champion at the Angus Futurity in Louisville. It was only the third time in history that a female won that latter distinction, a fact which leads Monsieur Flamb to declare, "There are male chauvinist cattle as well as pigs in this world."

Because of international breeding restrictions, once Gourmet Delight has set foot on French soil, she will not be permitted to return to the United States. So after the exposition Flamb will sell her to a French cattle breeder. Thus Gourmet Delight may gain a crown but will be banished from her native land forever.

We think Flamb's unusual combination of interests as well as Gourmet Delight's unfortunate fate might make a good story for *Manhattan Today*. I'll give you a call in a few days to discuss the idea further.

Cordially,

Archie Flagler

Archie Flagler
Account Executive

Note that we have an insubstantial story here without a clearly defined angle, and that Flagler makes light of the facts. But the idea of a prize-winning Black Angus flying across the Atlantic to Paris and then, because of breeding restrictions, not being permitted to return is just crazy enough to interest a feature editor. And since Flagler is pitching a Manhattan publication, he tries to capitalize on the uniqueness of a New York restaurant owner who is also a breeder of cattle. Flagler includes with the letter a captioned photo of Gourmet Delight posed inside of Flamb's N.Y.C. restaurant, The Flambé East. The photo took some trouble to set up, but Flagler knows that it's an original enough shot to warrant placement in its own right, possibly even without an accompanying story.

EXERCISES

Test Your Judgment

State whether each of the following would be best presented as news or newsworthy information:

1 A company appoints a new comptroller.

2 An environmental group tries to draw attention to the need to conserve water.

3 A new clothing boutique opens in town.

4 An automobile manufacturer reports the discovery that the brakes are faulty on its latest model.

5 A company which manufactures disposable diapers wants to emphasize the convenience of their product as well as counter the perception among some mothers that disposable diapers are unhealthy for newborns.

PR Workshop

1 The following press release (which was mailed to the press on April 18) contains many errors. Suggest improvements in form and style and note where reorganization and clarification are called for. Be prepared to critique the release in class.

CONTACT: Bernie Frank/Susan Wolfe
Floram Public Relations
122 East 61 Street
New York, NY 10021
(212) 555-1212/1211   FOR RELEASE: April 18

WREN LETS FLY WITH A NEW PERSONAL COMPUTER

CHICAGO.—Wren Computer Company demonstrated its new personal computer on April 18 at the Electronic Fair being held in Chicago. The new computer expands the Wren family machines to ten, ranging in price from $49.50 to $200.

-more-

-2

The new computer, which costs $200, is called the Wren Phillips 200. It has a number of unique features, including an expanded memory capacity, an added "soft-touch" key-word data entry capability, and more characters can be displayed on its monitor.

James Roe, executive vice president of Wren, said the computer was developed after surveying consumers and retailers about what they felt was needed in a home computer.

"We gave the Wren Phillips 200 a unique key-word entry that allows a faster entry than many other machines on the market today. Also, to make it easier to use, we made the keyboard larger. It also has a bank switching capability that is new to the personal computer," Roe said.

The computer's memory of 200,000 bits is readily expandable. A high-speed printer may be added, as well as a device that makes it possible to access databanks via telephone lines.

The combination of features makes the Wren Phillips 200 an excellent tool for education, entertainment, and productivity enhancement. "We felt that productivity use is the next growth area for the personal computer," Roe noted.

Wren will also be introducing a new series of computer games in the fall.

# # #

2   Choose a partner in the class and, for each situation below, take turns making a simulated telephone pitch to him or her. Decide in advance whom (or what media department) you will be calling, how you'll grab the editor or reporter's attention, what information you'll include (and what you'll

omit), and what kind of follow-up you'll be doing (press release, media kit, follow-up letter, invitation, and so on). In playing the role of editor or reporter, be as tough and challenging as you can in responding to your partner's pitch.

a You are PR director for the American Chemical Association. You are pitching the association's upcoming annual convention where the keynote speaker will be former Association president, Harvey Rosensweig, whom some believe to be this year's strongest contender for the Nobel Prize in chemistry. The convention will be held three weeks from now in Chicago. You'd like advance stories, if possible, and coverage at the convention.
   (1) Call a chemical trade publication.
   (2) Call the AP wire service.

b You are the public affairs officer of Karloff University, a small engineering college in New Jersey. You are pitching the fact that Karloff has just received a $3 million grant from Datap Corporation (a data processing company) to develop its robotics department. The endowment is a windfall for the university. However, some faculty have expressed reservations about it; they're afraid that corporate funding on such a large scale might limit their freedom as independent researchers.
   (1) Call the campus newspaper.
   (2) Call the *New York Times*.

c You are an account executive with Marston Associates, a New York PR agency which handles the Filco Drug Company account. You are pitching Filco's new arthritis drug, Protex, which tests show to be 10 percent more effective than other arthritis drugs on the market. Keep in mind that the company marketed an arthritis drug several years ago which was implicated in the deaths of several diabetic users. Protex has been rigorously tested, and the company hopes it will dispel the negative image created by its association with the former drug.
   (1) Call a magazine aimed at people over 65.
   (2) Call a TV talk show dealing with health and consumer topics.

d You are public information officer for General Telephone Company. You are pitching the company's latest underwriting venture, a traveling exhibition dealing with the history of communications technology. The exhibition is beginning its tour with a five-week stint at the Air and Space Museum in Washington, D.C. A gala opening and press party are being staged for June 5.
   (1) Call a technology journal.
   (2) Call the *Washington Post*.

e You are an account executive for Jon Elman, Inc., a Philadelphia PR agency which has just won a major account: the Tourist Board of St. Teresa Island, an island in the Caribbean which has recently overthrown its Marxist government and replaced it with a pro-Western government that desperately wants to improve the island economy by promoting tour-

ism. You are pitching the fact that St. Teresa's is now eager to welcome tourists and offers a good value vacation in a beautiful, natural setting.
(1) Call a travel magazine.
(2) Call the *Wall Street Journal.*

f You are public information director for Fairview Hospitals, a privately-owned group of drug rehabilitation centers which have just decided to open a new clinic in Marlton, New Jersey, a suburb of Philadelphia. Fairview specializes in treating cocaine addiction and has centers in or near New York City, Chicago, and Los Angeles. You are pitching the move in order to attract more patients and assist fund-raising. Keep in mind that there is some opposition to the center from the local community.
(1) Call a local radio station.
(2) Call the *Philadelphia Inquirer.*

PR Case Studies

1 You are the public information director for the Cranville School System and the following information comes to your attention:

Herbert Macey, a 55-year-old former math teacher, has been principal of Cranville High School for three years. When Macey first took the position, the school was in bad shape. Reading scores were among the lowest in the area and absenteeism was an enormous problem. Teacher morale was poor, especially after there had been a number of incidents in which teachers were verbally abused in the classroom. Macey had grown up in the neighborhood, had attended Cranville High, and had taught math there for more than 20 years. Five years ago, he went back to school to become certified as a high school administrator. Although he loved to teach, he felt that his skills were more needed in the administrative area. Three years ago, he was appointed to the principalship, despite the opposition of a number of teachers who felt he was too rigid and old-fashioned. After only two years as principal, reading scores improved by 30 percent, and now, at the end of his third year, 75 percent of the student body is reading at grade level.

Macey has made a concerted effort to recruit "tough" teachers. By tough, he means people who have high academic standards and who aren't afraid to discipline disruptive students. In his second year as principal, he was the focus of controversy when he arranged for ten Cranville teachers to be transferred to other schools because he felt they "weren't in step with what Cranville needs right now."

Macey says his philosophy of education is simple: He doesn't believe in "wishy-washy liberal" tactics. "Students go to school to learn, not to be coddled," he says. He has turned Cranville into a school of strict regimentation: "Absenteeism is simply not tolerated. We threaten suspension, then we suspend, and if the problem continues, we expel the student. That's how it was when I went to school," he says, "and it works."

Write a pitch letter to the *Cranville County Times* suggesting that a feature story be written on Macey and/or Cranville High School.

2 You are director of communications at Memorial Hospital, a 200-bed community hospital in Deerbrook, Pennsylvania. The hospital, which is a principal primary-care facility outside of Pittsburgh, has plans to expand its cardiac care unit by 15 beds in September.

On June 2 the director of the hospital, Stanley Cartwell, announces the appointment of Dr. Alan Stewart as the new chief of medicine upon the retirement of Dr. John Revson in August. Cartwell hands you a photo of Stewart (which you can have duplicated if you wish) and Stewart's résumé (see below).

Write a news release and photo caption aimed at the local Deerbrook paper. Also write a memo to the director of the hospital explaining where else you plan to send the release and the photo.

CURRICULUM VITAE

NAME: Alan Stewart, M.D.
BIRTHDATE: October 15, 1921
BIRTHPLACE: Morristown, New Jersey
FAMILY DATA: Married (Susan Schneider Stewart); 3 children (Lisa, John, Paul)
HOME ADDRESS: 30 Oak Drive, Pittsburgh, PA 15260. Telephone: 412/555-4121

Education and Training

1939–43   B.A., Yale University, New Haven, Connecticut, 1943, Chemistry
1946–50   M.D., Yale University, 1950
1950–51   Internship, Hospitals of the University Health Center of Pittsburgh, Internal Medicine
1951–53   Residency, Hospitals of the University Health Center of Pittsburgh, Internal Medicine

Appointments and Positions

1953–57   Assistant Professor, Medicine, University Health Center of Pittsburgh
1957–60   Associate Professor, Medicine, University Health Center of Pittsburgh
1961–83   Professor, Medicine, University Health Center of Pittsburgh

Certification and Licensure

1951   National Board of Medical Examiners
1951   State License, Pennsylvania
1954   American Board of Internal Medicine

148 Developing Visibility I: Engaging Media Interest

Memberships in Professional Societies

1953 Member, New York Academy of Sciences
1954 Member, American College of Physicians
1957 Fellow, American College of Physicians

Publications

Over 100 publications and contributions to textbooks, with original research in the fields of hypertension, cardiovascular disease, and the influence of prostaglandins on coronary artery disease.

Full list of publications available on request.

---

3 Reread the Model Case Study in this chapter about handling a non-event. Make a rough sketch of what you think the photo of Gourmet Delight posed in Otis Flamb's restaurant might look like; then write a caption for your photo-sketch (using Archibald Flagler as the contact). Assume that the photo and caption will be sent to New York feature-oriented publications like *Manhattan Today*.

4 You have been hired as PR consultant for The Sumptuary, a restaurant in Hoboken, New Jersey. Select from the background material given below, and write a pitch letter to *Big Apple News*, a monthly magazine aimed at young, "upscale" New Yorkers, suggesting that a feature story be written on The Sumptuary.

Hoboken, across the river from Manhattan, used to be a decaying industrial town until it was "discovered" by young New York City professionals. Deciding to take advantage of the city's low rents and proximity to the big city, they began renovating brownstones and turning Hoboken into a trendy little community. The proprietor of The Sumptuary, Michael Dougherty, is interested in capitalizing on Hoboken's new image and wants to attract clientele not only from among new residents of the area but from among Manhattan-dwellers as well. (Hoboken is only a 15-minute train ride from N.Y.C.) The Sumptuary is in a landmark building (dating from 1799) and has been tastefully decorated in a country French style. Moreover, Dougherty has recently hired Jacques Doumier, a celebrated French chef, to oversee the kitchen. Doumier is the former chef at La Petite Maison, a restaurant in the south of France which, under his supervision, received two stars in the *Guide Michelin*. (The guide is the authoritative source for restaurants in France. Two stars—out of a possible three—means that the food at La Petite Maison was excellent.) Among Doumier's specialties are a duck dish with currants and apples, a salmon souffle, and frogs legs in garlic sauce. His desserts are especially noteworthy, and he was awarded French Pastry Prize from the Academy of French Chefs in 1978.

5   You work in the public relations department of Warners, Inc., a textile manufacturing company in Dallas, Texas. You are told that the company is interested in publicizing its manufacture of Linel, a new synthetic fabric which looks like linen but has none of the natural fiber's inconvenient characteristics: It doesn't crease easily and it's inexpensive.

In gathering information about the fabric, you speak first with Jim Kolb, head of the Warners Research Group which developed the fabric.

"We've been working on Linel for five years now," he tells you. "I think we have a good product. Its only drawback is that it isn't as cool as linen. But it sure is a lot cooler than most synthetic fabrics."

You also speak to a New York designer, Ken Miles, who you know is familiar with the fabric.

"Linel may revolutionize women's ready-to-wear clothes," says Miles. "Linen has always had a wonderful look but it's very difficult to wear. It wrinkles so easily that it's not practical for the average person. Linel solves that problem."

The vice president of sales at Warners, Edward Keon, tells you that sales are moving briskly and that most major designers have put in at least sample orders for the fabric. He tells you that Linel garments will be on the market in major department stores by next fall and will probably be retailing at about half the price of linen.

Write a press release about Warners' new fabric.

6   You are public information officer for Southeast Air, a small Florida-based domestic airline. Early in the afternoon of May 5, you receive a frantic call from an air traffic controller saying that a Southeast Boeing 727 bound for Miami has been hijacked to Cuba. The plane, which took off from Atlanta at 1 P.M., had 75 people aboard. The controller, Noel Jobbs, says the captain, Robert Free, relayed the following message to him about ten minutes ago: "It's a hijacking. The guy's got a gun to my head. We're going to Cuba."

After speaking to Jobbs, you immediately mobilize your special emergency task force and get Jeff Rosselli, president of the airline, on the phone. He says, "I can't understand how this could have happened. We stepped up security three months ago after the other two hijackings. We doubled the number of baggage checks and we just installed a better X-ray screening unit."

The plane is expected to land in Havana in two hours, but you know that the phones will start ringing in half an hour with questions about the delayed flight. You want to prepare a preliminary release for distribution by your task force to local radio and TV stations which will be airing their news programs before the landing. What will the broadcast release look like?

NOTES

1. See Alan R. Raucher, *Public Relations and Business 1900–1929* (Baltimore: The Johns Hopkins University Press, 1968), p. 6.
2. Henry C. Rogers, *Walking the Tightrope: The Private Confessions of a Public Relations Man* (New York: Berkley Publishing Group, 1980), p. 43.
3. *New York Times*, November 14, 1975, p. 1.
4. *The Associated Press Stylebook and Libel Manual* (New York: The Associated Press, 1984), p. 277.
5. Linda P. Morton, "Use of Photos in Public Relations Messages," *Public Relations Review*, X (Winter 1984), 19.
6. Walter Guzzardi, Jr., "How Much Should Companies Talk?" *Fortune* (March 4, 1985), p. 66.
7. *New York Times*, February 23, 1986, p. 1.
8. *New York Times*, July 30, 1985, p. 1.
9. Edward L. Bernays, *Crystallizing Public Opinion* (1923; reprinted New York: Liveright Publishing Company, 1961), p. 183.

6

Developing Visibility II: Planning a PR Event

Sometimes alerting the media by phone or in writing may be only the beginning of your responsibility in relation to a news or newsworthy story. It may also be your job as a PR practitioner to conceive of and organize an event which requires media attendance. PR events have become increasingly important components of public relations programs in recent years, since they represent a more dramatic and concentrated method of transmitting a PR message to a client's target audience.

A public relations event is like a theatrical production—it should be well-conceived, carefully rehearsed, and dramatically rendered. As the organizer of an event, you are its director, responsible for seeing that the various parts of the production mesh properly for the desired effect.

Like a theatrical event, a PR event also carries with it a degree of risk. When something is "live," it is impossible to be sure that all the variables involved are under control. News conferences, for example, always run the risk of coming up against late-breaking big stories which are liable to steal away attendance at the last minute. Outdoor special events always run the risk of bad weather.

But risk, if it can't be entirely eliminated, can be minimized through good planning. This involves, first, choosing a place and time that are convenient for those you want to attend. If you are inviting a variety of local media and businesspeople, you will want a midtown location that has proximity to most of your audience's place of work. If you are eager to have a story appear in next morning's paper, you will want to be sure that reporters have time to attend and then return to write their stories before deadline; this means scheduling the event in the early afternoon, or even the morning (hence, the growing popularity of press breakfasts).

	June	July	August	September
Media kits	XXXXXXXXXXXXXXXXXXXXXXXXXXXXX			
Invitations		XXX		XXXXXX
Presentation format		XXXXXXXXX		
Speeches	XXXXXXXXXXXXX			XXX
Arrangements (room, menu, equipment)	XXXX			XXX
Follow-up				XXXXXXX

FIGURE 6-1 Timetable for News Conference Scheduled for September 5

The next important step in planning a PR event is developing a method for keeping track of and coordinating the various tasks involved. Perhaps the simplest such method is a task timetable—a grid which plots the major tasks involved in the event against a list of dates leading up to it (and continuing beyond in the case of follow-up).

The timetable should be divided into major category headings, as in Figure 6-1, plotted against the dates specifying when each task should be begun and completed. This timetable indicates that while sustained effort must be devoted to developing the media kits, other activities will need attention only at specific points in the planning period. Speeches, for example, will be written early, but practice readings will also have to take place a week or so before the conference. Plotting the time necessary to perform these major tasks helps you see each in context and makes it easier to assess the time, energy, and expense involved in the overall effort.

In addition to the general category timetable, it's also a good idea to prepare a number of mini-timetables, which break down major tasks into specific tasks and assign an appropriate time frame in which these should be completed. Figure 6-2 is a detailed mini-timetable for the development of media kits.

In addition to timetables and mini-timetables, practitioners may sometimes find it useful to employ more formal "road maps" for planning purposes. Among the more commonly used such methods is the Program Evaluation and Review Technique (PERT) diagram,[1] in which each supporting task involved in an overall event is laid out graphically in its relation to preceding and succeeding tasks. The interval between tasks is then labeled with three figures representing the *optimistic*, *probable*, and *pessimistic* number of days necessary to get from one task to the next.

	June 1–15	June 16–30	July 1–15	July 16–31	August 1–25
Collect quotes	XXXXXXXX				
Draft releases		XXXXXXX			
Research fact sheet	XXXXXXXXX				
Draft fact sheet		XXXXXXXX			
Research backgrounder	XXXXXXXXXX				
Draft backgrounder		XXXXXXXX			
Select still photos		XXXXXX			
Caption photos			XXXX		
Select kit cover			XXXX		

FIGURE 6–2 Mini-Timetable for Preparation of Media Kits for September 5 News Conference

153

	June 1–15	June 16–30	July 1–15	July 16–31	August 1–25
Get final approval on materials		XXXXXXXXXX			
Estimate volume				XXX	
Have materials duplicated				XXXXX	
Assemble kits					XX
Mail kits					XXXX

FIGURE 6-2 *Continued*

The advantage of a PERT diagram is that it allows you to visually assess how various tasks interconnect and to identify the series of tasks (or *Critical Path*) which will take the longest time to accomplish. The Critical Path can then be targeted for special attention and additional resources to improve the probability of completion within the desired time frame.

In Figure 6-3, a special event has been plotted in a PERT diagram. Each circle designates a task (see accompanying list of tasks), and the three numbers leading from one task to the next represent the optimistic, probable, and pessimistic time estimated for the task's completion. The Critical Path (the series of tasks requiring the longest probable time to completion) has been traced in heavy ink.

If you are responsible for the budget of a PR event, you will also want to prepare at the outset a list of necessary and optional expenditures. (This might include a low-budget version and a more expensive version of the same item.) The list should be reviewed by your supervisor and your client as early as possible and an agreement reached as to the leeway you are permitted in the optional area. To establish approximate costs, a few preliminary calls to vendors, hotels, and caterers are advisable. Since it is often impossible to cal-

1. Receive assignment
2. Develop press lists
3. Mail invitations
4. Make call-backs
5. Book location and speakers
6. Design invitations
7. Confirm menu and set-up
8. Draft media kits
9. Obtain approval on kits
10. Compile kits
11. Hold news conference (Sept. 5)

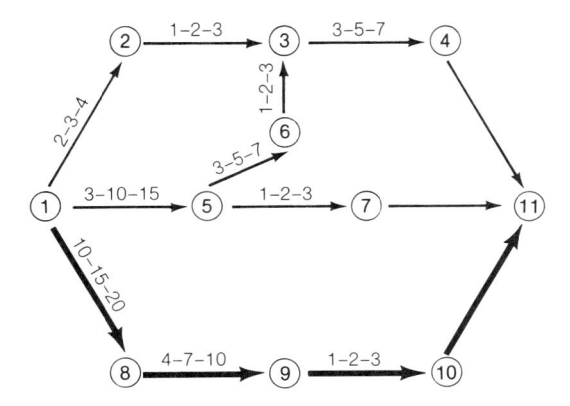

FIGURE 6-3 Plotting a Special Event with a PERT Diagram

culate the miscellaneous expenses which crop up in organizing an event, you will usually want to submit a contingency expense figure (make this about 10 percent of your total estimated expenses).

Always confirm arrangements several times before an event. Don't leave anything to chance, and don't expect that something will be taken care of unless you specify that it should be. Moreover, in reserving space for an event, never assume that the same conditions hold at all times. A pleasant enough space during the day may become a wind tunnel at night, or a rock group may hold its rehearsals next door to the auditorium where you plan to hold your senior citizen's ballroom-dancing competition. If you are hiring a bartender, find out not only the charge per drink, but also the bartender charge for a given duration of time. Discuss payment arrangements in advance with vendors and hotel people so that they know when they can expect to be reimbursed for their services. Make sure to ask if there is a rental fee for the room or space you plan to use. Finally, remember that the only sure way to get all the information you need about services and arrangements is to draw up a list of questions and make sure you get the answers in writing. Do this as early as possible in the planning stages so that if arrangements need to be altered, this can be done before invitations and media materials are printed and mailed.

Here are some basic *before*, *during*, and *after* steps to follow when organizing a PR event of any kind:

BEFORE

1 Prepare and maintain timetables for the completion of tasks.
2 Update media lists to be sure you invite the right people. (You don't want to address an invitation to Frank King, Energy Editor, when he is now City Editor or went to work for a rival paper six months ago.)
3 Make an initial telephone pitch informing the media about the event. These calls should serve to spark the interest of reporters and editors and alert them to the arrival of invitations. Try to get a tentative head count of media attendance at this time.
4 Send out invitations about two weeks before the event and ask guests to R.S.V.P.; for those who don't, call to confirm attendance several days before.
5 Make sure you have checked out all facilities and equipment in advance.
6 Know to whom you can go if something breaks or fails to arrive on time. (Meet personally with custodians, technicians, caterers, store managers, and so on.)
7 Meet with the event's participants and explain their roles to them. (Review this again at intervals in the planning stages and directly prior to the event. If possible, arrange for a dress rehearsal.)

8 Make sure that written materials are accurate and are in keeping with the content and style of the event. Leave enough time for the review of all materials by supervisors and clients.

DURING

1 Provide media representatives with name tags and have them sign a guestbook as they arrive so that you have a record of who showed up.
2 Be sure someone is available to assist photographers in setting up shots and identifying participants. Know in advance whom you want to have photographed and which individuals should be grouped together. Give the photographer a list of these instructions before the event.

AFTER

1 Contact media if you come up with any additional information or background material that might assist them in preparing a story.
2 Keep track of coverage of the event through clipping services or by monitoring the media in which you think stories might appear.
3 Write thank-you notes to all participants and special guests.

THE NEWS CONFERENCE

Probably the best known of all public relations events is the news conference—the ceremony at which an important story is formally announced to the media. There are some obvious advantages to a news conference over a simple press release. The conference dramatizes the news announcement by giving it a live presentation and by linking it to a specific time and place. It also capitalizes on the media's desire for a *scoop* (getting a story first), since a newsperson who is absent from a news conference must, by definition, get scooped by the reporters who are present. Finally, a news conference gives an organization the opportunity to explain in person any technical or controversial information which might be subject to misunderstanding. When, in 1963, the mayor of New York City decided to favor the fluoridation of the city's water supply, he held a news conference to announce and explain his position on this volatile issue.[2] When, in 1985, Procter & Gamble Company found that leaflets had been widely distributed claiming that its logo was an emblem of the devil, the company held a news conference to deny the accusation.[3] As different as these two situations were, both required explanations which were of considerable public interest. A news conference was the most direct and efficient means of delivering these explanations.

Deciding Whether to Hold a News Conference

Since not all stories warrant news conferences, holding one indiscriminately can damage your credibility. Before deciding to organize such an event, ask yourself the following questions:

HOW IMPORTANT IS THE INFORMATION TO BE ANNOUNCED?

If you ask the media to attend a news conference, they generally assume that the information to be announced is important—or at least important within their special interest area. Don't waste a news conference on a mediocre story. Remember that crying wolf once is usually enough to keep the media away the next time when the story might really deserve attention.

WHO WOULD BE INTERESTED?

It's a common error to assume that your story has a broader appeal than it really has. Take an objective look at your material and decide who would be interested. For example, a company that develops a new insulation material might want to hold a news conference for people in the building construction and energy media but bypass the more general consumer media—at least until the material has been tested on the market and some dramatic energy-saving statistics can be made available. Clearly, the narrower the field, the greater the chance that any new product or development will be considered important within that field. This is why organizations with specialized functions tend to hold more news conferences than groups of a more diversified nature. A special-interest news conference is also easier to organize since it assumes a shared vocabulary and background among those who attend.

WOULD A NEWS CONFERENCE ENHANCE THE CREDIBILITY OF THE ANNOUNCEMENT?

Sometimes a news conference can be built less around the announcement itself than around the individual making the announcement. If your company has just come up with a new tennis shoe and a top-seeded tennis player believes that it represents a major improvement over existing shoes, the news conference can become a vehicle for the player's first-hand testimonial. In a new product announcement of this kind, the president or sales director would probably announce the development of the shoe and details concerning its marketing; the director of research and development would explain its special features; and, finally, the tennis pro would attest to its superiority on the tennis court. The addition of a celebrity has been recognized as a boost to what would otherwise be a standard new product announcement, but the willingness of companies to pay often exorbitant fees for such testimonials has, in recent years, detracted from their credibility. Sometimes the presence of the president or executive vice president of a large company is enough of a media draw—especially if the official is a well-known figure in the business community. However, new product announcements, unless they involve truly unique features, are often better served by sending out news releases and working with the media individually in the development of feature stories.

An important instance when a news conference tends to lend considerable credibility to an announcement is in the event of an accident or a crisis. Here, the presence of experts to answer questions on behalf of the organization and to explain technical or medical issues can help put the lid on panic and prevent a distorted version of what happened from being reported.

ARE THERE ANY SUPPORTING MATERIALS WHICH COULD HELP DRAMATIZE THE ANNOUNCEMENT?

The use of slides, diagrams, and films are often included as part of the news conference format. Supporting materials make sense as a means of taking advantage of the live presentation. They also give TV newspeople something to put on tape besides the "talking heads" of company presidents and sales directors. However, audio-visual materials should be used judiciously; be careful not to let a jazzy presentation or unusual graphics eclipse the content of your announcement.

Pitching a News Conference

A public relations practitioner will often want to pitch a news conference over the phone before sending out invitations. This pitch should give some idea of what will be announced, but should hold back the details or key information since this must serve as the lure for media attendance. A typical press conference pitch might run like this:

PR Practitioner: We thought you might be interested in attending the Sun Corporation news conference on Friday, April 10th at noon at the Sheraton. Sun will be announcing the details of its new government contract. The contract's a big one.

Media Representative: How big?

PR Practitioner: It's a multi-million dollar contract, but we can't release the details until the conference. The president of Sun will be there to make the announcement and answer questions. You'll be receiving an invitation, but we'd like you to mark your calendar now.

Most media people understand that information can't be released prematurely, but they may try to wheedle it out of you anyway. Make sure to let them know that experts and/or top officials will be present to comment or answer questions. After the telephone pitch, a mailgram and follow-up call can serve in lieu of an invitation where an added sense of urgency or importance is called for.

Question and Answer (Q & A) Sessions

A good news conference is a dramatic occasion which offers advantages to both public relations and media people. As a staged event, it provides its organizers with a degree of control over the proceedings which they do not have in a more informal interview situation. At the same time, it provides media people with the convenience of receiving both written materials and live statements at once. It also gives them an opportunity to ask questions directly of the participants after the formal announcements have been made.

Question and answer sessions are a standard part of news conference format and are often considered by the media to be the most important part. Remember that these sessions are not subject to your complete control. For this reason, many practitioners hold formal practice sessions (*media training*) with their clients prior to the conference to help them develop responses to difficult questions (see the discussion of the speech in Chapter 8).

The Press Party

A familiar variation on the news conference is the press party—a more social, less news-oriented event which is often held to mark the opening of an art exhibition, or a music, theater, or dance production. The press party can provide an informal means for those involved in the event, including its sponsors, to mix with media representatives and with each other. Since press parties are usually given to generate feature articles or for purely social reasons, they need not be scheduled to take into account newspaper deadlines for that day. Hence, press parties are often late afternoon or evening affairs where cocktails and even dinner may be served.

Increasingly, characteristics of the press party are showing up at news conferences as well. Cocktails, hors d'oeuvres, even full meals and entertainment may sometimes accompany an important announcement to the media. Some public relations people frown on this trend and stick by the rule that news conferences should concentrate on announcing news and that refreshments should be confined to coffee and donuts. Others feel that a news conference that incorporates elements of the press party will provide an added incentive for media attendance.*

---

*Despite variations in format, food and drink are usually not served until after the formal announcements have been made.

It is probably best to reject any general rule on news conference format and instead choose the format which meshes well with the particulars of your situation. Try to match food, drink, and presentation to the nature of the announcement, the personalilty of the client organization, and the image it wishes to project with the media. A nonprofit organization with a public service image, for example, will probably not want to hold a news conference at a posh downtown restaurant; a lavish display would seem inappropriate to both its image and its financial capability. Such a setting, however, might be perfectly appropriate for a real estate company announcing the opening of a midtown luxury condominium.

THE SPECIAL EVENT

Unlike a news conference which announces news, a special event makes news. The sponsoring organization, by attaching its name to the event, grabs the attention of the media and gains publicity for itself.

A special event can take an infinite number of forms. It can be a grand-opening celebration for a shopping mall, a seminar held by a city on industrial development, a fashion show to publicize a new line of swimwear, an insurance company's sponsorship of a marathon run, and so on. One of the great advantages of a special event is that it can generate media coverage at the same time that it communicates directly with its target audience.

Special events may explicitly promote specific products or services. A shopping mall opening or a fashion show of a designer's clothes are examples of such events. Other special events may be less obviously promotional while nonetheless maintaining a clear link to their sponsor. Take the case of the pet shop owner who decided to hold a competition in which neighborhood dogs were invited to perform their best tricks. The competition had good visual content and was picked up by the local TV news stations. It also drew direct participation from local dog owners—the shop's present and potential customers. And because the shop owner held the contest in her shop, both the TV viewers and the participants had no trouble connecting the show with its sponsor. Similarly, a car dealer who sponsored an antique car show was banking on the assumption that people who like antique cars are also interested in buying new cars. In order to connect his business more clearly with the event, he chose to begin and end the show with a display of his latest models and to distribute backgrounders comparing features of the old cars with features of cars in his showroom.

A more innovative example of a special event which indirectly helped to market its sponsor's product was the Twinings Tea Company promotion of "afternoon tea." The company hit on the idea of promoting teatime as an alternative to dinner, lunch, or breakfast as the best social context for businesspeople to meet. As part of the promotion, Twinings held a series of "press teas" in major cities across the country and, without pitching its product directly, succeeded in linking its name to the new businessperson's social event which it had helped to create.[4] People would now be more likely to drink Twinings when they met for tea.

In the case of some special events, however, it is not always possible or desirable to maintain a direct link to the sponsor's product. When Macy's Department Store underwrites the Fourth of July fireworks in New York City each year there is no clear relationship between the fireworks display and the store (after all, Macy's doesn't sell fireworks). Nonetheless, the mass appeal of the event outweighs the need for a direct connection. Macy's is supplying entertainment to an enormous number of people and is gaining widespread recognition for its public-spiritedness as a company, if not for its products directly. Moreover, the annual fireworks are a New York event and Macy's is eager to be thought of as *the* New York store. The best special events have such a rationale behind them. Thus, Hertz, the car rental company whose slogan is "We're Number One," sponsors a program in which sportswriters throughout the country pick the top high school athletic performances of the year. The culminating event is an awards dinner at which the "Number One" presentations are made by company spokesman O. J. Simpson.[5] Like Macy's and Hertz, more and more organizations are recognizing the benefits attached to underwriting events which capture the spirit of how they want to be perceived. They know that a good public relations practitioner can publicize the sponsor with the event so persistently that the two become permanently entwined in the public mind, even if there is no direct connection between the event and the sponsor's line of buisness. David Finn, throughout his years as chairman of the public relations firm Ruder Finn & Rotman, has championed the position that corporate sponsorship should arise "naturally out of the genuine interest of the executives who happen to be in top management positions at a particular time." Although a direct link to the sponsor is certainly to be welcomed, he says, when no such link is possible the reasons for sponsorship ought to be "the establishment of meaningful bonds between the corporation and other segments of the community which in one way or another share a common destiny."[6]

Special events sponsored by nonprofit organizations are usually fundraisers or vehicles for relaying a public service message or both. A popular way of getting the most mileage out of such events is by dedicating a day, week, or month to a specific issue and organizing a series of related special events during this period. "Employ the Physically Handicapped Week," for example, might lend itself to a series of fund-raising and awards dinners, a wheelchair marathon, and a crafts fair featuring the work of handicapped artists. The observance of this special week would focus media and public attention on the employment needs of this segment of the population and, at the same time, lend impetus to a fund-raising drive.

Pitching a Special Event

While you may want to make preliminary calls to the media, alerting them to the date, you will usually need to follow up with invitations that communicate the nature and atmosphere of the event. Edward Bernays provides a classic (if unwieldy) example of effective invitations when he recalls the organization which, for a banquet held on behalf of its building fund, sent invitations out on large bricks.[7]

If possible, the invitation should also suggest a story angle and, when addressed to TV reporters and editors, should stress any visual aspects of the event. Thus the pet shop owner who is sponsoring the pet show sends out an invitation which promises some provocative visuals:

Media Alert

The First Annual Canine Talent Show

SEE DOGS:

Dance the Polka

Wash Dishes

Eat Ice Cream Cones

and more

Where: Janet's Pet Shop
49 Main Street

When: Saturday, April 9
4:30 P.M.

For more information call Janet Stern, 555-0909.

Nonprofit organizations sponsoring events may sometimes get extra publicity mileage by alerting media to the various stages in the development and implementation process. The decision to sponsor the event, the selection of a chairperson, the appointment of a planning committee, and reports on progress and new developments could each warrant a short news story along the way.[8] Where a public service is involved, the media tend to be more willing to consider printing stories based on less-than-world-shaking announcements. And local media will always be interested in information involving prominent local citizens.

Setting Up a Newsroom for a Special Event

When an event promises to bring in substantial out-of-town media, it is good public relations practice to provide these newspeople with a space which can serve them as a make-shift newsroom. The room should be a convenient distance from the site of the event and should be equipped with adequate telephones and typewriters, as well as an ongoing supply of coffee and water. A public relations person should be on hand in the newsroom to distribute media kits and assist reporters in obtaining interviews and other information as needed.

Variations on the Special Event

While most special events are dramatic "happenings," we can also stretch the definition of a special event to cover other types of undertakings sponsored by organizations for the purpose of generating interest from both the media and the sponsor's target publics. The oral history project developed by a local nursing home is an example of an activity which was not linked to a specific time and place but which ultimately served the same purpose as a special event. For this project, the nursing home staff taped the personal histories of all the home's residents, then had the tapes transcribed and distributed in book form throughout the community. Local newspapers and magazines wrote a series of stories based on the oral history, and a local TV news show did a feature on the nursing home and its occupants. The project thus became a means of increasing the home's visibility within the community and was ultimately valuable in assisting fund-raising and the recruitment of volunteers.

Certain kinds of product promotions also resemble special events in that they manage to arrest the attention of the target audience and the media, and associate the product with a larger concept or cause. An example of this kind of innovative product promotion was Jockey International, Inc.'s decision to give underwear to the needy, singling out members of the Solidarity labor union in Poland, flood victims in Ft. Wayne, Indiana, and earthquake victims in Italy for donations.[9] Jockey turned the standard give-away promotional technique into an original (and pragmatic) public service that won the company coverage in the *Wall Street Journal*. Procter & Gamble also developed an effective and newsworthy promotion when it put diamonds into selected boxes of its cleaning powder and liquid during its sixtieth anniversary year.[10] As tokens of durability and brilliance, the diamonds made a symbolic statement about the company's identity, and the product promotion took on special meaning in being linked to the anniversary celebration.

Model Case Studies

DEVELOPING A FORMAT FOR A NEWS CONFERENCE

All news conferences share certain general characteristics: They are live,* formal presentations in which important information is relayed by a noteworthy official, an expert, or by some combination of qualified individuals to a selected media audience. The formal presentation portion of a news conference usually runs 20- to 30-minutes (when there are audio-visual materials or multiple speakers this can be longer) and is followed by a 20- to 30-minute question and answer session. Following the news conference, personal interviews and photographic sessions are often scheduled, and participants mix socially with media people over drinks or refreshments.

Within this general format, however, the specific format of a news conference can vary depending upon the nature of the information being announced, the kind of organization or organizations involved in the announcement, and the image which the sponsoring organization wishes to project. It's a good idea to evaluate these factors early in the planning stages of the event, then develop a format which is consistent with them.

Alan Fuller is an account supervisor at a Manhattan public relations firm which handles Stellax Petroleum. The oil company has recently decided to underwrite a television series on trends in modern art entitled *The Modern Eye,* which will be broadcast in the fall on PRST, a New York–based station which is part of the nonprofit National Public Network (NPN). The host for the series is the noted art historian and social critic, Alexander Pym.

Fuller and his client decide they should hold a news conference a month before the series airs. Their rationale is that *The Modern Eye* represents an unusually comprehensive and insightful overview of modern art and that many representatives from a variety of media would be interested in seeing a preview tape.

---

*The exception is the teleconference which transmits a presentation by satellite to targeted locations.[11]

They also feel that Stellax's decision to underwrite a series on modern art, a subject which is largely misunderstood or ignored by the general public, deserves first-hand justification and explanation.

Once the decision to hold a news conference has been made, Fuller begins by evaluating the nature of the information to be announced and the kind of organizations involved in making the announcement in order to determine the best possible format for the conference.

Although a series on modern art would ordinarily have a limited appeal, *The Modern Eye* attempts to make modern art accessible to a wider public. Thus the information to be announced, while seemingly specialized, is of a broader and more popular nature than might be expected. Fuller feels the news conference should communicate that the series can be enjoyed by a more general audience than that of artists, intellectuals, and students.

Fuller knows that there are many contributing groups which must be considered in planning the news conference. One of the most important is the PRST station on which *The Modern Eye* will air and which will be responsible for helping to "sell" the series to affiliates in the NPN system. Fuller is well aware that PRST, like all the NPN stations, has a reputation for serious, educational programming. This reputation will enhance the series' credibility, though Fuller is also eager to capture viewers who might not normally watch NPN shows. An additional consideration is PRST's nonprofit status and the fact that it has suffered financial difficulties in recent years. A lav-

1. Receive go-ahead from Levy
2. Determine location
3. Establish and confirm equipment and set-up
4. Determine order and nature of presentations
5. Obtain copies of participants' speeches
6. Rehearse presentations
7. Develop media lists
8. Design invitations
9. Prepare media kits
10. Make preliminary calls to media
11. Do mailings
12. Make follow-up calls
13. Hold news conference (April 1)

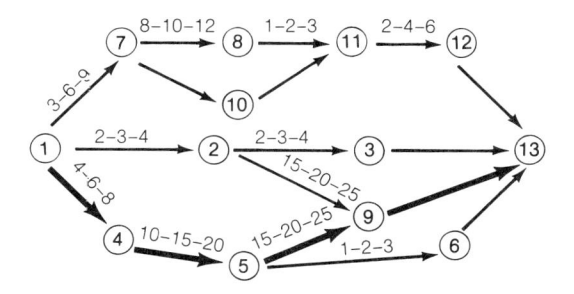

FIGURE 6-4 PERT Diagram for Stellax News Conference

	Jan.	Feb.	March	April
Media Lists	XXXXX			
Invitations		XXXX		
Calls, mailing, and confirmation			XXXXXXX	
Physical set-up	XX		XXXX	
Presentation		XXXXXXXXX	XX	
Media kits		XXXXXXXXXXXX		
Follow-up				XXXXXXX

FIGURE 6-5 April 1 News Conference

ishly staged news conference would therefore be out of keeping with the station's image, however much it might coincide with the image of the sponsor.

The series has been produced by an independent production company which developed the programs out of the original idea supplied by Stellax. The producers are the creative people responsible and their role must be duly acknowledged. In addition, Alexander Pym, the show's host, must be properly recognized. Pym's reputation in the art world gives him considerable drawing power with certain special-interest media.

Finally, there is Stellax itself, the series' sponsor. Stellax is a young oil company, formed only five years ago. Its enormous success is owed in large part to its chairman, Frank Levy, who helped streamline the company's refining process, making Stellax a world leader in this area. It is Levy, in fact, who originated the idea for the series. Along with being an innovative and highly successful entrepreneur, he is also well versed in modern art and a collector in his own right. His personal collection is said to be worth several million dollars.

Having reviewed this information carefully with his staff and with the agency vice president in charge of the account, Fuller first proceeds to draw a PERT diagram that will help him determine a Critical Path in the planning of the conference. He traces the Critical Path in heavy ink (Figure 6-4).

Then, in order to see the tasks in clearer relation to the dates at which they need to be executed, he constructs a general task timetable (Figure 6-5).

Finally, Fuller also draws up a series of mini-timetables for each of the tasks on the general list (Figure 6-6).

	January 1 2 3 4 5 6 7 8 9 10 11 12 13 14 15 16 17 18 19 20 21 22 23 24 25 26 27 28 29 30 31
Media Lists	
Update lists	xxxxxxxxxxxx
Develop new lists	xxxxxxxxxxxxxxxx

	February 6 7 8 9 10 11 12 13 14 15 16 17
Invitations	
Graphics	xxxxxxx
Copy	xxxxxx
Final Approval	xxxxxxx

	March 6 7 8 9 10 11 12 13 14 15 16 17 18 19 20 21 22 23 24 25 26 27 28 29 30 31
Calls, Mailing, Confirmation	
Telephone pitch	xxxxxxxxxxxxxxxx
Address invitations	xxxxxxxxx
Mail invitations	xxxxxxxxx
Messenger invitations	xxxxxxxxx
Call-backs	xxxxxxxxxxxxxx
Compile list of attendees	xxxxxxx

Physical Set-up

	January 1 2 3 4 5 6 7 8 9 10 11 12 13 _____ 15 16 17 18 19 20 21 22 23 24 25 26 27 **March**
Location	XXX
Menu	XX
Layout	XXXXX
Arrange for photos	XXXXXX
Confirm	XXXXXX XXXXXXXXXXXX

Presentation

	January 18 19 20 21 22 23 24 25 26 27 28 29 30 31 _____ 18 19 20 21 22 23 24 25 26 27 **March**
Format	XXXXXXXX
Speeches	XXXXXXXXXX
Final approval	XXXXXXXX
Rehearsal	XXXX

FIGURE 6–6 Mini-Timetables for April 1 News Conference

169

Media Kit Materials

	January 18 19 20 21 22 23 24 25 26 27 28 29 30 31	February 1 2 3 4 5 6 7 8 9 10 11 12 13 14 15 16 17
News release	XXXXXXXXXXXXXXXXXX	
Fact sheet	XXXXXXXXXXXXXXXXXXXX	
Backgrounder	XXXXXXXXXXXXXXXXXXXX	
Bios	XXXXXXXXXXXX	
Photos	XXXXXX	
Final approval	XXXXXXXXXXXXXXXXXX	
Production		XXXXXXXXXXXX

Follow-up

	March 26 27 28 29 30 31	April 1 2 3 4 5 6 7 8 9 10 11 12 13 14 15
Retain clipping service	XXX	
Call-backs		XXXXXXX
Follow-up mailings		XXXXXXXXXX
Final report		XXXXXXXXXX

FIGURE 6-6 *Continued*

TASKS INVOLVED IN DEVELOPING A NEWS CONFERENCE

To better understand what Fuller will have to do, let's run through each of the major tasks and explain the specific tasks involved under each:

Media Lists

In order to communicate the popular appeal of the series, Fuller hopes to attract as diverse a media representation as possible. He wants to invite selected feature writers, editors, and reviewers from the popular consumer and women's magazines and national and New York-based newspapers, but he also wants to invite the editors of specialized art, TV, and video publications, including in-house newsletters and bulletins devoted to these industries. Finally, he plans to invite business reporters and editors who might be interested in Stellax's underwriting venture from a business point of view or who might wish to do a feature story on Frank Levy, the innovative entrepreneur who also happens to be an art collector.

In developing media lists, Fuller updates existing lists of editors and reporters on the magazines and newspapers, TV and radio stations in his files by calling to see whether the names on the press lists are still accurate. He also creates new lists—for example, of art editors—which he didn't have before. He develops these lists by first checking *Bacon's* and other publicity directories and by consulting library indexes for the names of scholarly and specialized journals in the areas of art and education. He also consults directories for nonprofit associations and foundations that fall within the art and education areas, and calls these organizations to see whether they put out newsletters to members, employees, or customers in which an article on the series might be featured.

Invitations

Fuller wants to have invitations printed with a copy of a noted work of modern art on the front flap. However, he knows enough to discuss the idea with the show's executive producer and with Alexander Pym to be sure that a work is chosen which is consistent with the series' content and emphasis. For example, though he would like to choose a painting from Levy's personal collection, none of Levy's work is featured in the series. He and Pym finally settle upon Picasso's *Les Demoiselles D'Avignon*. It is featured in the series as one of the first examples of *cubism*. The final invitation, including the printed copy, is submitted to the client for review. It is also submitted to the PRST project director.

172 Developing Visibility II: Planning a PR Event

Calls, Mailings, Confirmations

About a month before the conference, Fuller proceeds to call all the names on the lists alerting them to the event and encouraging them to mark their calendars. Where possible, he uses these calls to set up advance interviews and to schedule interviews for the day of the conference. He suggests story angles that might appeal to a specific editor or reporter. He also stresses that a preview tape will be shown and that both Levy and Pym will be present to answer questions.

Formal invitations are mailed two weeks prior to the conference, leaving time for the recipients to R.S.V.P. or, if they don't, for confirming call-backs to be made. Local media have their invitations messengered to them a week before, since messengered invitations are more likely to arrest their attention. Call-backs on the messengered invitations are made a day after they are sent. When the final call-backs have been completed (three or four days prior to the conference), Fuller compiles a prospective attendance list. This will be used to draw up name tags for the media and will be checked against the sign-in book at the conference to evaluate attendance.

Physical Set-up

One of the first orders of business in preparing a news conference is to select and confirm a conference site. In this case, Fuller looks for a center-city location capable of holding 150 people (estimated media attendance is 120; this leaves room for a substantial number of non-media guests).*

Though Fuller feels that the site should be attractive and comfortable, he is against holding the conference in an opulent setting which would jar with the NPN nonprofit image. Moreover, many of the large N.Y.C. hotels with their ornate decorations and conservative atmospheres would not be in keeping with the series' subject matter or with the young, maverick image of Stellax. Fuller chooses, finally, the reception hall of a well-known artists' association for the site of the conference.

Food and drink will also be kept simple and will include an assortment of cold hors d'oeuvres and chilled white wine.

Fuller has checked to be sure that the room can be supplied with the appropriate equipment needed for the conference. This includes a microphone, lectern and table, adequate seating for 150, and lighting for photographers and TV crews. (The five large TV monitors for the presentation of the preview tape will be supplied by PRST, and Fuller maintains contact with

---

*Room size for a news conference is often tricky to estimate. It is important to have enough room for comfort, but a large space which is only half-filled leaves a poor impression. In general, overcrowding is preferable to the opposite.

their maintenance department to be sure that delivery occurs on the proper date.) All arrangements are confirmed and reconfirmed at intervals throughout the planning stages of the event. Several days before the conference, Fuller does a final check of all these items with the building's technical staff. He also talks to the caterer to confirm the amount of food and the manner of its presentation. On the day of the event, he or his assistant will be available at the site to give last-minute instructions during the set-up.

Fuller also arranges for the placement of a sign-in desk in front of the conference hall where the media will be welcomed, given name tags, and asked to sign a guest book. This will provide a record of attendance for use in call-backs and for reference in completing a subsequent report to the client concerning the success of the event. He also arranges for a private photographer who will be briefed thoroughly before the conference on which shots should be taken (Levy with Pym; Pym, Levy, and the president of PRST; the executive producer, Pym, and Levy; and so on). These photos will be captioned and sent to publications which do not send a photographer to the event. They will also be inserted into the media kits sent to news people who do not attend.

Presentation

The presentation is obviously the most important component of the news conference and must be carefully orchestrated. Fuller first decides upon an order of presentation and on the relative priority which each speaker should be given in the event. Ordinarily, he would have designated Alexander Pym as the featured speaker. In this case, however, Frank Levy seems a better choice. Levy's knowledge of art and his importance in the business world give him a broader appeal than Pym and allow him to bridge the gap between the series' specialized subject matter and the public's more practical interests. Levy can also reinforce Stellax's corporate identity as an innovative, creative company.

Once he has established Levy as the principal speaker, Fuller outlines the order and time allotment for each presentation. The opening remarks (five minutes) will be made by the president of the PRST station, followed by a five-minute statement by the series' executive producer. The senior vice president of Stellax will then introduce Frank Levy who will deliver his remarks on the relationship between art and business and on the importance of the series (twenty minutes). Finally, Pym will speak for ten minutes about the modern art movement and introduce the fifteen-minute preview tape. Fuller realizes that this will be an unusually long news conference owing to the number of speakers and the preview tape. He also knows that his time estimates are optimistic and that the speakers are likely to make longer presentations.

While he gives suggestions to all the speakers concerning what they should include in their remarks, he only takes an active role in developing the speech of his client, Levy. The others have their own staffs to help them or feel strongly about writing their own remarks (as in Pym's case). Nonetheless, Fuller asks that a draft of each speaker's statement or at least an outline be sent to him as early as possible so that he and his client can know in advance what is going to be said and can suggest changes if they feel these are called for.

In developing Levy's speech, Fuller holds several discussion sessions with his client in order to become familiar with Levy's ideas and personal style. The speech goes through several drafts as Levy edits, cuts, and makes suggestions for additions. Excerpts from the final speech are copied and inserted in the media kit.

Media Kit Materials

Besides excerpts from the speech, other materials in the kit include a news release announcing the series; a fact sheet containing information on the production dates, the independent production company, PRST, Pym, and Stellax; a backgrounder on the series' content and on modern art; bios of Pym and Levy; and captioned photos of Pym, Levy, and several pieces of artwork featured in the series. These materials will, of course, be approved by all parties involved prior to their final printing.

Follow-up

After the conference, Fuller will use the sign-in book to contact those who attended and ask them whether they are interested in previewing individual segments of the series or holding interviews with Levy or Pym. He will also send copies of the media kit to those who did not attend and make follow-up calls after the kits have been received.

Prior to the conference, Fuller retains a clipping service to monitor newspapers and magazines for articles on the series beginning on the day after the conference date. He also retains an electronic media service that will monitor TV and radio coverage and will send him transcripts of programs or news items in which the series is mentioned. Since this is an expensive service, he will retain it only for a limited length of time. In the first three weeks following the conference, he will use the clippings that have come in and the information from the sign-in book to compile an initial report for his client. He will also submit periodic updated reports in the months ahead and during the period when the series airs, listing the coverage that has been generated and outlining plans for additional publicity.

SELECTING THE RIGHT SPECIAL EVENT FOR A CLIENT

There are two general reasons why you might counsel your organization to sponsor a special event. One is that an event creates news and thus serves as an ideal means of generating publicity when there is no concrete news at hand. In this sense, a special event is a staged feature—lacking a newsworthy angle, it goes about creating one. Since special events usually have visual content and are pre-planned, TV news editors can shoot the footage and use it as "filler" when it's convenient.

The other reason why an organization might want to consider a special event is to make a contribution to the community. Such an event might be cultural (a music festival), diverting (a dance competition), or a public service (a free have-your-blood-pressure-taken booth). In these cases the publicity potential for the sponsoring organization is indirect but can be highly effective nonetheless.

Some special events manage to combine elements of direct publicity for their sponsors with elements of indirect publicity. The following case offers an example.

Jeremy Dawson is public information director of the Davis Port, a 30-mile stretch of port and undeveloped adjacent land near New Orleans. The Port has traditionally been used to ship coal arriving by rail from the Midwest, to Europe and Japan. The coal shipments keep the port financially solvent but do not contribute to the kind of growth that Dawson and Joe Sneed, the Davis Port executive director, would like to see for the area.

Sneed tells Dawson that coal is a large-volume, low-cost commodity and will never make the Port's fortune. Instead, he'd like to attract more diverse cargo, as well as encourage labor-intensive manufacturing companies to settle on the adjacent land. These companies would build up the area and bring more business to the Port. For several years now, Sneed has been seeking to attract these companies, but with little success. He now approaches Dawson for help. How can he convince manufacturers that locating a plant near a port area would be both convenient and economical? How can he convince them to come to Davis?

After considering the situation, Dawson decides that Davis Port needs to stage an unusual special event which will draw the attention of the media to the area. He knows that it is important to reach not only the standard port publications which tend to run regular stories on even the most trivial new developments at Davis, but also the more general industrial development, manufacturing, and business publications which are read by prospective managers who might be interested in relocating or opening up a new plant.

The PR objective, as Dawson understands it, is to explain the advantages

176 Developing Visibility II: Planning a PR Event

of a port location to manufacturing companies throughout the country and to associate these advantages specifically with Davis Port.

Dawson's first idea is to hold a gala riverboat party to which all new business prospects would be invited. The Port had staged such parties before to entertain visiting dignitaries and as tie-ins to local fund-raisers, and they had always been rip-roaring successes. But after thinking it over, Dawson concludes that such an event would be too social for the objective he has in mind. It would not focus on the Port's concrete advantages. Guests might have fun and get a tax write-off in the process, but they could hardly be expected to make relocation plans on the basis of a good party.

Another idea which occurs to Dawson is to make a promotional film about the Port which could be shown to targeted companies and to the media. But he quickly realizes that this too is an unpromising idea for a number of reasons. For one, it would be impossible to make a film that would be substantially different from other films which have already been made by other ports. Moreover, such a film could be easily dismissed by the media as self-serving due to its obvious promotional content. It would therefore never bring the Port the kind of wide-ranging publicity it needs.

Then a modified and seemingly more promising version of this idea occurs to Dawson. Why not make a series of film clips—one- to three-and-a-half-minute mini-documentaries—using Davis Port as a model for discussing the advantages of port-situated manufacturing? Each clip could be given a newsworthy angle, mailed to local TV stations throughout the country and picked up when a local news show needed a news filler. This approach would bring wide exposure and would downplay the self-serving aspects of the pitch by presenting the subject-matter as objective reporting (see the discussion of films and tapes in Chapter 7). But Dawson finally rejects this idea too because he feels the kind of exposure generated by a series of news clips would be too broad—not targeted enough to manufacturing companies, the Port's key audience. Moreover, the clip, owing to time limitations, would have to be a superficial treatment of the subject, not substantial enough to sell a manager contemplating relocation.

Finally, Dawson comes up with an idea which he feels has none of the drawbacks of his previous ideas. He proposes staging a special event that would take the form of a seminar on port-related industrial development. The seminar would be a day-long series of presentations and panel discussions on subjects dealing with ports and manufacturing. It would feature the following kinds of speakers: directors of other ports (non-competitive with Davis) to discuss the advantages of manufacturing near a port site; representatives from companies already located in the Davis area to give testimonials; land developers to explain how port-adjacent land can be prepared for industrial use; experts on new methods of containerization and shipping to discuss how these services can be exploited by manufacturing companies; and railroad representatives to explain rail-ship link-ups.

The seminar would be a state-of-the art look at the relationship between ports and manufacturing. It would have a general appeal since it would draw on experts from all over the country, but it would highlight Davis Port by making it the site of the seminar. Such an event would draw attendance from both the media and the top management of companies considering a port location. Without being an obvious sales pitch, it would help "sell" Davis Port by linking the Port to a topic of special interest to its target publics.

DEVELOPING TIE-INS AND SPIN-OFFS TO A SPECIAL EVENT

While the obvious publicity value of a special event resides in the happening itself, publicity benefits can also be derived from activities or materials attached to the main event. To assure that you achieve maximum value from an event, you need to consider the possible *tie-ins* and *spin-offs* which could be developed to prolong or enhance it.

A *tie-in* involves the linking of another, secondary activity to the main event. This is often done when other organizations want to tap into the resources already in place. The practical benefits of tie-ins are two-fold: They extend the range of your publicity by "adding on" to the main event, and they give you the opportunity to share material and labor costs with other sponsors. Of course, this also means sharing the spotlight with others. However, if the tie-in is of the right kind and the tie-in sponsor is not in competition with you, the results can be profitable to both parties.

A *spin-off* is an event, an activity, or a material subsequent to a special event which prolongs the event's publicity value over time. Sometimes a special event can set the stage for a series of sequel events; sometimes the proceedings of an event can be taped and turned into a book, brochure, or documentary film. Spin-offs are obviously more economical than events initiated independently since they draw on the resources and build on the momentum generated by the original event.

For three years the Fairfield Medical Center, a community hospital, has sponsored an annual health fair. The fair, which is held in the spring on the hospital's grounds, features a variety of booths offering free advice on such subjects as nutrition, exercise, and emergency medicine, as well as free blood-pressure readings, blood typing, and vision and hearing testing.

Jane Durang, the hospital's information director, has helped organize the event since it was first introduced. This year, however, she feels that the hospital can get more extensive and long-term publicity out of the fair than it has in the past. For this purpose, she decides to develop a program of tie-ins and spin-offs for the event.

Her first move is to draw up a list of local organizations and businesses which might be interested in developing tie-ins to the fair. Of the list of groups, three, when contacted, express definite interest: the local health food store, women's club, and shoe store. Through meetings with representatives from each group, Durang is able to develop tie-ins which are suited to the sponsoring organizations and which would be of definite value to the hospital. The following tie-in events and activities are agreed upon for each of the three sponsors:

THE HEALTH FOOD STORE

A week before the fair, the store agrees to hold a series of lectures to be delivered by a trained nutritionist. The nutritionist will demonstrate and discuss healthy recipes using the store's products and will encourage listeners to attend the health fair for more nutritional information and diet tips. The hospital will supply the nutritionist, and the store will defray all other costs, including the publicity for the lectures.

THE WOMEN'S CLUB

The club had expressed interest in pursuing a fund-raising activity for the hospital which could be linked in some way to the annual health fair. After speaking to the hospital director, Durang is told that funds are presently needed for the renovation of the pediatric play area. The renovation is important but not terribly expensive and could be accomplished for $5,000. The women's club decides to kick-off a fund-raising effort for this renovation when the health fair opens on Saturday morning. Durang arranges a kick-off ceremony in which the director of the hospital, the mayor of the town, and the president of the club will speak on the hospital's role in the community, its priorities in general, and the renovation project in particular.

THE SHOE STORE

At Durang's suggestion, the store decides to hold a "Run for Health Mini-Marathon" on Saturday morning, preceding the fair's kick-off. Durang arranges that the six-mile run begin at the store and end at the hospital, and that traffic be blocked off along the marathon route between 8:30 A.M. and 10 A.M., when the kick-off ceremony is scheduled to take place on the hospital grounds. The store will print several hundred T-shirts with the slogan "Jordon Shoes' Run for Health—Run for Fairfield," to be worn by marathon participants and to be sold at the fair.

Along with these tie-in activities, Durang feels the fair lends itself to spin-off materials which could help publicize the hospital after the event has taken place. One of her spin-off ideas is to compile a collection of health tips from the many specialists who will be participating and to publish these in a manual for distribution at supermarkets, drugstores, and in the hospital's reception area. Another spin-off idea which Durang decides to implement is a series of short public service announcements, taped for radio and videotaped for TV. Each of the series of clips will discuss some aspect of health and safety endorsed by a hospital spokesperson. Since the experts will be assembled for the fair, the making of the clips will be facilitated.

Finally, Durang develops a health and safety survey to be administered at the fair. The survey is a short questionnaire asking people what they know about their health and in what areas they feel they need more instruction. The questionnaire will be administered randomly to visitors, and the results will be compiled by research specialists on the hospital staff. From the results, Durang plans to write a series of press releases for the media highlighting some of the more interesting data.

EXERCISES

Test Your Judgment

In your opinion, which of the following items of information should be announced by means of a news conference? Where a news conference does not seem like a good option, suggest an alternative means of publicizing the information.

1 A car manufacturer puts out its new model; features include bucket seats, slightly improved gas mileage, and a more streamlined exterior.

2 A Nobel prize–winning physicist claims that a new vitamin supplement will help prolong life.

3 The local charity launches its annual fund-raising drive.

4 A small computer company appoints a new vice president of sales.

5 A national arts foundation appoints a new director who intends to shift foundation giving from group grants to individual grants.

6 A hospital opens a special obstetrical unit to handle high-risk pregnancies.

7 A senior official in a large publicly owned company is arrested on drug-dealing charges.

PR Workshop

Brainstorm with the class to come up with a special event which would be appropriate in the following case:

A local brewery which has been making beer in the Northwest for several decades finds itself losing business to imported beers which are being aggressively advertised. A limited survey shows that the beer remains a favorite with the area's old-timers, but that younger people tend not to know about it or to associate it with their grandparents' tastes. The president of the company would like to woo the younger market without deserting the beer's old-fashioned image. As a kick-off to a new PR program, he wants to stage a special event which will set the tone for the ensuing campaign.

PR Case Studies

1 You are the public information director of Marshall Aeronautics, a major aeronautics company which has just received a large government contract to design and build a new type of special missile. The missile is strongly opposed by a number of anti-war and environmental groups, but government defense experts claim that it is crucial to national security. The contract will be a financial boon to the company and will permit the creation of hundreds of new jobs. It will also turn the plant and the surrounding area into a high-security zone.

You want to hold a news conference to announce the contract to the media. Write a memo to the company president, Michael Schmidt, justifying the need for a news conference and describing the format which you think the conference should follow.

2 You handle public relations for an environmental group which favors solar energy. The group decides to hold a seminar entitled "Solar Energy and the Future" in which experts in the energy and environmental fields will be invited to participate. The seminar will feature papers on solar energy and exhibits of solar equipment and designs.

Write a list of possible spin-offs and tie-ins for the seminar.

3 As publicity director of a book publishing company, you want to promote a new book scheduled to go on the market in six months. It is entitled *Get Rich Quick: Everybody's Guide to a Fortune* and is written by a famous self-made millionaire.

Write a memo to the company president, Felicia Schell, in which you enumerate several special-events ideas and suggest a format for a news conference to promote the book.

4 Select a project which you know you need to complete in the coming year. (Possible projects might include writing a term paper, applying to graduate school, applying for a job, planning a large party, or renovating a house.)

Develop a PERT diagram, a general task timetable, and a series of mini-timetables for the project.

NOTES

1. See Charles A. Sengstock, Jr., "How to Apply PERT to PR Planning," *Public Relations Journal*, 26 (June 1970), 14-16.
2. *New York Times*, April 3, 1963, p. 1.
3. *New York Times*, April 18, 1985, sec. C, p. 3.
4. Hanna Rubin, "What's Hot and How It Got That Way," *Public Relations Journal*, 41 (June 1985), 23.
5. Art Stevens, "What's Ahead for Special Events," *Public Relations Journal*, 40 (June 1984), 31.
6. David Finn, "Modifying Opinions in the New Human Climate," *Public Relations Quarterly*, 17 (Fall 1972), 15.
7. Edward L. Bernays, *Crystallizing Public Opinion* (1923; reprinted New York: Liveright Publishing Company, 1961), p. 197.
8. See Howard and Carol Levine, "Your Role in Building Interest," *Effective Public Relations for Community Groups* (New York: Association Press, 1969), pp. 167-71.
9. *Wall Street Journal*, March 25, 1982, p. 1.
10. *Wall Street Journal*, January 21, 1985, p. 8.
11. See Alvin M. Hattal and Daniel P. Hattal, "Videoconferencing," *Public Relations Journal*, 40 (September 1984), 21-24.

7
Developing Visibility III: Controlling the Message

In Chapter 1 we explained that a major difference between public relations and advertising is the degree to which the client tends to control the message directed at the target audience. In PR, we explained, the control is generally less: When a story is pitched to the media, it is up to the media to decide what to do with it. This lack of control over the final message greatly enhances credibility—it implies that what is being reported is objective and true. But it can also be risky.

Take the case of a public information director at a neighborhood youth center who wants the local newspaper to write a story about the center's service to the community. Let's say a reporter agrees that this might make a good feature, proceeds to do research on the center, and discovers, in the course of research, that the center is badly mismanaged. There is nothing now to prevent the reporter from straying from the original angle and printing a story criticizing rather than supporting the center.

The risk of seeing an effort backfire like this is built into much public relations work. Therefore, it's not surprising to learn that sometimes public relations practitioners prefer to avoid this risk and use controlled messages; that is, they choose to communicate directly with their target audience, without passing through the potentially transforming filter of the media. At such times, public relations resembles advertising, with the difference that PR practitioners tend to use controlled messages within the context of a larger PR program—as one strategy among many designed to further the client's overall PR objectives.

The following are several reasons why a client might choose to control the message as part of a public relations effort:

Developing Visibility III: Controlling the Message   183

1. Client-prepared materials for hand-out or direct mail can provide easy reference data for the target audience, and accompanying graphics can add a visual reference that helps reinforce the client's identity.
2. Client-prepared materials assure that complicated or delicate information gets relayed in the precise terms the client wishes to use.
3. Where the law demands that certain information be made public, client-prepared materials can place emphasis where it will be of most advantage and can explain potentially damaging information or place it in a less damaging context.
4. Client-prepared materials can be a vehicle for artists and writers to give the client's message a creative and original presentation.

In this chapter we will discuss some of the most common tools employed by public relations practitioners for relaying controlled messages.

CONTROLLED MESSAGES IN PRINT

Flyers and Posters

Both flyers and posters should be developed around an *organizing idea* which informs the choice of written and graphic elements. Establish an appropriate organizing idea by asking yourself what your public relations objective is and how the flyer or poster can help achieve it most effectively. For example, a radio station whose PR objective is to increase its listener base among 18- to 22-year-olds might send out flyers to college students which are designed like party invitations. The organizing idea would be: "Listening to WCTU Is Where the Action Is!" The best organizing ideas are simple and lend themselves to easy-to-grasp visual presentations.

Also remember that flyers and posters, like all materials produced on behalf of a client, should reflect an "identity system"[1]—those elements which visually and verbally separate one organization from another. This means that color, graphics, and slogan references should tie in, wherever possible, with a larger PR program, thus allowing the flyer or poster to be instantly associated with a specific organizational identity.

Before deciding to produce flyers, you need to know your target audience and how it can be reached. This means obtaining comprehensive, up-to-date mailing lists (specialized mailing lists can be purchased from list houses for fees, which vary depending upon the size and nature of the list) and/or having access to locations frequented by your target publics where the flyers can be handed out. Once you've determined the target audience and the method of distribution, you can begin thinking about how you want the flyer to look. While you will need to suit the presentation to the interests and personality of your target audience, all flyers should contain some type of arresting content, either in the way of color, unusual graphics, or witty copy. Since most people receive an enormous volume of junk mail, a flyer without one or more of these distinctive qualities will be automatically overlooked. Be careful, however, not to let graphic elements clutter the presentation and eclipse the information you want to get across.

The typical flyer is printed on 8½-inch by 11-inch durable paper for easy mailing. (Check the weight of the paper stock in advance to be sure that it won't raise mailing costs beyond your budget.) Where economy is necessary, flyers can be addressed and stamped on a blank flap and thus mailed without an envelope. R.S.V.P. information can also be included by designing a self-addressed, perforated flap which the receiver merely fills out and mails back. (If you want to prepay return postage, find out if your organization has a franking number or contact the post office about obtaining one.) If you are mailing flyers which you want the receiver to post on bulletin boards or walls, be sure to mark "Please Post" in bold letters.

Where a flyer can offer some elaboration on its message, a poster doesn't have this luxury. It has to be extremely simple and brief (requiring no more than a 20-second reading time and, ideally, much less), since it must be comprehended by people who are passing quickly and who may be distracted when they do so. Color and graphics are most important—many of the best posters have few words (although in some cases, a message of unusual wit or shock value can be more dramatic if presented in simple lettering without accompanying graphics).

There are two possible approaches to relaying the message in a poster. You can present the message directly, leaving nothing to the imagination of the viewer. Or you can deliver it indirectly, demanding that the viewer "fill in" for what's missing. A poster which displays a crushed cigarette and the caption "Stop Smoking" would be an example of the first approach, while one which shows a row of matches with the matchheads removed and the caption "'Cause We Care"* would be an example of the second. Whatever the approach taken, a poster should never be cluttered, and intricate artwork and delicate print are rarely acceptable options. Colors should be chosen and coordinated to reflect the mood that you wish to project, and size and shape should be selected to complement the space and situation in which the poster will be displayed (unlike many European countries, the U.S. specifies no standard dimensions for posters).

While you will want to oversee and suggest copy and graphic ideas for flyers and posters, you will need a graphic designer for the execution and a printer for the production if you are interested in a polished final product (see the following discussion on brochures for details on these support func-

---

*An actual matchheadless matchbook displaying this slogan was a promotional item developed by the American Cancer Society for a recent campaign.

tions). Posters to be produced in bulk (more than 1,000 copies) are usually printed by photo offset, while a less extensive run may be silk screened, a method which works especially well in reproducing solid, bold colors.

Brochures

Brochures are staple public relations materials which organizations usually find themselves employing on a periodic or an ongoing basis. These can be *special purpose brochures* devoted to specific events, issues, operations, or campaigns, or *general background brochures* designed to introduce an organization in a general way to its target publics. General background brochures are especially important because they serve as the basic calling cards for organizations. They are the back-up items which organizations send out in conjunction with other materials when they pitch a story to the media or engage in direct mail campaigns with their target publics. Most organizations also make such brochures available at their reception desks or service counters as a resource for visitors or customers. PR agencies and other businesses which depend on clients will mail general background brochures (often accompanied by a personalized cover letter) to new business prospects (see Chapter 9).

Like a flyer and poster, a brochure should be based on an organizing idea which lends it coherence and makes it compatible with the client's overall PR effort (in preparing a brochure, you should always know the target audience, PR objectives, and PR message of your client's larger PR program). The organizing idea can then be translated into a memorable sentence or phrase to be used as a title or running theme in the brochure copy. A local tenant's organization, for example, establishes an organizing idea for its brochure: "The West Side Tenants' Association wants to introduce itself and explain its value to you and your community." It then reduces this to a simpler, more memorable message in the brochure's title: "Meet Your Best Neighbor: West Side Tenants' Association."

Once you have established the organizing idea for the brochure, you will want to determine an appropriate format. Length, paper stock, typeface, graphic elements, and color are all aspects of format. If your budget is limited, it's a good idea to start with a listing of the format elements you'd like to include, determine the cost of these elements, and then eliminate elements or revise the format until you meet your budget estimate.

Keep in mind that a general background brochure is an important element in your client's "identity system" and should therefore carry through slogans, graphic elements, and logos which have been used in the larger PR campaign. Once produced, it generally requires only periodic updating so long as a given PR program remains in place. When a new program is initiated, a new brochure should be prepared that reflects the new target audience, PR objectives, and PR message.

Here are some guidelines for developing effective brochures for organizations:

GIVE THE BASICS UP-FRONT

Like a good press release, a good brochure gives the basic information first, then goes on to include additional, less important material. The address and telephone number of the organization should, of course, appear prominently. While other priorities will vary from organization to organization, the opening copy of a general background brochure usually identifies the organization and what it does and offers a brief statement on why the organization, its product or service, is valuable to the target audience. This may be followed by a short history of the organization and a list and short biography of the principal officers. Specific information concerning operations, case studies, employees, community service, and so on, generally come later. Information should be divided using appropriate headings. Where possible, try for simple parallel structure which logically groups ideas while reinforcing the organizing idea. Thus, a brochure developed for a local health club entitled "Invest in Your Body's Future" carries through the idea of "investment" by presenting its subject matter in two parts:

The Investment (a listing and explanation of the various activities available at the club):

Swimming
Running
Machine exercise and weight-lifting
Aerobics and yoga

The Pay-off (an explanation of the effects these activities will have on your health):

Your heart
Your lungs
Your muscles
Your body profile
Your emotional well-being

USE APPROPRIATE DICTION

In brochures aimed at nontechnical audiences, diction should be simple and easy to follow. If the target audience is more specialized, the terms chosen should be those commonly used by that audience. Thus, the brochure put out by a heat-pump manufacturing company and directed at engineers would be different from the brochure by the same company directed at the general consumer. If you do not have the appropriate expertise yourself, consult an expert inside the organization who can explain technical operations or terms to you and who can review your copy to be sure it is accurate and sounds authentic.

BE AS SPECIFIC AS POSSIBLE

Platitudes about good service, fine community spirit, and quality control abound in most organizational brochures. Your audience has probably begun to distrust such claims, or at least to pay little attention to them. A front-page article in *The American Lawyer* described the expensively produced brochure of one prestigious law firm that was so filled with unsupported platitudes and generalizations that the reporter found it not only unpersuasive but insulting to its readers.[2] The best brochures give concrete examples of achievements and detailed descriptions of how their organizations' operations differ from those of the competition.

BE DISCRIMINATING IN DETERMINING FORMAT

Brochures can vary in size and length. The simplest brochures are four-page, 5½ inches by 8½ inches or 8½ inches by 11 inches. It's most economical to increase page numbers by multiples of four (four, eight, twelve, and so on). Size and length of brochures should be determined by your budget, the nature of graphic elements to be included, and the kind and abundance of material that needs to be covered. Think as well about how you want the recipient to handle the brochure. Should it be pocket-sized so that it can be carried around and consulted at will, or large and glossy for possible display on a bookshelf or magazine rack?

The use of color in a brochure is another important consideration. The most modest option is a simple black and white printing, or, for slightly more dash, a colored paper stock with standard black print or perhaps colored ink. Two-color printing allows you to differentiate logo or other graphic elements in an additional color; only four or more colors provides for full-color presentation of photos. Full-color printing will, of course, be the most eye-catching, but it may not always jibe with the client's target audience or larger PR objectives. If your organization is a traditional one which caters to a conservative public, a four- or more color printing may not convey a properly subdued appearance and you might do better with a two-color or black and white printing—even if the budget would allow more colors.

Be especially discriminating about which and how many photographs you choose to place in the brochure. If there are one or two principals in the company, you may want to include their pictures, but if there are four or more, it may be more visually effective to omit the officers' photos altogether and substitute some other, more interesting, photography—of employees at work, of the company headquarters if it's attractive, of a community project, special event, or underwriting venture which the organization has sponsored. While it's important for the brochure to reflect the personality of the organization, don't make the mistake of preparing a brochure that appeals more to the egos of management than to the interests and needs of the prospective audience.

MAKE SURE ALL COMPONENTS OF BROCHURE PREPARATION ARE PROPERLY OVERSEEN AND COORDINATED

If there is a graphics expert inside your organization, you will want to consult with him or her at intervals as you compile information and write copy. This person may have ideas about *layout* (the specific ordering of pictures and text) or artwork that may influence your research and writing of the brochure copy. If you are using an outside graphic designer, it's also advisable to trade ideas as early as possible. Try to have some notion of what you want before you meet with the consultant, and make sure you see a *mock-up*, or *dummy* (a scaled version of the piece that indicates where photos and printed material will go) before the brochure goes to the printer. After the copy has gone to the typesetter, you should be given the opportunity to see *galleys* of the typeset printed copy for proofreading. You can also ask to see a *press proof*—a sample of the entire piece as it comes off the press. If you make changes in the press proof, however, you will probably be charged an additional fee.

PREPARE AND KEEP TO A TIMETABLE

Because the preparation of brochures involves the coordination of many disparate tasks, it is important that you work out a realistic time frame for the project and then decide in advance how long each task involved should take. Get time estimates (as well as budget estimates) from a number of graphic designers, photographers, printers, and typesetters, and ask them for references so that you can consult their past clients about the quality of their work and their reliability. (If you feel overwhelmed by the prospect of dealing with so many specialists, you can always hire a good graphic designer who will find the photographer, printer, and typesetter, negotiate fees, and oversee their work for you.) Finally, be sure that each component of the brochure is properly approved by your supervisor along the way, or you may end up with a press proof that has to be radically altered at the last minute, entailing an unnecessary expenditure of time and money.

Annual Reports

Publicly owned companies and nonprofit organizations are obliged by law to file yearly statements with the federal government and with shareholders

Developing Visibility III: Controlling the Message **189**

to disclose certain financial data specified by the Securities and Exchange Commission (SEC). Most companies choose to turn this obligation into a public relations tool by "packaging" the financial data in an appealing format and offering commentary on the statistics. This document, called an *annual report*, is used to communicate information about the organization, not only to government officials and stockholders, but also to financial analysts, consumers, potential investors, contributors, employees, students, and others interested in knowing more about the organization. In a sense, an annual report is simply a more elaborate and specialized brochure, but it is governed by so many formal conventions that it needs to be treated separately.

While the financial data for an annual report is compiled by the accounting and legal departments of an organization, it is often the job of the public relations practitioner to coordinate the report's production. This means that the practitioner, without being a financial expert, must have a working knowledge of what an annual report contains and how this material can be collected, edited, and, in some cases, written.

The standard contents of an annual report include the following:

Summary table(s) of financial results or "highlights" (comparing last year to this year).

A list of the organization's officers and board of directors

A letter to shareholders from the top executive (director or president/chief executive officer).

A story describing the company's operations, its direction for the future, and/or its role in the community (emphasis here will vary depending upon the nature of the company and its priorities for the year).

Related photos of officers, workers, the work environment, new equipment, buildings and plants, and so forth.

A brief financial analysis in prose form, often accompanied by simple graphs and charts to illustrate trends.

Financial data (the hard figures, usually left to the accountant).

According to one financial communications expert, the best annual reports present their material in "layers," so that each element, from the cover graphics to the hard financial data, communicate the same information at different orders of complexity.[3] This way, readers with varying amounts of financial expertise will be able to derive the same essential message from the report. In order to assure this kind of unity, you should work closely with the graphic artist so that the visual elements reflect the report's orientation and mesh well with the written copy.

If you are expected to write the preliminary draft of the letter to stockholders, you will want to meet personally with the president, or if this is not feasible, ask him or her to jot down notes that can start you thinking in the right direction. The feature story which follows should complement and extend points made in the letter. If there are a number of distinct points of interest, you may want to divide the feature into a series of short mini-features, each dealing with a key issue, such as personnel, retail operations, or community service. However, the more these subdivisions can be shown to relate to each other and reflect an overall emphasis, theme, or organizing idea, the better.

In writing the feature material, be simple and direct, and use vivid, concrete examples wherever possible. This is not the place for technical language or flowery prose. Don't avoid discussing obvious problems or setbacks; such omissions will look like a cover-up. While you want to present the organization in the best possible light, you also want to appear as honest and upfront as possible. Even a financially naive reader can sense when the presentation is disguising or distorting information.

Since an annual report is the organization's most important financial and legal document, it will have to go through an elaborate series of reviews before being ready for final production. It's a good idea to establish as early as possible how the review process will be accomplished and who will grant approval on what information. Try to discuss ideas in advance with the appropriate individuals. You will certainly want to meet with your client's accountant and lawyer several times during the year to be sure that written copy accurately reflects statistical information and conforms with SEC guidelines.

According to specialists in the field, there promise to be many new developments in annual report preparation over the coming years. Reports seem likely to grow thicker in pages and more sophisticated in appearance (better quality paper stock, more innovative design, more interesting if not more overall use of color).[4] Sid Cato, an expert in this area, predicts that video annual reports (following the lead of video newsletters) are options for the future and that reports will soon be put on-line for computerized access.[5] He also foresees annual reports becoming more accessible and "human" in their presentation, working harder to relay the feel and personality of an organization as well as its objective position in the marketplace.

CONTROLLED MESSAGES IN THE ELECTRONIC MEDIA

For a long time, public relations activity was aimed primarily at the print media. This was because many PR people were former newspaper reporters, more familiar and comfortable with the conventions of print. In the past few decades, however, a new kind of public relations practitioner, attuned to the publicity opportunities inherent in TV and radio and familiar with the latest trends in technology as well, has extended the range of PR activity to include the electronic media. Today, access to radio and TV (including the rapidly expanding area of cable TV) is pursued as vigorously by PR practitioners as access to print. Many of the larger public relations agencies and departments have initiated in-house broadcast departments which produce their own films, videos, and audio tapes. Meanwhile, smaller agencies and departments are becoming increasingly interested in retaining independent consulting firms to work in this area with them.

Obviously, controlling the message in the electronic media involves different variables than those which are important in print. Although preparing a brochure demands the coordination of visual elements with written ones, broadcasting adds the element of time (duration) and in the case of film and videotape, incorporates dynamic rather than static visuals. Copy must also be prepared to be spoken rather than read, a consideration which is especially important in radio where there are no visuals to assist meaning.

Films and Tapes

The most common type of film* produced by PR departments and agencies is the standard promotional film which describes and illustates the company's general character and range of operations. Such films will often involve a *voice-over* (in which the individual speaking is not seen on the screen) as explanatory narration for the visuals. At its most conventional, these films follow the same general format as the company brochure, merely revising the copy to conform with the spoken style of voice-over and using film versions of the scenes and people featured in the brochure's still photography. Such films obviously will never win Academy Awards, but they can be a practical way to orient new employees or provide an introduction to visitors.

While conventional promotional films continue to be important PR tools, these are being supplemented or replaced in many cases by films which are both more original in format and less blatantly promotional in content. Often having the style of documentaries, such films take a more in-depth look at a specific operation, individual, or activity, seeking less to promote the organization as a whole than to produce a newsworthy or human interest feature to increase the visibility of the organization indirectly. Such films, when well done, can have considerable mileage: Not only can they serve as in-house orientation resources for employees and visitors, but they also can be marketed for use on TV or shown at association or club meetings when the membership has an interest in the film's topic.

Some public relations agencies with their own broadcasting departments

---

*We use *film* here to refer generically to both film and videotape. In fact, most TV news shows use three-quarter-inch tape, but since film can easily be transferred to tape, TV editors will usually accept either medium. Film still assures a better final product and is preferable for materials being prepared for organizational meetings or movie theaters where 16-mm film projectors are more likely to be in use than VCRs. But as VCRs improve in quality and drop in price, tape may eventually replace film as the preferred medium.

have also begun to produce short (one- to three-and-a-half-minute) documentary-style film and audio clips for placement as news or features on TV and radio. (These are often made by chopping a full-length documentary into a number of edited shorter segments.) These news or feature clips, also called mini-documentaries (*mini-docs*) or video news releases (*VNRs*), either are mailed to a number of selected TV or radio stations whose demographics match the client's target audience or are transmitted via satellite (with news directors at the targeted stations alerted by mailgram to the time of the transmission).[6] To be picked up, the mini-doc must contain news or newsworthy information; that is, it must reflect an interesting but objective relationship to the topic and must not be an obvious sales pitch for the sponsor organization. Although it is difficult to track whether or not a mini-doc has been shown on a local station, many organizations feel that the potential advantages of getting a controlled message placed as part of a news show are so much greater than buying space on TV or radio for a designated number of assured advertising spots that they are willing to risk the uncertainty involved. The mini-doc, when it *is* picked up, is much more credible than an advertisement, and since it runs as news, there is no charge for space.

TV mini-doc scripts follow a standard film script format. The clip usually begins with a short introductory narration to be delivered by a reportorial figure. Then, the left side of the page (labeled video) begins a description of the visual scene or action, while the right side of the page (labeled audio) transcribes the spoken text and the description of sound effects as they occur simultaneously with the visuals. A *cumulative time* notation is given at intervals to mark the time passage within the clip. (See Exhibit 7-1, a mini-doc written for a clothing designer to help publicize a newsworthy line of sportswear.)

Radio mini-doc scripts are written with the reportorial commentary interspersed with the interviewee's statements (presented in indented bold type or capital letters). The duration of the interview material is usually noted in the margin so that adequate space can be left for its insertion after the reportorial commentary has been taped.

Public Service Announcements (PSAs)

Public service announcements are messages prepared by nonprofit organizations to be read by broadcast announcers free of charge as a public service. They are most commonly sent to radio stations, although videotapes or scripts with accompanying slides can also be prepared for use by TV. Announcers are obliged by law to air a certain number of PSAs during a specified period, but they can choose which announcements they will air and when they will air them.

PSAs can be prepared as 10-, 20-, 30-, or 60-second spots. Sixty-second

EXHIBIT 7-1 Sample TV Mini-Doc Script: Bang, Bang—You're *Not* Dead. (Reprinted with permission of the Broadcast Division of Ruder Finn & Rotman, Inc.)

STUDIO ANCHOR OPEN:

A new line of designer sportswear—a little different than most—is being introduced that will protect you from more than just the elements. Correspondent Dick Cunningham has a report . . . . .

VIDEO	*CUMULA-TIVE TIME*	*AUDIO*
MARKSMAN EMPTIES CLIP AT MANNEQUIN	:06	Wild sound—gunshots
GARMENT INSPECTED TO SHOW BULLET FAILED TO PENETRATE	:16	It's the bullet-proof line—fashionable and *extremely* functional—designed to stop a .38 special at close range, and even a .44 magnum.
LS OF FASHIONS BEING MODELED	:23	The fall fashions were unveiled at a press reception called by EMGO U.S.A., Limited.
CU OF INDIVIDUAL GARMENTS	:29	Jumpsuits, hunting and flight jackets, and even vests.
SUPER: JON JOLCIN DESIGNER	:55	BASICALLY, I WANT TO MAKE FASHIONS WHICH ARE NOT ONLY ATTRACTIVE, BUT ALSO PROTECTIVE. I TRIED TO CREATE A FASHION THAT WOULD NOT LOOK LIKE A BULLET-PROOF PRODUCT BUT WOULD BE A FASHIONABLE PRODUCT. WE TRIED TO MAKE A PRODUCT THAT WOULD APPEAL TO THE PEOPLE FROM A PROTECTIVE POINT OF VIEW AS WELL AS FROM THE HIGH FASHION POINT OF VIEW.

-more-

REPORTER SYNC		THE SECRET IS THIS LIGHT-WEIGHT KEVLAR, TUCKED UNOBTRUSIVELY INSIDE THE FRONT AND BACK PANELS OF THE GARMENT. IT WILL STOP MOST BUL-LETS—THIS THE COMPANY
	1:07	GUARANTEES.
SUPER: ABRAHAM SILBER-SHATZ PRES., EMGO U.S.A.		ABSOLUTELY. IN FACT EACH OF OUR GARMENTS CAR-RIES WITH IT AN UNCONDI-TIONAL $500,000 GUARAN-TEE, SHOULD THE BULLET PENETRATE THE GARMENT. THIS ASSURANCE IS BACKED UP BY PAST EXPE-RIENCE AND INCREDIBLE TIGHT QUALITY CONTROL
	1:25	STANDARDS.
RIFLE RANGE TEST OF TEFLON BULLET		The company has also devel-oped a special alloy that, in initial tests, has stopped the controversial armor-piercing teflon-coated bullet—a bullet which already has gone through 40 layers of Kevlar and a half-dozen phone
	1:39	books.
REPORTER CLOSE — SYNC		HOPEFULLY THE NEED FOR THIS SPECIAL ALLOY WILL BE A THING OF THE PAST AS THERE'S AN EF-FORT IN CONGRESS NOW TO BAN THE TEFLON BUL-LET ALTOGETHER. BUT FOR JUST ABOUT ANY OTHER TYPE BULLET, AN INVEST-MENT YOU CAN LIVE WITH. DICK CUNNINGHAM, NEW
	1:52	YORK.

spots are less likely to air, since free intervals of this length are not plentiful. Thirty-second spots are probably most common and most effective, although you may want to send several different-length spots to provide the station with a choice. Begin by writing down everything you want to say, then cutting and rewording to fit your time allowance. The reading time of the spot, along with contact information and airing dates, should be clearly marked on the script.

Remember that your PSA will be read by a station announcer who has whipped it out of a file, usually without having read it ahead of time. This means that the spot must be easy both to read and for the listener to grasp after one, usually rapid reading. Try to repeat the place, date, and time of an event at least twice in the spot. If time permits, you can also include a phone number (repeated twice, if possible). Like broadcast releases, PSAs should be double- or triple-spaced with wide margins. Diction and sentence structure should be kept simple, and difficult names should be spelled out phonetically.

Slide Presentations

Everyone has been present at a slide presentation where the speaker loses his or her place, the projector breaks down, the script is halting and monotonous, and the slides are boring, illegible, and add nothing to the talk. Such presentations have given slide shows a bad name and, certainly, there are pitfalls to the medium which seem to be accentuated as more and more high-tech alternatives become available. Even so, many organizations use slides effectively at sales meetings, client presentations, employee orientations, and other events. There are obvious budgetary advantages attached to using slides, and when well conceived and carefully prepared, slide presentations can have a dramatic, personalized impact that cannot be duplicated with films or tapes.

There is no set formula for matching words and visuals in preparing a slide show. Which comes first may depend upon whether the verbal or the pictorial element is the most important in the presentation, or upon practical determinants (if existing slides need to be used, or if the script needs to be approved before the slides can be shot). Words and pictures can also be developed together by means of *storyboards*—cardboard sheets which match sketches of the intended visual image on the left with scripted material on the right.[7] By this method, you can edit spoken material so that it fits with pictures and, at the same time, get a clearer sense of which pictures would best fit the script. Ideally, you will want the script to present a series of "thought passages"—or idea units—to match each picture. Remember that the script must be written to be read aloud, and that visuals must be simple enough to be grasped quickly by the audience but original enough to add a new dimension to what is being said. The best slides illustrate verbal points rather than repeating them. An explanation of light refraction, for example, could be made by using slides to illustrate the phenomenon through a pictorial analogy. A first slide might show how large waves in an ocean are broken up and scattered into ripples as they collide with a concrete obstacle. A second slide might show a diagram of light rays confronting obstacles in the atmosphere. Using the slides as referents, the speaker would simply make the analogy explicit.

In working with the photographer in the preparation of slides, make sure you provide a detailed written order of what you want and go over that order in person to be sure your specifications are understood.

Once script and visuals have been developed, you need to make sure that the presentation will be effectively delivered. If possible, you will want to know who will be delivering the slide show *before* you prepare it, so the script can be fit to the style of the presenter. When this is not possible, it becomes necessary to fit the speaker to the show, rather than vice-versa. This involves, at the very least, finding someone with a good speaking voice, a sense of timing, and an even modulation to deliver the presentation. Don't underestimate the importance of the presentation technique; even the best script and the most sensational slides can fall flat if the voice that accompanies them is dull and uninspired (see Chapter 8, p. 222).

Slide scripts should be clearly marked to indicate when a slide should be changed, and both speaker and projectionist should practice the coordination of slide changes and script-reading before the final presentation. Better still is to arrange for remote control attachments to the projector so that the speaker can change the slides without having to rely on a projectionist. The projector should of course be checked in advance, as should the order of the slides and the script pages. During this rehearsal session, have someone stationed at the back of the room to be sure that the slides can be read at that distance. (It's worth spending more to assure that slides have good color contrast and a crisp, legible image.) During the slide show, the presenter should stand to the left of the screen from the vantage point of the audience. This means that each time a slide has been read, the audience's eyes will travel back to the speaker for more information (since we read from left to right).

Alternatives to Slides

Where you haven't the time or money to prepare top-notch slides, other, more modest alternatives exist in the form of *overhead projection* or simple *flip charts*. Indeed, according to communications consultants Marya W. Holcombe and Judith K. Stein, overheads and flip charts are preferable when the audience is smaller (about 100 people for overheads, under 20 for flip charts) and the presentation more informal.[8] When you are interested in focusing attention more on yourself and your verbal presentation than on accompanying visuals, these options may also be a better choice.

Overhead projection, which magnifies images drawn in colored markers on clear sheets of plastic (*transparencies*), offers several additional advantages over slides. For one thing, this kind of projection rarely requires turning off lights to display images, which means you can use the projector at a set interval during the presentation to clarify a point graphically, and then turn it off without drawing undue attention to the fact. You can also highlight details on the screen by pointing directly to the transparency as it lies under the projector. The transparencies themselves are easy to make and can even be created as you speak to your audience by drawing directly on the clear plastic as it is being projected.

Where overhead projectors are not available or desirable, more basic accompaniments to verbal presentations are flip charts. These oversized drawing pads don't run the risk of mechanical breakdown and can be easily flipped back to re-emphasize a point made earlier in your talk. Flip charts can be prepared ahead of time or written on spontaneously as you speak. They work well in training seminars or other educational forums where you want your audience to participate actively in developing ideas or where you wish to ingrain key words or simple images in their memory.

Model Case Studies

PREPARING AN ANNUAL REPORT

Unfortunately, many practitioners rush the preparation of the annual report in the last months of the year or fail to properly gather and evaluate their resources along the way. As a result, they end up wasting valuable time toward the end of the project—when they ought to be revising and polishing final copy.

For organizations which run on the calendar year, financial information should be available by late January. Since general projections will be known considerably before this time, most of the report should be completed before the actual statistics become available. And even before the general projections are known, a graphic artist should be selected who can help you get many of the more basic decisions out of the way. Decisions concerning paper quality, typeface, number of colors, approximate number of pages, and number of copies of the report to be printed should be made as soon as you have some idea of your overall budget. The number of reports to be printed can be calculated according to the number of stockholders, security analysts, employees, customers, and financial press who will need to receive copies. Since annual reports are always printed in bulk, a "short run" is usually under 10,000 copies. Remember that the more copies you print, the cheaper each individual report will be.

During the early planning period, you can also make initial contact with the various individuals who will be important resources for information in the report and who will supply approval on copy. These will probably include the organization's lawyer and accountant, the heads of company divisions or departments, and the senior organizational official (chairperson and/or president or executive director) whose name will be attached to the letter to stockholders at the front of the report. How you make contact with these people and how extensive this contact is will depend on the size and nature of the organization you work for.

Larry Pagano is public relations director for Drug Products, Inc., a company that operates a chain of 100 drugstores across the country. Among his public relations responsibilities is the preparation of the company's annual report.

Pagano is especially concerned about the report for the upcoming year since the company has recently diversified into a number of areas which do not directly relate to its drug-retailing operation. It has purchased two private hospitals, a nursing home, and a vitamin manufacturing company, and these new investment areas have not been as profitable as had been expected. Moreover, while a number of new stores have opened in urban areas, some of the suburban stores have closed in the past year, a trend that promises to continue in the years ahead. While none of this is necessarily catastrophic, it does represent a shift in orientation for the company which will need careful handling in the annual report.

Pagano is therefore especially interested in gathering his resources for the preparation of the report as early as possible so he can concentrate on writing the letter to stockholders and the feature material in the last months.

Drug Products' fiscal year ends with the calendar year in December, and financial statistics for the year are made available by the accountants on February 1. Pagano begins planning next year's report almost a year in advance of this date and, as a first order of business, draws up a timetable (Exhibit 7-2).

In consultation with the graphic artist, Pagano decides that, given the allotted budget and the company's simple and straightforward image, the annual report should be the standard 8½ inches by 11 inches and have a two-color format: white paper, black print (one color), and grey border design (second color).

The questionnaires which Pagano administers in August to the company's division heads include questions like the following:

EXHIBIT 7-2 Timetable for Annual Report

March

1. Select graphic artist and photographer.
2. Calculate approximate number of copies of report needed this year.
3. Have graphic artist begin negotiations with printers.
4. Evaluate last year's annual report and discuss changes in size, paper, color, layout, photos with graphic artist.

April-May

1. Meet informally with division heads to discuss questionnaire preparation.
2. Meet with lawyer and accountant about projections. Discuss review procedure for copy.
3. Make appointment for September meeting with chairperson.

June-July

1. Draw up preliminary questionnaire for division heads.
2. Do research in company archives to gather information and ideas for feature story.
3. Make preliminary photo assignments.

August

1. Meet with accountant and lawyer and gather fiscal trend information.
2. Finalize questionnaires.
3. Administer and evaluate questionnaire.
4. Draw up statement of objectives reflecting the emphasis of the report to discuss with chairperson.

September

1. Meet with chairperson.
2. Write preliminary draft of letter to stockholders.

October-November

1. Write draft of feature article.
2. Send drafts for review.

> 3 Make additional photo assignments.
> 4 Meet with graphic designer and printer.
>
> **December**
>
> 1 Meet with accountant and lawyer for confirmation of projections.
> 2 Make additional revisions.
> 3 Send out second review of copy.
> 4 Finalize photo selection and layout.
> 5 Finalize order with printer.
>
> **January**
>
> 1 Get approval on final copy.
> 2 Get dummy approved.
>
> **February**
>
> 1 Receive final financial information (February 1).
> 2 Review galleys.
> 3 Receive press proof.
>
> **Have reports printed (March 1).**

1 Has there been a change in orientation within your division in the past year? If yes, how do you view this change?
2 What are the strengths of your division? What are the weaknesses?
3 What are your long-term goals for the division?
4 In what direction do you feel the company is heading?
5 Do you feel your division reflects the style and direction of the company as a whole?

He finds, after evaluating the responses, that most division heads see the company's diversification as a healthy extension of its original activities. They say the drug-retailing operation was getting into a rut and needed revitalization. In researching the company, he finds that it has always expressed a commitment to health care and that most of its private donations have been to health care institutions and foundations.

In his September meeting with the chairman, Henry Brancusi, Pagano presents his findings as well as the following summary statement which he proposes should serve as the organizing idea for the report: *Drug Products has extended its traditional commitment to health care through its latest acquisitions.* Brancusi approves this statement and explains that diversification in health-related areas has indeed always been the long-term goal of the company and that present activities are finally fulfilling the original hopes of the company's founders. Brancusi also notes that owing to the company's conservative management, it is to be expected that the new operations will take several years before they become profitable. (This, he says, was generally the case for each new retail store which the company opened in the past.) As for the shift from suburban to urban stores, the chairman argues that this follows a simple demographic trend. In the fifties, the shift had been to the suburbs; now there seems to be a reversal of that trend as people return to the cities. The stores, which have always served a middle-class population, are merely following their customers.

On the basis of his research and his meeting with the chairman, Pagano decides that the best way to express the report's organizing idea is to place the company's present activities in the context of its history. Although he knows that a historical overview is generally saved for a tenth, twenty-fifth, or fiftieth anniversary report, he feels that the recent shift in operations warrants a historical orientation this year. Such a focus, he concludes, will provide a sense of continuity and logic to the diversification and will help place the losses of the new operations into a context which will show them to be temporary. With this in mind, he proceeds to draw up the following early draft of Brancusi's Letter to Stockholders. (The letter will, of course, be scrupulously reviewed by company lawyers and edited by Brancusi himself before being approved; it will also be suitably revised once the final statistics for the year become available.)

To Our Stockholders:

During the twelve months ended December 31, 198-, Drug Products entered upon a new phase of growth and development. The opening of three new urban stores marks a demographic shift in our retail operations. New acquisitions in health-related businesses represent a new trend toward diversification. These events signal Drug Products' commitment to keeping pace with the changing health-care needs of middle-class America.

In 1939 the first Drug Products retail store opened in Albany, New York.

Instead of copying the general store format which characterized so many small retail outlets of the period, company founder Edward Ferraro recognized the value of limiting product selection to basic drugstore items. With that first store we established a format for drug retailing that would prove enormously successful in the years ahead.

Drug Products developed as a chain during the 1940s as 20 of our stores opened their doors in major urban centers throughout the Northeast. In the 1950s we began to shift our concentration from urban to suburban markets, paralleling a trend in American life which saw the middle-class consumer moving to the suburbs. By 1975, 70 percent of our stores were situated in suburban areas, and these stores grossed 92 percent of all Drug Products' earnings.

The 1980s has been a period in which changes in middle-class America have once again dictated changes in our business. Last year saw a drop in the income from suburban stores of 11 percent and an increase in urban store sales of 14 percent. These figures support general demographic findings that middle-class Americans are rediscovering the cities as a place to live as well as work.

Determined to capitalize on this trend, Drug Products has this year opened three new stores in urban centers and closed two of its least profitable suburban stores. The new stores—in center city Philadelphia, the Chelsea section of Manhattan, and downtown Baltimore—are all situated in areas experiencing rapid growth and revitalization. Start-up costs for new stores generally exceed income, and it often takes several years for new retail outlets to become entrenched in the community. Losses registered for new stores this year are therefore in keeping with the general trend of start-up operations. Nevertheless, we are gratified to see how quickly sales have picked up as reflected in the increased earnings recorded for our fourth quarter.

The decision to expand into urban markets has also been accompanied by the decision to diversify. Our long-time sponsorship of nonprofit health-education programs naturally led us to consider becoming more directly involved in health care in a profit-making capacity. An approaching saturation of retail markets and the increase of stiffer competition from discount retail drug stores made it seem feasible to pursue this kind of diversification now.

In January Drug Products purchased Vita, Inc., a distinguished manufacturer of multi-vitamins for children, which we have long carried in our retail outlets. Sales in Vita totaled $5 million this year, showing a 5 percent profit, and we expect this to quadruple within the next five years.

In addition to the manufacturing company, this year saw the acquisition of three health care facilities—two hospitals and a nursing home—in New York State. Unfortunately, these operations have been hardest hit by the recent recession. Gross revenues from all three facilities totaled $30 million, while cost of operations exceeded this amount by 25 percent. However, with renovations of the two hospitals almost completed, we expect to see a substantial reduction in expenses and a decrease in operational inefficiencies which should positively affect profitability.

An overview of the year's financial picture is predictable in light of the allocation of resources to new acquisitions. Net fiscal earnings were $27 million, a decline from $35 million in 198-. When new acquisitions are excluded, our earnings were up 11.5 percent for the year, despite the closing of three suburban retail stores. Although the dividend this year did not equal that of previous years, a 2 percent increase in the fourth quarter reflects an optimistic trend which we expect to continue.

This has been an exciting year for Drug Products, demonstrating our adjustment to the needs of our customers and to the economic climate in which we find ourselves. We would like to commend our stockholders for seeing us through this period of change. We anticipate substantial dividend increases in the year's ahead as reward for their patience and support.

Henry Brancusi

Henry Brancusi
Chairman of the Board and President

Note that the letter explains the company's present direction in light of its past history and places the year's decline in profitability into a context which makes it seem like a temporary set-back. All information is presented in the best possible light, yet there is no attempt at cover-up. Also note that the letter alludes directly to stockholders' interests in the last paragraph. The stockholders must be convinced to stay with the company as it moves in a new direction.

Once he has drafted the letter, Pagano next sets to work on the feature material. He decides that the feature article will be presented in the following three parts: (1) a discussion of the traditional aspects of Drug Products' business that have remained in place over the years; (2) a discussion of present new operations as they link up with traditional ones; and (3) an assertion of the continuity between Drug Products' past and present customers. In discussing the feature material with the photographer and graphic designer, Pagano hits on the notion of using old pictures of early company stores and products in a timeline arrangement leading into pictures of more recent developments. Underlying the choice of all graphics and copy material is the organizing idea of Drug Products' continuing and expanding commitment to health care as it concerns the middle-class consumer.

PREPARING A PUBLIC SERVICE ANNOUNCEMENT

Though public service announcements are controlled messages that, like advertisements, are broadcast in the form in which they are produced by their sponsors, they are uncontrolled in the sense that you cannot know when they will be aired. A broadcaster may decide to read your PSA only at 3 A.M. or fail to read it at all. To help improve the chances of frequent pick-up, offer a station at least three different-timed versions of the PSA (10-, 20-, and 30-second versions are probably the best choices). At the top of the page, clearly mark all necessary client and contact information, along with information concerning the time frame (airing dates) within which the PSA should run. The running time of each announcement should also be designated.

Jennifer Silk is public relations director for the Retro Movie House, a non-profit theater in the Delaware Valley specializing in old movies and avant garde productions by young artists. In three months the Retro will be featuring a series of films produced by students and local filmmakers from the area. Silk sees the series as an important cultural event. She is also convinced that the local population will find these films more interesting than the theater's usual features, which tend to appeal to only a small, homogeneous audience. To get the word out to those who normally wouldn't think of going to the Retro, Silk decides to prepare a number of PSAs and mail them to the local rock and country music radio stations which attract the majority of local listeners. She also plans to make two 35-millimeter slides of interesting scenes chosen from the films to be shown in the series and send these, along with the PSA audio script, to the local TV station.

Before Silk begins work on the announcements, however, she calls the stations and gets the names of the individuals who handle PSAs. She also inquires about station deadlines. (She is told that PSAs for the radio stations must be sent five weeks in advance of the desired airing date; PSAs for the TV station must be sent seven to eight weeks in advance. These are standard deadlines for both media.)

With this information in hand, she sets to work writing the announcements. She begins by simply jotting down in sentence form all the information she has relating to the upcoming event. Her rough notation reads as follows:

> Starting on October 15th, the Retro Movie House in Fulton Hill off Rte. 70 will feature a week-long series of films produced by local Delaware Valley filmmakers. The films will deal with the trials and tribulations of life in the area and should be of special interest to local residents. Among the featured films will be Jon Miskovitz' "Southern New Jersey Blues" and Katharine Forrest's "Weekend in Philadelphia." Young filmmakers from area university film departments will also be featured. You can pay at the door or buy a week-long pass to all ten films being shown. For details, call Jennifer Silk at the Retro Movie House at 555-0495.

Silk uses this rough copy as the basis for developing three (10-, 20-, and 30-second) PSAs. First, she fashions a suitable "hook" which can serve as the lead for the two longer versions of the announcement:

Funny, sad, intimate films about life in the Delaware Valley by local filmmakers—that's the featured entertainment at the Retro Movie House in Fulton Hill off Route 70 starting October 15th.

She then starts the process of adding and editing information to construct three PSAs of appropriate length. The final copy, approved and ready for mailing to the stations, looks like this:

Retro Movie House
Fulton Hill, N.J. 08034

Public Service Announcement

Contact: Jennifer Silk, PR Director
(609) 555-0495

For Immediate Release
Kill Date: October 22, 198_

(10 seconds)
For a week of films about the Delaware Valley by local filmmakers—come to the Retro Movie House in Fulton Hill starting October 15th. For details call (609) 555-0495.

(20 seconds)
Funny, sad, intimate films about the Delaware Valley by local filmmakers—that's the featured entertainment at the Retro Movie House in Fulton Hill off Route 70 starting October 15th. Enjoy a week of films about life in and around Philadelphia. Pay at the door or save by purchasing ahead. For details, call Retro at (609) 555-0495.

(30 seconds)
Funny, sad, intimate films about the Delaware Valley by local filmmakers—that's the featured entertainment at the Retro Movie House in Fulton Hill off Route 70 starting October 15th. Enjoy a week of films like "The Southern New Jersey Blues" and other features about the trials and tribulations of life in and around Philadelphia. Pay at the door, or save by buying a week's pass in advance. For full details, call Retro at (609) 555-0495. That's (609) 555-0495.

PREPARING A MINI-DOC

In producing a mini-doc, the objective is usually to develop a news or newsworthy angle as a means of publicizing your client indirectly. Like the op-ed article which will be discussed in the next chapter, the mini-doc must not be an overtly commercial message. Experts in the broadcasting field say that one or at most two client "plugs" (direct references to the client) are all that can be included in most mini-docs without damaging the credibility of the message. Only in cases where there is exceptional human interest (a crisis involving the organization or a revolutionary new product) can a mini-doc afford to focus on the client organization exclusively. Although news conferences are now acceptable subjects for mini-docs (since they provide TV and radio stations not present at the conference with useful footage), such footage is usually edited by the stations if it is used.

To discover a newsworthy angle for a mini-doc, think about ways in which your client could be linked to a recent current event, trend, or public concern. Then build a story that introduces the general topic first and incorporates the client's involvement indirectly.

TV mini-docs are admittedly expensive. When budgets are tight, radio mini-docs, which can be developed at a fraction of the cost, may be the better choice.

Michael O'Neal, a public relations officer with Boyd and Co., a Chicago architectural firm, has been having problems generating publicity for his client. While the firm has been doing well enough with small contracts, it has not obtained any of the large contracts recently that would interest the media. Meanwhile, some of O'Neal's best media contacts have dried up as several newspapers and specialized architectural publications folded this year.

Lacking other alternatives, O'Neal pins his hopes on the upcoming Boyd Awards Ceremony. This event is held annually to honor the three architects who have created the best designs for the firm that year. In the past, O'Neal had been satisfied to get cursory mention of the award-winners in some of the architectural magazines. This year, however, he wants to see the event yield its full PR value. For this purpose, he decides to investigate the winning designers and their designs in more depth in the hope of finding a newsworthy angle.

Interviewing the three winning architects, O'Neal discovers a common thread: They all have designed structures which include special energy-saving features. Since energy-saving continues to be a newsworthy topic, O'Neal decides that this might be a good angle for a mini-doc on the prize-winning designs.

To develop a mini-doc that would exploit the energy-saving angle as a means of indirectly publicizing the firm, O'Neal brings in Dan Stuart, an outside consultant who is a professional broadcaster and producer. Since the firm has a limited public relations budget, O'Neal and Stuart decide that a radio mini-doc would be the best choice.

To prepare the mini-doc, Stuart first discusses the angle for the clip with O'Neal and frames the following statement that will serve as the organizing idea for the piece: *With energy-saving now on the minds of all Americans, energy-saving design has become an important architectural consideration not only for residential structures but also for commercial structures.*

Stuart then proceeds to tape interviews with the contest winners. These interviews will be edited for insertion at appropriate intervals in the mini-doc script once the narrative copy has been written. Since there is no video component to this mini-doc, each architect can be interviewed and taped over the phone at minimum inconvenience.

O'Neal helps Stuart write the mini-doc script and choose segments from the taped interviews for insertion at appropriate intervals. The finished mini-doc script follows. (The duration of each interview segment has been marked in the margin so that when Stuart tapes his own reportorial overview he can leave adequate space for their inclusion in the final editing process.)

Saving Energy Through Design: A Common Sense Solution

As winter approaches and the temperatures drop, all of us begin to think about keeping warm. We turn up the heat at home, and we expect a warm and comfortable environment at work. But we've learned that the energy needed to keep us warm costs money. Many of us have started to dress like Eskimos in our own homes rather than pay astronomical heating bills. In the office, the cost of energy affects us more indirectly, but you can bet that when employers have to pay landlords higher heating bills, the money to pay them comes out of our paychecks. On top of it all, energy costs continue to skyrocket while energy supplies for the future remain a question mark. No wonder many states have imposed energy-saving restrictions—aimed at business and industry especially—to keep the energy situation in check.

I'm Dan Stuart and a full 30 percent of the energy use in the U.S. and Canada goes to the heating and cooling of buildings. But some architects say that between 25 and 50 percent of that total can be saved through energy-conscious design of these same buildings. Three of those architects were recently honored by their firm, Boyd and Company, for producing the firm's three best architectural designs for the year. All the winning designs happen to have energy-efficient features. Rachel Kinsey, one of the award-winners, explained the principles behind her design for a life insurance company in northern Pennsylvania:

:25   WE USED CANTILEVERING ON THE SOUTHEAST FACADE SO THAT EACH FLOOR SHIELDS THE FLOOR BELOW IT FROM THE INTENSITY OF THE SUN AND WE PROTECTED THE TOP FLOOR WITH A STEEL SUN LOUVER. THIS KEEPS THE INTERIOR COOLER DURING THE SUMMER BUT ALSO LETS THE SUN ENTER DURING THE WINTER WHEN THE SUN IS LOWER IN THE SKY.

208 Developing Visibility III: Controlling the Message

> While most of the attention paid to energy saving has been focused on residential structures, the Boyd architects are demonstrating that energy is a factor in the design of commercial and industrial structures as well.
>
> Jeffrey Finley, another winner in the competition, explained the rationale for his design of a computer company in Minneapolis:
>
> :19 WE REALIZED THAT BY ADDING A NUMBER OF INTERIOR FEATURES WE COULD CUT ENERGY CONSUMPTION BY 10 TO 15 PERCENT. WE USE A HEAT RECOVERY SYSTEM WHICH REUSES WASTE HEAT GENERATED BY THE COMPANY'S COMPUTERS.
>
> And not all the energy saving has to come from new buildings. Old buildings can also be rejuvenated or, in the language of architects, "retrofitted," to be energy savers. In fact, one of the prize-winning designs was for an ingenious retrofit of a 20-year-old packaging manufacturing company in Detroit. Steven Wilson, who designed the retrofit, explained some of its features:
>
> :22 WE REPLACED SOME OF THE GLASS WITH MASONRY, WHICH CUT HEAT LOSS CONSIDERABLY, AND WE REPLACED THE ROOF WITH A BETTER INSULATED MATERIAL. WE ALSO RETROFITTED SOME PARTS OF THE INTERIOR TO IMPROVE AIR FLOW. IN SOME CASES, WE MERELY RECOMMENDED CHANGES IN WINDOW MATERIALS AND CARPETING.
>
> Beauty and practicality—that's what these prize-winning designs have to offer. And that's the future for our commercial and industrial architecture. I'm Dan Stuart.*
>
> *This fictional mini-doc is based on an actual mini-doc prepared by Dick Cunningham and Bernice Molina of the Broadcast Division of Ruder Finn & Rotman, Inc.

Stuart tapes himself reading the script and splices in the taped interview segments. Fifty copies of the finished mini-doc are then made and mailed (*bicycled*) to 50 selected radio stations. (Stuart includes not only local Chicago stations but also stations serving the cities where the prize-winning buildings are located as well as other northern cities which would be concerned with energy-saving.) With each tape he includes a self-addressed, stamped postcard asking the station news director whether the tape has been aired and, if so, when. After about a month he begins to get some of the postcards back. Unfortunately, many stations simply do not respond, making it impossible to determine precisely how much airing the mini-doc has received.

EXERCISES

Test Your Judgment

1 List the best communication tool or combination of tools (poster, flyer, brochure, promotional film, mini-doc, PSA) for relaying each of the following controlled messages:
a New techniques in microsurgery have revolutionized the field of reconstructive surgery, according to surgeons at Memorial Hospital.
b The local women's auxiliary will host its first annual dinner-dance.
c The law firm of Stern and Rowe Associates has a superbly trained and experienced staff and offers a wide array of services tailored to the needs of small businesses.
d The Hard-Sole Manufacturing Company has an excellent system of quality control by which it oversees all phases in the production of its Hard-Sole shoes.
e Drinking and driving don't mix.
f A day-long seminar on the city's historical landmarks will be sponsored by the Preservation Society, a local nonprofit organization.

2 State whether slides, overhead projection, or flip charts would be best to use in each of the following situations:
a A meeting in which the 10 basic personality traits necessary for success in the company are explained to a small group of new trainees.
b A presentation by a city parks official on the kinds of flowers and plants present in the city's parks.
c A presentation to a town's zoning board explaining why a specific lot should be rezoned.
d A meeting in which a manager presents the company's newest venture to her 10 subordinates and solicits their input.
e A seminar for 100 executives in which one of the speakers wishes to dramatically demonstrate, on the spot, the decline in company stock in the past year.
f A new business presentation by a graphics company to a prospective client.

PR Workshop

1 As a class, work together to edit the following rough PSA draft into a polished *30-second* piece:
Spring is here and the flowers are blooming and so are our local poets. They'll be reading and discussing their poems on spring in a day-long poetry-reading

at the Morristown Public Library located on the Green starting at 10 A.M. on April 29th. Josephine Filstein will launch the day of rhymes with her prize-winning poem, "April's First Surprise." Other poets who will be reading their poems will be Jeffrey Billstock, a former editor of *Poetry Review*; Joan Lister, a well-known writer of poems for children; and Stefan Karkov, the Russian émigré poet. Following their readings, the poets will discuss their poems and the effect of the seasons on their writing. They will also run a poetry-writing workshop from 1 to 2 P.M. Support our local poets and our local library by attending "Poems for Spring." Tickets available from Marcia Briggs at the library. (*now runs about 45 seconds*)

2 As a class, choose a simple "how to" task (how to bake a cake, change a tire, ride a bike, do the breaststroke) and together turn an explanation of the process into a draft for a slide show. Use the chalkboard to serve as the storyboard where you sketch out the relationship of pictures to script. Under the direction of the entire class, have one person be responsible for making rough sketches of the visuals on the left, and another for putting down the scripted material to be read with them on the right. After a full draft of pictures and script has been made, go back over it and discuss adjustments that would improve both sides of the storyboard.

PR Case Studies

1 You are a public information officer for a university that has just introduced a new microcomputer program. The program, which is at the forefront of a national trend, requires all incoming freshmen to own a personal computer and have the opportunity to use it in all their courses.

In researching the program as background for developing a PR campaign, you are struck by the many ways in which the microcomputers will be used across the curriculum. A particularly interesting application is in the area of English composition where special "invention" programs have been developed which help students master the writing process. The computers are programmed to ask students leading questions that help them come up with and develop topics for essays.

You believe that there is an opportunity for generating indirect publicity for the program by producing a mini-doc dealing with the application of computers to the teaching of writing. Develop a specific angle for the mini-doc based on the above information and prepare a short (one- to three-and-a-half-minute) radio script which could be taped and sent to local stations as a potential news or feature story. (Try to find someone in your college English department to interview for the quoted sections.)

2 You are the public affairs officer for Optimum, Inc., a company based in Washington, D.C., which manufactures pollution control equipment for industry. The problem is that big business and many government officials in

the present administration would like to ignore environmental issues in general and are suspicious of your company in particular. They feel you are in league with radical environmentalists and are only interested in subverting business interests and turning the economy over to the "commies."

You feel it's time to design a new company brochure that communicates directly to your target audience—big business—and seeks to dispel some of these impressions. Write a memo to your supervisor proposing that a new brochure be written, explaining what you think its organizing idea should be, and outlining the kinds of information it should contain.

3 You are director of communications for a large, publicly owned publishing company, F. S. Filler and Son, Inc. In preparing the annual report, you have just interviewed the chairman of the board and president, John Catlin. The following is an edited transcript from the interview:

Filler and Son has steadily grown since its beginning 25 years ago. This year saw major growth in the paperback division, Disc Inc., and the adolescent book division, Teen Books. In these two divisions together, we have generated $25 million in sales (before taxes). Hardcover sales decreased by 25 percent and our international book division also saw a decline of 35 percent. In total, earnings were down by $3 million, although if we were to exclude the international book division (entering only its third year), earnings would be up 10 percent. We had three best-sellers this year, including the runaway hit, *Confessions of a Love Addict*, which has already sold 1.5 million copies and promises to be one of the biggest selling books in our history. We also opened two more Filler and Son retail bookstores, to join our one N.Y.C. store. These stores, in Chicago and L.A., are doing well and we hope to continue expanding our retail operation in the next few years.

Given the current general decline in hardcover sales, we plan to build up our existing paperback divisions by adding new specialty departments. Among those which will be initiated beginning next year are a science-fiction department, a historical romance department, and a "how-to" department.

We feel business is going well. Though there will be no dividend increase this year, last year's increase showed a spurt of growth which we think will be continued next year. The company has come a long way from being a small privately owned publisher of specialty gift books. Since going public ten years ago, it has expanded to offer a full range of titles and has become a quality contender in the publishing field.

Select from the above material to develop a Letter to Stockholders for the chairman's signature.

NOTES

1. See Elinor and Joe Selame, *Developing a Corporate Identity: How to Stand out in the Crowd* (New York: Lebhar-Freedman Books, 1977).

2. Steven Brill, "Tin Rhetoric, High Gloss," *The American Lawyer*, VI, No. 4 (April 1984), 1.

3. Richard A. Lewis, "Printed Financial Communications," *The Investor Relations Handbook*, ed. Arthur R. Roalman (New York: AMACOM, 1974), p. 102.

4. See Rose DeNeve, "The Graphic Edge," *Public Relations Journal*, 41 (July 1985), 19–25.

5. Sid Cato, "The Annual Report: Here I Come World," *Public Relations Quarterly*, 30 (Spring 1985), 17–21.

6. See Alissa Rubin, "Video News Releases: Whose News Is It?" *Public Relations Journal*, 41 (October 1985), 18–23.

7. See James R. Jeffries and Jefferson D. Bates, *The Executive's Guide to Meetings, Conferences, & Audiovisual Presentations* (New York: McGraw-Hill Book Company, 1983), Chapter 14.

8. Marya W. Holcombe and Judith K. Stein, *Presentations for Decision Makers* (Belmont, Calif.: Lifetime Learning Publications, a division of Wadsworth Publishing Co., 1983), pp. 74–76.

8

Dealing with Issues

When our modern industrial state began to take shape in the nineteenth century, the first great capitalists built their empires without regard for public opinion. These robber barons, as they were called, might have helped the public incidentally but, if they did, it was not through conscious intention but as a by-product to money-making. During this period of expansion, big business saw no need to account for itself or justify its actions.

But the twentieth century saw the emergence of a new business philosophy that was to have important effects on the field of public relations.[1] Industrialism had given rise to a complex and multi-faceted society, and business—the engine which helped set this society in motion—began to inhabit a position of responsibility in the public imagination. If a train went off the tracks or a bridge collapsed, the public pointed the finger at business. When a larger disaster struck in the form of the stock market crash of 1929, the public outcry against big business became clamorous. In the face of emerging consumer advocacy groups, labor unions, and government regulation, business could no longer afford to neglect public opinion and hold its tongue.

Thus the public's hostility to business fueled by the Depression brought into being the concept of *corporate social responsibility*. The consumer public would no longer tolerate the existence of big business as an anonymous money-making machine. Heads of industry were now expected to define their goals, justify their policies, and chronicle their achievements. With this new mandate, public relations practitioners had their work cut out for them.

Yet, up until recently, the public relations profession did not wholly fulfill the comprehensive function which modern society seemed to require. This failure was largely due to a business community which continued to assign public relations practitioners individual tasks to perform without encouraging them to deal with the larger context encompassing these tasks. It was not until business began to view its relationship to the public more holistically that the PR practitioner was invited to act as a partner to management in dealing with the complex and controversial issues which are an ongoing part of doing business in a modern society.

Unlike products, issues are intangibles; they cannot be seen or held on to, and yet they condition the way we perceive organizations and their products. The concept of monitoring and explaining issues is based on the assumption that the relationship of an organization to its social environment involves many points of view and kinds of information; thus research, evaluation, and program planning must be an ongoing process. This process clarifies management's sense of its own position, gives external publics a clearer understanding of why business decisions get made, and makes long-term planning and policy-making more just and consistent. Much of the emphasis on issues in recent years has developed in an effort to deal constructively with media, legislators, and consumer action groups whose perception of how a particular company or industry handles an issue of public interest can have an enormous effect on the laws that get passed and on public opinion in general. This is why, for example, the chemical industry has been struggling for years to convince legislators and the public that it is doing all it can to deal responsibly with the issue of toxic waste disposal. It wants to win goodwill and curb the enactment of strict government regulation of the industry.

The concern with issues in public relations has become so popular that a formal method of dealing with them, called *issues management*, has been developed. W. Howard Chase, now director of the Institute of Public Issue Management at the University of Connecticut, launched this concept in 1977.[2] Chase advocates a "systems approach" to solving business problems, arguing that issues affecting an organization should be identified, grouped, prioritized, and handled by mobilizing the appropriate resources and talent to deal with them. Taking Chase's ideas a step further, other theorists have suggested that public relations issues management should be *catalytic* as well as reactive, helping to bring issues forward, not just dealing with them after they have begun to have influence.[3] Thus, a local PTA, wishing to see the school budget increased, might want to catalyze the issue of the decline in public school education by publicizing test scores and arranging media interviews with students and teachers. The alternative would be waiting until the public came to a recognition of this issue on its own, which might mean waiting until after the upcoming school referendum was over.

Of course, many practitioners argue that issues management is not new. According to William E. Duke, a former chairman of the PRSA's Issues Identification Committee, "the process is nothing more than a systematic, practical, and effective approach to what they [practitioners] have been doing for many years."[4] What is new, however, is the attempt to make this kind of thinking a more explicit part of public relations practice and to move beyond the task-orientation which so often used to limit PR work. The concept of issues management represents an impulse to bring public relations responsibilities into closer proximity to management decision-making, a precinct where it has not traditionally been welcome.

In general, the key to dealing with issues is to maintain an ongoing dialogue with internal and external publics and be willing to continually update and revise information as new facts and points of view become available. A single issue may, over time, break down into multiple issues or may change shape entirely. This is why research and evaluation as well as planning and implementation must be carried on simultaneously. Moreover, recent theorists in the field note that "issues become 'resolved,' but never 'solved' once-and-for-all"; they move into a state of dormancy until their potential as issues are once again activated.[5] Take the issue of alcohol abuse, which became such a national concern in the 1920s that the enactment of Prohibition resulted; now, after a period of relative dormancy, this issue has been reactivated, while an issue like drug abuse seems to be moving toward dormancy. The recognition that no issue is ever definitively dead or persistently alive must always be part of the issues management process.

In the following pages we will first discuss how present and potential issues can be identified, and then outline some of the implementation tools with which they can be effectively managed. Since the information relating to issues tends to be more complicated than information relating to events or products, the tools used to manage them are what we call *depth tools*—communications methods that are capable of supporting an argument in some depth by presenting evidence, acknowledging and rebutting points on the other side, and offering access to experts and objective sources where necessary. In enumerating these tools, we have made a distinction between those which are *impersonal* (which argue a point of view without using a subjective voice) and those which are *personal* (which depend for their effectiveness upon the distinctive style of the writer or speaker or on personal interaction between speaker and audience). Keep in mind that the tools being described in this chapter are also commonly used in situations which are not issue-oriented. (Fact sheets, for example, are standard components of media kits, and speeches can be given on all sorts of topics, not just issue-oriented ones.) We present these communications tools here, however, because they are especially well suited to the task of dealing with issues.

IDENTIFYING ISSUES

To identify issues affecting or potentially affecting your client organization, you need to thoroughly understand the context in which the organization operates. This means knowing how it interconnects not only with other, similar organizations, but also with the entire economic, social, and political environment of which it is a part. Here are some guidelines for identifying issues:

1 Read trade publications relating to your client's industry, and newspapers (national and local) which can provide an ongoing context for understanding industry trends.
2 Do periodic research on your organization—its products, services, industry, competition, and other, related topics. Use card catalogs and periodical indexes, or on-line data bases if you have access to these.
3 Discuss (*brainstorm*) with colleagues concerning the possible repercussions of recent current events or fads as they could affect your client, your client's industry, and the economy in general.
4 Periodically review trends and events which have affected another industry (not your client's). Consider how these changes could conceivably affect your client, or how your client would react if it were undergoing similar experiences.
5 Carefully analyze all survey data. If your client has administered a survey or taken a poll, no matter what the objective of the study, examine the research data carefully. Often scrutinizing results from a new perspective brings potential issues into relief which would otherwise be overlooked. Also keep abreast of more general surveys and polls reported in the news or available from public information agencies. Under certain circumstances, you may want to suggest that a communications audit be done in order to get a direct reading on an issue as it relates to your client (see the discussion on public relations opinion audits in Chapter 3).
6 Keep an ear open to ideas and complaints arising within your client's organization. Employees are often able to sense an issue's importance as it affects them before experts have caught on to the connection. One practitioner also suggests having lunch with your client's lawyer on a regular basis and, by this means, keeping posted on what's happening in the courts that might affect the organization in the long run as well as the short run.[6]

DEPTH TOOLS

Once an issue of importance to your client's organization has been identified, you will then want to prepare a public relations program to deal with it. As with any PR program, this should be an operational plan which offers a rationale, outlines a general strategy, and enumerates appropriate tools for implementation (see Chapter 4). The tools that follow are those we feel are most often employed and best suited to implementing PR programs devoted to issues management.

Impersonal Depth Tools

THE FACT SHEET

Generally no more than a page long, the fact sheet serves to present important information in a convenient, readable fashion. Fact sheets are staple media kit items because they provide an easy checklist to the media of key facts or personalities relating to the event, product, or service being promoted. In the case of an issue, a fact sheet represents a short-hand compilation of relevant facts and statistics which can serve as a supplement to a more analytical backgrounder (see the discussion of the backgrounder that follows).

The following are some practical tips for constructing a fact sheet:

1. Label the fact sheet clearly. Title the page "Fact Sheet" or "Facts about X" so that readers know immediately that this is *hard* data.
2. Make sure you have established an organizing idea before you begin developing a fact sheet. The organizing idea of a fact sheet should govern which facts are included and which are omitted. (This same organizing idea will be refined into a more specific issue statement in the accompanying backgrounder.)
3. Number or use bullets to present points in a fact sheet directed at the media. The presentation should be easy to read and should allow the reader to easily differentiate one fact from another. If the fact sheet is directed at the general public, a question-and-answer format can sometimes be more appealing than a bulleted presentation.
4. Use simple graphics. Design should be subordinate to content unless the subject is a whimsical one. A fact sheet dealing with an important issue should be as ungarnished and straightforward as possible.
5. Avoid jargon or technical language. If it's necessary to use some specialized language (in a fact sheet about a medical issue, for example), include a glossary at the bottom where starred technical terms are defined.
6. Check facts carefully to be sure they're accurate. An inaccurate fact sheet is the worst type of public relations.

THE BACKGROUNDER

Usually a companion piece to the fact sheet, the *backgrounder* (or position paper as its longer version is called) sets the facts in context and supplies a reasoned argument for a client's position on a particular issue. Underlying the backgrounder is an *issue statement* which constitutes the organizing idea or focus of the argument. Thus a backgrounder prepared by a community group concerned about public school education might frame the issue statement: *Teachers must be paid higher salaries and given more incentives if we are going to revitalize our local public school system.* The backgrounder would support this statement by perhaps citing evidence concerning the importance of good teacher morale to good teaching and then relating low salaries and the lack of incentives to the low quality of education in the community. An accompanying fact sheet might be prepared around the less specific organizing idea. *We need to improve public school education in our community.* The broader focus of the fact sheet would allow for the inclusion of supplementary information not addressed in the backgrounder. The fact sheet might list the average number of college-bound students from the community (as compared with the number from another community of comparable size); the number of Merit Scholarship winners that year (as compared with the number from another community of comparable size); the present school budget (as compared with the budget of another community of comparable size); the drop-out rate; the average teacher salary (as compared with the average salary in other professions); the number of teachers who have left the system within the past five years; the average number of students in a class; and so forth. Thus, the fact sheet supplies a collection of information which implicitly supports your position and which a reporter or individual concerned with the issue might want to know. The backgrounder explicitly directs the reader to embrace a specific point of view.

Some backgrounders tell the story of how something happened, hoping that a detailed account will correct any misperception which may exist about the events in question. But a narrative backgrounder should also be organized around an issue statement. A chemical manufacturing company responding to an inquiry by an environmental group, for example, might decide to write a corporate history to support the issue statement: *Since its beginnings, our company has played a responsible role in dealing with the problem of toxic wastes.* Note that the issue statement here is a positive formulation, not a defensive one. Even if someone has attacked your client or client's industry, the backgrounder should not be written defensively. In those instances in which a client *is* at fault, the best public relations strategy is to be forthright about assuming blame for the situation in question. After doing so, you can then move on to focus on the organization's positive accomplishments in other, related areas.

Personal Depth Tools

THE OP-ED ARTICLE

An effective way to air a client's opinion on an important or controversial issue is with an *op-ed article* (named for its placement opposite the editorial page in a newspaper). Op-eds are relatively short opinion essays on topics of general interest to a newspaper's readership. They often have the by-line of officials or experts whose views are judged to carry weight. While an op-ed is never a direct sales pitch, it can be excellent publicity for a client since it sets up the writer as an authority in a given area and, by extension, enhances the reputation of the organization with which the writer is affiliated. (In most op-eds, a short blurb at the end of the article identifies the writer, thus making this affiliation clear.) When a controversial issue is concerned, an op-ed can be a means of disseminating the point of view of an organization in a personalized way. This was the case in an op-ed appearing in the *New York Times* which carried the by-line of the president and chief executive officer of IBM Corporation.[7] The writer used the op-ed to explain his company's continued economic involvement in South Africa. Although some readers might not have found the argument persuasive, the op-ed did attempt to provide a reasoned justification for the company's policy and made clear that IBM, despite its presence in South Africa, did not support that government's policy of apartheid.

The idea for an op-ed article often comes from a public relations person who recognizes that a subject in the news or an issue of public concern has bearing on a client. The PR practitioner may also recommend that a particular official in the organization lend his or her by-line to the piece.

The writing of an op-ed can be a cooperative effort, with the practitioner arranging to interview or chat informally with the individual who will by-line the article, and then preparing a draft for review. As with a speech, an op-ed piece will usually go through several drafts as additions and revisions are made so that the article will justly express the ideas as well as the style and tone of the individual whose by-line it carries. The finished article will then be sent to the op-ed editor of a targeted newspaper (or newspapers) for consideration.

Here are some tips on how to write and place successful op-ed articles:

1 Know your audience. Newspapers have different readerships, editorial styles, and political slants. You will be more successful in placing op-ed pieces if you take these variables into account. Remember that a local paper will be interested in different sorts of topics than a regional or national paper. Also, count the number of words in typical op-eds in your target publication to be sure that your submission is the conventional length.

2 Don't make the article obviously self-serving. An article offering management tips for high-tech industries would be a suitable op-ed piece; an article telling how a specific management consulting firm can help improve management techniques would not. Most editors will reject obvious sales pitches out of hand. As a rule, the only direct mention of the client should be in the blurb at the bottom of the article which identifies the writer (for example, "John Smith is president and CEO of Smith and Stern Consulting, Inc., in Providence, R.I."). Be sure to include this blurb with the op-ed article when you mail it to the editor. (Emphasize the

writer's link to your client in the cover letter as well.) Mention your client in the body of the article only when this is crucial to the development of the argument and would be of genuine interest to readers.

3 Don't be afraid to use *I* in an op-ed piece. Unlike the fact sheet and backgrounder where an objective style is important, the op-ed should relay the personality of the writer and, if possible, should humanize the topic being discussed. This is especially important when the article is arguing the unpopular side of an issue.

4 Use concrete examples to back up generalizations. Draw upon history, current events, and personal anecdotes. (You can pick these up in an interview with the individual for whose by-line you are writing, or you can suggest that he or she add them in designated places when reviewing the rough draft.)

5 If you send the op-ed to more than one newspaper, make sure the papers are not in competition. (This means that the papers do not service the same geographic or demographic groups.) If you are offering the article to one paper at a time, specify in your cover letter to the editor that you are offering it on an "exclusive basis." If that paper rejects it, you can offer it as an exclusive to another paper.

6 If you come up with an idea for an op-ed, decide in advance who in the organization would be most suitable to by-line the article. Choose someone who has an interest in and a knowledge of the subject and who has an appropriately high level of importance within the organization. Use your judgment. For a technically oriented article, the director of research and development might be a better choice than the president of the company. In determining the best individual to by-line an op-ed, you might also want to have an alternate in mind in case your first choice is not interested or not available to work with you on the piece.

ADVOCACY ADVERTISING

This variation on the op-ed article dispenses with the problem of placement by treating the opinion piece as an advertisement. That is, to assure placement, the sponsor organization pays for space in a newspaper, magazine, or TV or radio broadcast in order to air its opinion on a given issue. Recently, sponsors of advocacy advertising, or *advertorials* as they're sometimes called, have had difficulty purchasing broadcast time. This is owing to regulations requiring that stations give equal time to both sides of an issue, thus demanding that free TV or radio space be given to the other side. Meanwhile, however, advertorials are flourishing in the print media, following the lead of Mobil Corporation's brilliantly successful series of advocacy ads in major newspapers. (Mobil not only wrote the ads in the form of opinion pieces but also purchased space opposite the editorial page in which to run the ads.)

Experts also foresee increased use of advertorials on cable TV where the equal-time stipulation is not judged to be applicable.[8]

THE BY-LINE ARTICLE

A variation on the op-ed article, the by-line article is generally a longer piece prepared for placement in a technical, business, or other special-interest publication. Some by-line articles do not mention the name of the client organization in the body of the piece; others are more obviously self-promoting and take the form of a company profile or an in-depth analysis of a company operation. The president of a public relations agency, for example, might by-line an article describing how her agency developed a public relations program for a nuclear power plant. The article might be placed in a public relations or communications journal, or in a trade publication aimed at the nuclear power industry. These publications would not mind the fact that the article was self-promoting because their special-interest readership would genuinely want to know the specifics of how such a program was handled.

Before preparing a by-line article, investigate the magazines and journals in your client's trade area. Check to see which ones accept by-line pieces, the sorts of articles they tend to run, and the general length. If you have a good idea for a by-line article, you might want to write a query letter or make a phone call to the editor of the publication before you begin working on the piece. Tell the editor that your client is thinking of preparing an article on a given subject and ask whether the publication would have an interest in running it. The editor might suggest an approach or specify information which should be included.

THE LETTER TO THE EDITOR

Although written in the first person like an op-ed article, the letter to the editor differs from an op-ed in that it is usually a highly specific rebuttal or response to an article, a statement, or an issue. If, for example, a publication runs a story which directly or indirectly criticizes your client or argues a position harmful to your client's interests, you may wish to refute specific points made in that article in a letter to the editor of the publication in which it appeared. Or if a story which has bearing on your client contains faulty facts or references, a letter can enumerate the errors and provide correct information. A good example of this kind was a letter to the *New York Times* signed by a vice president of ABC News which objected to a *Times* editoral criticizing network coverage of the recent presidential election.[9] The writer cited the title and date of the editorial, briefly summarized the newspaper's argument, and then went on to refute it.

While letters are not the most dramatic editorial tools, they are a sensible way of letting the readership of a publication know that your client is on top of things and alert to inaccuracies. Letters to the editor can also be a relatively simple means of getting your client's name attached to a desired issue in a publication where you might otherwise have difficulty placing stories.

To write effective letters to the editor, keep in mind the following guidelines:

1 Check the standard length of the letters to the editor in the target publication before you write your letter. Some publications publish letters of variable length, others prefer brevity. If you write too long a letter, it may be cut and points you feel are important may be omitted.
2 Decide in advance what point or points will be the focus of the letter. If you are addressing more than one point, begin with a summary statement which encompasses all points; then proceed to deal with each in turn.
3 Clearly identify up-front the article, individual, and/or issue which your letter will address. (For example, "I would like to refute three points made by John Dove in his December 30 article, "The Errors of Viet Nam.")
4 Use rational argument, not name-calling or inflated language, to refute points.
5 Choose the most appropriate individual within the organization to sign the letter. For a letter responding to a recent article dealing with new directions in plastics research, for example, you would probably want to have the research director of the client company sign the letter. Occasionally, it may be appropriate for you as an organization's public relations officer to sign your own name to a letter to the editor written on your client's behalf.

THE SPEECH

Like the op-ed and by-line article, the speech is a personalized method of explaining a complex or important issue to a target public. The difference, of course, is that a speech is also a live, oral presentation. This can represent an advantage from a public relations standpoint since in-person communication has been found to be more persuasive than other forms of communication. According to experts in the field, "it is harder to say no to someone face-to-face—no matter what is being said—than it is to reject a broadcast or print message."[10]

To take full advantage of the medium, however, you need to think of the speech as an integrated process that involves research, writing, and delivery, as well as other related activities.

Preparing the Speech When preparing a speech for a client, keep in mind that what you are preparing is meant to be spoken rather than read. The audience will not have the advantage of going back over the material as it can with a written text (although in some cases a written version of the speech can be included in a media kit or provided as a hand-out). Even when printed versions are available, the effectiveness of a speech depends largely upon its ability to hold an audience's attention and be understood at the moment it is being delivered. This means that it should be written in the style of the spoken word. Vocabulary should be kept simple and examples should be vivid and concrete. Most important, a good speech should be built around a single, clearly defined message: an organizing idea which ideally can be distilled into a repeated word or phrase. A speech which wanders far afield or tries to make too many points is likely to leave the listener bored and confused.

In preparing a speech, begin by asking yourself the following questions:

How much time is available for the speech? Twenty to thirty minutes is the standard speech length, but certain occasions may call for shorter or longer speeches. Where a time limit has been specified, it should be respected. As a rule, shorter speeches are appreciated—especially following a meal.

What is the occasion? A good speech should take into account the setting and occasion of its delivery. This may involve no more than an opening remark thanking the host for the invitation to speak at, say, the Second Annual Men's Club Dinner. But where the occasion is especially noteworthy, it may be possible to incorporate it into the theme of the speech. For example, at a chamber of commerce luncheon celebrating a town's centennial anniversary, the president of a local company might speak about advances in his industry over the past 100 years.

Who is the audience? Some understanding of audience is crucial in determining the proper tone and content for a speech. A speech delivered to a group of bankers about the need for constructing a nuclear power plant in a given community would certainly not be the same speech delivered to a group of college students on the same subject. While there could conceivably be a certain amount of overlap in the two presentations, the speech to bankers would probably focus on positive economic factors relating to the facility, while the speech to students would be more concerned with refuting arguments relating to risk of accident and availability of alternative energy sources.

What is my client's objective in making the speech? When an organization receives an invitation to give a speech, acceptance should not be automatic. Evaluate what will be specifically achieved through the speech and how well this objective fits with the PR objectives of the organization. In some cases, it may be worth turning down an invitation rather than spending time and money preparing a speech that won't help accomplish your PR objectives or might even dull the thrust of a larger PR program.

Answers to the above questions will help you decide whether a speech is worth giving and, if it is, to focus on a suitable subject and approach. But even with these questions answered, you should not begin writing until you have some knowledge of the speaker. A speech is only as good as its presentation, and matching the speech to the speaker is crucial to the art of good speech writing. To do this, you should ideally meet personally with the speaker and tape the interview for future study. The meeting will give you a chance not only to learn the speaker's opinions on the proposed topic, but also to become familiar with his or her interests, sense of humor (or lack of it), and distinctive mannerisms. With the tape, you can do more in-depth analysis of speech patterns, intonation, and vocabulary. The speech you eventually write should be one which the speaker feels comfortable giving and which places his or her personality in the best light. Commonly, the final speech is the result of three or four drafts reworked over a four- to six-week period.

Here are some pointers for preparing an effective speech:

1 Begin with a salutation (greeting) of the various dignitaries present and the audience in general (for example, "Ms. President, Members of the Board, Respected Alumni").

2 Include a clear statement of the speech's organizing idea early on, usually in the first or second paragraph. It used to be a standard suggestion that speeches begin with a quotation. Experience has shown, however, that this can seem contrived unless the quote is carefully chosen and suited to the speaker's style. When in doubt, leave out the quote and get straight to the point.

3 Frame your organizing idea in vivid, concrete language, and try to repeat a memorable word, phrase, or image that evokes this idea throughout the speech. For example, a political candidate who wishes to stress the idea of community solidarity in diversity might use references to "the ethnic American family" throughout the speech as a way of relaying this idea in a way that speaks personally to the audience.

4 Avoid jokes unless the speaker has a real comic gift.

5 Include personal anecdotes which link directly to the main points. Don't use them if they are digressive or overly long.

6 Be sure the speech is easy to read. It should be double or triple spaced with wide margins. Use phonetic spellings for words which risk being mispronounced (instead of "Dr. Goldstein's remarks," write "Dr. Goldsteen's remarks").

7 Keep the general organization of the speech simple. New ideas should be prepared for by marker statements that tell the audience what to expect. (For example, "Now, let me give you three reasons why we need

to amend this law. The first and most obvious reason is . . . .") Use parallel structure where you can, since parallel ideas tend to be easy to follow and remember. The parallel paradox ("Ask not what your country can do for you, but what you can do for your country") can be an especially effective way of making an idea quotable. Summarize your major points in the conclusion, repeating them in the same order in which they were presented in the body of the speech.

Although these same organizational and rhetorical devices might seem simplistic or redundant in a written document, they are desirable in a speech where the audience does not have the luxury of going over the material a second time.

Delivering the Speech Speech preparation should not end with the writing of the speech but should extend to the delivery. Too often good speeches are spoiled by untrained speakers who never make eye contact with the audience, swallow their words, lose the dramatic potential of a point by failing to pause long enough in appropriate places, and engage in other inexcusable but common errors of delivery. Probably the best way to cure such mistakes is through practice and critique. This process can be facilitated by videotaping the speaker and having him or her critique the tape with you.

While it is not necessary that a speech be learned by heart, it is important for the speaker to be familiar enough with the text to make eye contact with the audience at regular intervals. For a speaker to achieve this degree of familiarity generally means reading the speech over 15 to 20 times prior to the presentation. Some of these readings should be part of practice sessions in which gestures and voice modulations are perfected.

Responding to Questions A final aspect of the speech which should not be ignored is the question-and-answer period which generally follows the delivery. Some public relations departments have developed media training programs which specialize in preparing speakers to answer questions on radio and TV talk shows or at news conferences. Even under more ordinary circumstances, it may be a good idea to stage a practice question-and-answer session in which the speaker is asked difficult or hostile questions. Videotaping such a session can help the speaker see how he or she comes across and how certain responses work better than others.

Here are some rules for clients to follow on how to effectively handle questions:

1 Be calm and friendly in dealing with your questioners, no matter how hostile they may become. A good-humored, though forceful reply will appear to advantage against a surly questioner.

2 Use simple analogies and metaphors to help explain complex points. Avoid technical terminology unless your audience is a technical one. If part of the audience is technical and part isn't, keep technical answers brief and try to follow with a summary in nontechnical terms.

3 Maintain a degree of control in determining the flow of the discussion. In general, speakers should be equipped with a number of pre-planned answers. Speaker and lecturer Don Hill advocates preparing a "mini-speech of positive points."[11] Speakers can then learn to use transitions (*bridges*) which allow them to work in this material even if they are not asked about it directly.

4 If you don't know an answer to a question, say so rather than attempt to cover up your ignorance. If circumstances permit, take the name and address of the questioner and promise to get back to him or her with the answer once you've researched it.

Selecting a Spokesperson and Organizing Spokesperson Tours Where an issue needs to be disseminated to a number of different groups, an organization may choose to appoint a spokesperson—an expert who is adept at giving speeches and answering questions. Choosing the right spokesperson for such a task is important. The individual must be well acquainted with the subject and able to explain it gracefully, clearly, and succinctly. Moreover, the image of the spokesperson must be compatible with the image of the organization, since he or she is the organization's public representative, acting in the organization's interest in explaining its opinions and priorities.

A common problem in choosing a spokesperson involves finding someone who fits all the above criteria—who has the technical knowledge, the communications skills, and the right image for the job. Some organizations choose to train in-house spokespeople. (Depending upon the issue, this might mean drawing upon technical staff, top management, or public relations practitioners themselves.) Another alternative is to hire a spokesperson who combines the necessary qualities and who can be briefed on the organization and the specific issue in question.

Organizations use spokespeople in different ways. A common procedure is to organize a spokesperson tour, arranging for speaking engagements in targeted cities. To place a spokesperson (that is, book a speaking engagement), you should decide first what audience you wish to reach, then determine what forums are likely to bring this audience together. Local club luncheons and dinners, and trade and professional meetings and conventions are always looking for good speakers who would be of interest to their members. Make a list of all such organizations in the areas you wish to target, and make a telephone or written pitch, describing the topic your spokesperson can address and the competence of the spokesperson to address it. Explain why you think the presentation would be of special interest to the organization's membership.

Organizing a Speakers Bureau   Where the presentation of speeches is an ongoing part of an organization's public relations activity, a speakers bureau may need to be established in order to systematize the process. The bureau may consist of specialized communications personnel who prepare and deliver speeches themselves, or it may simply be a coordinating unit which draws on personnel from different divisions and levels within the organization to give speeches on specialized topics as needed. In large organizations, the bureau may involve the coordination of specialized writers and researchers with a technical staff team, each group contributing its expertise to the preparation of a speech which will be ultimately delivered by a top management official or appropriate spokesperson.

Whatever form it takes, the bureau concept implies that speech-making is an organizational priority and that all speeches delivered on behalf of the organization are consistent with larger PR objectives. A corporation with a diversified product line, for example, might feel that speeches made to community groups help it to project a more unified image. Or a company which manufactures a variety of innovative drug products might find that having its technical staff deliver lectures and poster sessions at medical conventions enhances its credibility with the medical establishment. In both cases, speech-making represents an ongoing PR contribution which could not be made as effectively through other means.

Speakers bureaus also routinely handle advance and follow-up publicity for speeches. This may involve the preparation of reprints, speaker biographies, and photos for selected media mailings or for use in direct mail campaigns to the public. Speeches which contain news or newsworthy information can be given more publicity mileage by serving as the basis for news or feature releases, and speeches which express a controversial or noteworthy opinion can be edited into op-ed or by-line articles.

Model Case Studies

PRESENTING AN ISSUE THROUGH A FACT SHEET AND BACKGROUNDER

One of the most popular uses for fact sheets and backgrounders is as a lobbying tool. Lobbying—the act of trying to persuade government officials to vote in a particular way on a legislative issue—has become an increasingly

228 Dealing with Issues

important part of public relations activity as more and more organizations realize the extent to which their interests can be affected by government regulation and other forms of legislation. As a result, many of the larger public relations agencies now have Washington branches founded for almost the sole purpose of lobbying government officials on client-related issues.*

Carla Robinson is a writer and researcher for the nonprofit activist group, Citizens Against Intervention in the Third World (CAITW). A week ago she was instructed by the organization's director to research an issue which had been in the news the previous week. The issue concerned the marketing of infant formula products to Third World countries by multi-national corporations.

The issue had already arisen some years ago when a number of nonprofit health organizations led a protest against the promotion of infant formula in the Third World.[13] These organizations had argued that the marketing of such products was sometimes deceptive, that many Third World mothers did not know how to use infant formula properly, and that the advertising of formula in the Third World discouraged many mothers from breastfeeding (the form of infant nourishment which medical experts agree is by far the healthiest and safest). Based on these findings, the World Health Organization (WHO) had voted in May 1981 to adopt a voluntary code restricting any kind of promotion of infant formula which was liable to discourage breastfeeding in Third World countries. Despite the lobbying efforts of many pro-breastfeeding groups, however, the U.S. voted against the code under the assumption that it represented a curb on free speech and free trade.

Now CAITW's director tells Robinson that WHO is considering re-opening the debate and staging another vote, this time for a stricter code. At the time of the 1981 vote, CAITW had not yet been formed, so there had been no opportunity to engage in lobbying activity then. With the resurrection of the issue, the organization now has the opportunity to become active in the debate and to prepare lobbying materials before the formal announcement of a new vote is made.

Robinson immediately sets to work researching the topic so that materials will be ready for distribution to U.S. health officials and the media as soon as possible. Her intention is to write a brief fact sheet and backgrounder which can introduce the issue in general terms. If and when a new vote is approved, these materials can be revised and expanded accordingly.

In preparing the fact sheet and backgrounder she first researches the topic in the library where she consults the following resources.†

---

*Although Capitol Hill is obviously the most concentrated site of lobbying activity, intensive lobbying also takes place on the state and local levels. In addition, according to the *Wall Street Journal*, multi-national firms are increasingly using PR people to lobby foreign governments and their ambassadors.[12]

†If Robinson had access to appropriate on-line data bases, her research would be greatly facilitated (see the discussion on additional research in Chapter 3).

The New York Times Index for 1981   This leads her to articles on the issue and on the original vote. She discovers, as she expected, that the *Times*, a newspaper with a liberal orientation, favored the code and thus can provide her with a number of relevant points to support CAITW's position.

The Wall Street Journal Index for 1981   This leads her to articles with the opposition viewpoint. The *Journal,* a conservative business daily which favors free enterprise, provides her with probably the most condensed and best articulated argument available for the other side.

The Reader's Guide to Periodical Literature for 1981   This leads her to magazine articles summarizing the controversy. Articles in weekly news magazines like *Time* and *Newsweek* are especially helpful.

The Social Science Index for 1981   This leads her to articles in scholarly journals in the social sciences that deal with the issue in more depth. Although most of the articles in the index are too technical and complex to serve her purposes in writing a preliminary fact sheet and backgrounder, they give her a more in-depth understanding of the subject, which may be useful later on.

Card Catalog   Here she searches for titles of recent books on breastfeeding which could provide further support for CAITW's position that this is the healthiest and safest form of infant nourishment.

Robinson takes notes on her reading and carefully jots down the sources (name of publication; name of author, if given; volume; issue; and/or date and page numbers). Although she will not include footnotes in her fact sheet and backgrounder, she will keep the information in case a fact is challenged and she needs to return to the source for verification.

Reviewing her notes, she then composes the following issue statement to serve as the basis for her backgrounder: *Breast milk is the healthiest form of nourishment for an infant. All promotional activities which directly or indirectly discourage Third World mothers from breastfeeding their babies should be discontinued.* She then constructs a short, informal outline for the backgrounder.

    I. Statement of immediate problem.
   II. Background on the value of breastfeeding.
  III. Background on the use of infant formula.
  IV. Call to action.
   V. Conclusion—brief refutation of opposition.

For the fact sheet, she compiles a list of concrete information to support this organizing idea: *Restrictions should be placed on the marketing of infant formula in Third World countries.* The information in the fact sheet will be objectively stated, but selected to conform to this organizing idea and to complement the backgrounder.

The two documents end up looking like this:

FACT SHEET
Breastfeeding vs. Bottle-feeding

Medical experts agree that breastfeeding is the healthiest way to nurture an infant. Human milk is nutritious, safe, and helps immunize against disease.

Almost all mothers can nurse their children. The notions that some women "do not have enough milk" or "lose their milk" are artifacts of culture.

Breastfeeding reduces the chances of ovulation, providing, in some cases, a natural form of birth control.

Recent clinical data suggest that the second generation of non-breastfed children are more psychologically vulnerable and insecure than their breastfed counterparts. This is because they have not experienced satisfactory "bonding" with the mother during early infancy.

Aggressive marketing of infant formula in Third World countries has influenced many mothers to abandon breastfeeding.

Health authorities in Third World countries have become alarmed by increasing numbers of non-thriving babies.

Where clean water or refrigeration is unavailable, sterilizing costly, and illiteracy widespread, formula food is apt to be misused.

Contaminated formula can cause gastrointestinal disease. Excessive dilution of formula to stretch supply can cause malnutrition.

—Prepared by Citizens against Intervention of the Third World

---

The Marketing of Infant Formula:
History and Background

For years many manufacturers of infant formula have marketed their products in developing countries. This practice has had dire effects on the health of infants whose mothers lack an understanding of how to use the formulas properly. Reports by health specialists that Third World mothers often over-dilute formula to make it last or mix formula with contaminated water supplies support this conclusion.

Human milk is the healthiest way to nurture an infant. It is nutritious, safe, and helps immunize against disease. There are also psychological arguments that favor nursing. It appears that the comforting closeness of mother and child during breastfeeding has a positive effect on personality development and that an infant who is breastfed is more likely to thrive emotionally as well as physically.

Infant formula first gained popularity in America during World War II when many mothers worked in the war effort and could not nurse their babies on a regular basis. Social attitudes during the 1950s and 1960s continued to encourage the use of formula in this country until, by the end of the 1960s, only one out of four American infants were breastfed.

In the 1970s, however, the trend changed and breastfeeding made a strong comeback in the United States. Physicians began to understand the nutritional benefits of breast milk and child psychologists began to encourage parents to let children develop naturally.

The declining market for infant formula in the U.S. led manufacturers to redirect sales strategies toward developing countries. Aggressive promotional campaigns began to be implemented which urged Third World mothers to abandon breastfeeding and join the "modern" world—ironically, when the modern world was returning to more traditional nursing methods.

Health authorities in the Third World have become alarmed as they witness the growing number of non-thriving babies. In case after case, misused formula seems to be the culprit. To stop such abuses, we need to

1. Stop media advertising directed at mothers in Third World countries.
2. Assure proper education and supervision by qualified health care personnel in the use of infant formula products.

There are those who argue that restrictions of any kind inhibit free enterprise and violate the concept of freedom upon which our country was built. But such arguments seek to pervert out most sacred ideas in order to support self-interest. What is at issue here is not profit or loss but the health and well being of future generations. A freedom pursued at the expense of human life can hardly be a freedom worth preserving.

—Prepared by Citizens against Intervention in the Third World

PRESENTING AN ISSUE THROUGH AN OP-ED ARTICLE

Deciding when to write an op-ed article and what subject to address requires good public relations judgment. As mentioned earlier in this chapter, the best op-eds, while they discuss issues from a personal point of view, are not direct sales pieces. Nonetheless, for an op-ed piece to be a public relations tool it should have definite *indirect* value to your client; that is, it should help accomplish the PR objectives of your program by increasing the organization's visibility with a target public and by connecting the organization to an issue with which that public is potentially concerned.

In preparing an op-ed, remember that its effectiveness depends on an implicit reciprocity: When you explain a complex issue or give advice to readers, they respond by offering you their goodwill. For this reciprocity to take place, the information offered must be clear, honest, accurate, and of genuine value and interest to the targeted readership.

Joan Goodman is the director of public information of Montgomery Medical Center, a university hospital which has been losing patients in recent years to nearby suburban hospitals. Through her discussions with hospital administrators and patients, Goodman has acquired a fairly good understanding of the problem. As an urban teaching hospital, Montgomery Medical isn't as plush as the nearby suburban hospitals. Montgomery has also suffered public relations damage from the complaints of patients who say they are being used as "guinea pigs" in the training of interns and residents. They are tired, they tell their friends, of being examined 20 times a day and nagged to take part in experimental protocols.

Goodman understands these complaints, but she also knows there is another side to the story which would be worth publicizing. To get the answers she needs, she speaks with Dr. Anthony Carr, the hospital's chief of medicine. Carr agrees that university hospitals like Montgomery are not as comfortable as many community hospitals. But comfort, he says, does not have much to do with good medical care.

Carr goes on to describe to Goodman the advantages offered by a university hospital, and he even gives some examples of patients who wouldn't have survived had they not had access to the hospital's special resources. That evening, Goodman ponders Carr's remarks. What patients need to know, she realizes, is not the particular benefits of Montgomery Medical so much as the general benefits of going to a university teaching hospital instead of a community hospital. In other words, she can tackle the problem of the declining census at Montgomery Medical by dealing with the *issue* of what constitutes good medical care in general.

What would help Montgomery most, Goodman concludes, is an op-ed piece in the local paper, the *Montgomery Times,* that explains the value of being treated at a university hospital. Carr, who had argued the position so eloquently, seems a logical choice to by-line the piece. As the hospital's chief of medicine, his name carries weight. And since Montgomery would not be mentioned in the piece itself, Carr's position, which would be mentioned in the identifying blurb, would serve as an indirect "plug" for the hospital.

On the basis of his remarks the day before (which she had put on tape), Goodman feels capable of drawing up a draft for an op-ed piece which can then be sent to Carr to edit and supplement where necessary. Before beginning the draft, however, she calls Carr to explain her idea and find out whether he is willing to pursue the project. He agrees and she sets to work. First, she checks the length of the op-ed articles in the *Montgomery Times*. These appear to average from 600 to 750 words, which means that the final piece must fall within this range. Next, she composes the following PR message to serve as the organizing idea for the article she is about the write: *While lacking the amenities of smaller community hospitals, university hospitals are on the cutting edge of new developments in medicine and therefore offer patients the best medical care.* This, she decides, is the essential message that the op-ed must get across to its readers. With this statement to guide her, Goodman proceeds to develop the following draft for review by Carr:

The Benefits of University Hospital Care

by Anthony Carr, M.D.
Chief of Medicine
Montgomery Medical Center

As a physician, I'm frequently approached at social gatherings by people who want to tell me about their latest experience in the hospital. Commonly, the most enthusiastic stories come from those who have spent time in suburban community hospitals. They sing the praises of these hospitals as though they were recounting the highlights of a Caribbean vacation. They tell me how plush and comfortable their rooms were, how good the food, and how well-mannered and cheerful the staff. Inevitably, they ask me why university hospitals can't provide them with such good service. My response is to ask what these amenities have to do with the real function of a hospital—the practice of medicine.

As hospitals are now in the business of competing for patients, stress is unfortunately placed upon peripheral services rather than the core service of health care. Many university hospitals are admittedly older structures with smaller rooms and fewer private rooms. Usually they are located in cities, making parking more difficult and more expensive. They also tend to be larger institutions whose size entails a more formal, bureaucratic relationship among departments and between staff and patients.

However, the key to fine medical care has always depended upon the training of the professionals who administer it and the kinds of specialized knowledge and resources available to these professionals. Comfortable, esthetically pleasing surroundings, and "nice" people, while they may offer temporary solace from pain, have little to do with actual healing.

Patients often lose sight of the fact that university hospitals are on the cutting edge of medical advances in this country. By definition, they are the clinical arms of medical schools, places where researchers and clinicians work hand in hand not only to advance the state of medical science, but also to provide the most up-to-date medical care for patients. In such a setting, even the most conventional protocols are constantly reassessed, and experts in every area are available to handle unique and difficult problems.

In addition, university hospitals are engaged in ongoing research programs and can therefore offer patients with unusual or extremely serious diseases the option of taking advantage of the latest experimental therapies and diagnostic techniques.

Finally, university hospitals have the advantage of a full-time house staff—interns and residents who provide minute-to-minute care for patients while they themselves are advancing through various degrees of medical training. In community hospitals, where there is no house staff, doctors cannot possibly be present 24 hours a day but have to commute from home, often traveling considerable distances to handle emergencies.

Of course, there are also the disadvantages of university health care. Being a patient in a teaching hospital may mean being subjected to repeated examinations by medical students, interns, residents, and even attending physicians. I feel, however, that the benefits which patients derive from these multiple examinations strongly outweigh the inconveniences. A patient's care may be discussed at many conferences and with ten or more different specialists who can, through their collective knowledge, add greatly to the patient's management. In medicine, as in most highly technical and complex fields, there is rarely one right solution but many possible solutions which need to be compared, weighed, and discussed in an effort to find the best one for a given patient in a given situation.

Recently, I treated a woman who complained to me toward the end of her stay at the hospital that she had been examined by three different medical students in the space of a week. How, she asked me, did these repeated examinations by such green apprentices benefit her treatment? I replied that, indeed, the examinations might not be of direct benefit to her, but that the process of training new physicians was important and that someday these same students would be experienced doctors with the knowledge and skills necessary to care for her children and grandchildren.

Carr likes the draft and suggests only minor revisions to make the piece more consistent with current medical usage and with his own style. Goodman then sends the article on for final review to the hospital director. After receiving the necessary approval, she mails the piece to Steven Barney, the op-ed editor of the *Montgomery Times* with the accompanying cover letter:

Dear Mr. Barney:

Please consider the enclosed article, "The Benefits of University Hospital Care," for publication on the op-ed page of the *Montgomery Times*. The article, which we are offering the *Times* on an exclusive basis, is by Dr. Anthony Carr, Chief of Medicine of the Montgomery County Medical Center. Dr. Carr, who practices internal medicine and hematology, has served as Chief of Medicine at the center for 15 years. He is an eminent practitioner, teacher, and researcher. We feel the information contained in the essay would be of special interest to *Times* readers.

I will give you a call sometime next week to discuss. Please feel free to get in touch with me at the Medical Center should you have any questions or comments you'd like to talk over before then.

Sincerely,

Joan Goodman

Joan Goodman
Director,
Public Information

Goodman also encloses a copy of Carr's resumé, and clips the following blurb to the article:

Anthony Carr, M.D. has served as Chief of Medicine of the Montgomery Medical Center for 15 years. He is a board-certified internist and hematologist who has made significant advances in the treatment of acute leukemia.

PRESENTING AN ISSUE THROUGH A SPEECH

At its best, the speech can be the most valuable of all public relations tools for dealing with a complex issue. A good speech matched with a good speaker can charm, if it cannot persuade, almost any audience.

Since a speech is a personal presentation, the character of the speaker accounts for a large part of its effectiveness. The best speakers do not step straight out of rhetoric texts but tend to be people with highly individualized personalities. Thus, instead of working against the idiosyncrasies of a speaker's personal style, good speechwriters learn to work with, even exaggerate, some of these idiosyncrasies so that the audience is made aware of the particular man or woman behind the words.

In some organizations a public relations writer may have to write speeches for a variety of individuals; in others the writer may be assigned a particular person whose speechwriting he or she always handles. Ideas for speeches may originate in the PR agency or department or may be suggested by an outside organization or group which invites your client to speak. In the latter case, a general topic is often proposed that can be shaped by the speechwriter to suit the PR objectives of the client.

Speeches can be edited into op-ed or by-line articles or distributed to the press verbatim to provide quotable material for a related story. If a speech is given on an important enough topic or to an important enough audience, a press release can also be prepared announcing the fact that the speech has been given and summarizing and quoting major points.

Bernie Long is the public relations director for the U.S. Division of Ino, Inc., a Chicago branch of a computer manufacturing firm whose headquarters are in Tokyo. Long, who has been with the company three years, has become concerned with the image of Ino in the United States after reading a spate of articles criticizing Japanese companies operating in this country. The articles indicated that many American businesspeople see the Japanese as encroaching on U.S. turf and stealing business away from U.S. companies. Recent scandals involving the theft of high-technology information from American companies by Japanese computer "spies" has made matters worse.

Long concludes that while there is certainly nothing he can or would want to do to hide the fact that his firm is operating successfully in this country, there are strategies that could be taken to enhance the image of the firm with an American audience. One of the major problems with the Japanese from a PR standpoint, Long feels, is that they lack the outgoing expressiveness of American businesspeople. Top Japanese executives like to keep a low profile and, even when they do appear in public, tend to efface any aspects of their personality that could be called distinctive. This self-effacing style does little to endear Japanese businesspeople to their American counterparts.

In developing a corporate identity program for Ino's U.S. division, Long specifies on his list of PR objectives the need to improve the image of Ino in the eyes of American business. As part of this program he suggests that speeches to selected target publics by top Ino executives be delivered more frequently. He identifies the target publics as American businesspeople, specifically the members of American business associations and clubs.

To get this facet of the identity campaign off the ground, he writes to national and local business associations to inquire about interest in having an Ino executive address their membership. He quickly receives a number of favorable responses, among them an invitation from a Chicago business club asking Ino to supply a speaker for its September luncheon meeting. The club secretary explains in her letter that the group, which consists of managers from area companies, would like a top executive to speak briefly (7 to 10 minutes) and be prepared to answer questions on American-Japanese business relations. Long feels that this is just the kind of opportunity which his company needs to take advantage of.

As a first step in preparing a speech for the occasion, Long jots down a number of topics which he feels might be appropriate. These include

1 Japanese vs. American business styles.
2 A history of Japanese vs. American business growth.
3 Japanese and U.S. productivity techniques.
4 The computer industry: its future in a world market.

While Long feels that each of these topics could be developed into a satisfactory speech, he decides that the first topic offers the most promise. It is most compatible with Ino's PR objectives and is also most likely to appeal to the general business membership of the club.

Before setting to work on the speech, however, Long first has to consider who at Ino would make a suitable speaker. He wants, if possible, to use a top executive from the U.S. division. Such a person would be easily accessible during the preparatory stages of the speech and would be more familiar with the American style of business than a higher level executive in Japan. Unfortunately, the president of the division, Mr. Fuji, seems to project that stereotype of surface formality and stiffness that the corporate identity program wishes to dispel. Though Long has grown to respect Fuji's honesty and devotion to the company, he doesn't feel the man would be an effective spokesperson.

The executive vice president of the U.S. Division is another story. A man in his seventies, Mr. Nakama has worked at Ino for 50 years (35 years in Japan, 15 years in the U.S.). Nakama has a wise, grandfatherly air that evokes a warm response from everyone he meets, and he speaks with an old-world charm that turns formality into graciousness.

After gaining approval at the necessary level to develop the speech for Nakama (the approval process takes time, for it is an elaborate ritual in Japanese firms), Long proceeds to meet with Nakama for a number of informal discussions. During the interviews, Long encourages Nakama to find examples and anecdotes from his own experience to illustrate his points. By taping these sessions, Long is able to free himself from taking notes, thus allowing a more spontaneous, informal atmosphere to prevail during the discussion. The tapes also give him a record of Nakama's speaking style which he can consult later. By the end of their first session, Long and Nakama have agreed on the following organizing idea for the speech: *Americans and Japanese would both profit if, instead of letting their different business styles divide them, they worked together to accomplish common business goals.*

238 Dealing with Issues

In addition to interviewing Nakama, Long researches the topic of American and Japanese business styles in the library. He finds numerous magazines, books, and textbook chapters devoted to the subject. But though Long incorporates some of the information gained from research, he tries to keep statistics and dry facts to a minimum. These are rarely appreciated by an audience and would seem especially out of keeping with Nakama's style. Instead, Long concentrates on using Nakama's personal anecdotes to get points across.

The following is Long's draft of Nakama's speech. (Note that Long uses extra space between lines to make the speech easier to read. Nakama will later add underlining and directions in the margins, after he has practiced the delivery and discussed his presentation style with Long.)

Remarks by Mr. Shigeru Nakama, Executive Vice President, U.S. Division, Ino, Inc., at a luncheon sponsored by the American Management Group: "Japanese and American Business Styles—A Comparison"

December 15, 198_
Chicago, Illinois

Mr. Chairman, Ladies and Gentlemen:

There is a proverb which is widely quoted in Japan that says: "In difference there is resemblance."

The proverb applies well to our two countries. Perhaps nowhere is it more applicable than to our respective business styles. On the surface, the American and Japanese business styles seem in direct contrast to each other. On a deeper level, however, we are more alike than we know. For us both, business is a necessary activity and a source of eternal fascination. We are both never satisfied with the accomplished goal; we are lured to strive further and achieve more. Finally, we are both believers in the business ethic: Business, we feel, is an improving activity both for our nation and for ourselves as individuals.

Surely, my friends, these similarities should be the basis for a strong and vital reciprocity. But though this has often been the case in the past, more recently it has not been so. The superficial differences have promoted suspicion and distrust, and we have failed to look beyond them to the greater harmony.

Let us examine what these differences are. For perhaps by understanding them we can diffuse their power to divide us.

When I first came to this country 15 years ago, I developed a friendship with an American named Jonathan Wise who was a manager in our company. We became and are still close friends. I consider Jonathan to be the very embodiment of the American businessman, and I believe that he sees me as the embodiment of his Japanese counterpart.

Let me explain why.

When we first met, Jonathan and I had both been with Ino for ten years. A year after we met, Jonathan left Ino and joined another electronics firm. Five years later, he joined yet another firm, where he was named vice president, and ten years after that, he joined a fourth firm, where he became executive vice president, the position he holds today. Meanwhile, I remained at Ino. Today, I too, occupy a position as executive vice president. But it is a position earned from devoting myself to one company during this length of time. Jonathan and my histories reflect the difference in how corporate success is engineered in Japan and in the United States. In America most executives chart their business success by navigating a successful course through different companies. In Japan our success comes through navigating successfully through one.

To cite yet another example of difference: Jonathan calls himself an idea man. I call myself a detail man. In fact, we often arrive at similar conclusions. But while Jonathan usually travels from the large picture to the small—from the "macro" to the "micro" view—I travel in the opposite direction. The Japanese are famed for their quality control—and this, I believe, is owing to our attention to detail, our refusal to be hasty or careless in completing a task. To amend a popular American saying, we never miss the trees for the forest. Americans, on the other hand, have a great reputation for innovation. Here, I believe, their success comes from that ability to leap out of the established frame of a problem into a broader or different context. This hardly means that Americans cannot produce quality products, or that Japanese cannot innovate. It is rather that each group seems to possess a dominant mode of thinking that lends itself best to a certain type of problem-solving.

When I first came to this country I was surprised by Americans' willingness to talk freely about things which we Japanese traditionally keep to ourselves: Problems with job, marriage, and children were popular topics of conversation at parties and over lunch. I found this same expressiveness operating in the work place: American managers were more flexible and open with colleagues and subordinates than their Japanese counterparts. In some cases the result of this openness was to encourage poor discipline and weaken the overall sense of purpose and authority. But I have also seen the positive effects of this style—for it humanizes the work place and, for certain individuals, helps produce an atmosphere conducive to creative thinking.

Many of the traits which characterize Japanese business are the result of our national character. We are a small country, with little ethnic diversity and few natural resources. Organization, efficiency, attention to detail, and loyalty to company have, in a sense, been conditioned into us by necessity. America, a larger country, with more diversity of labor and resources, finds the source of its business vitality in change, variety, and big ideas.

Yet we have only to discuss the attributes of the two countries side by side to see how they in fact represent a drive to achieve the same thing: economic success and the well-being of people. Moreover, these attributes complement each other in a way which neither side can afford to overlook. For if both our countries work together through joint ventures, patent exchanges, licensing, and the utilization of each other's skills and resources for manufacturing, people all over the world can enjoy better products.

As you know, I have spent my life working for a Japanese company. Yet for the past 15 years I have lived in America and grown to love this country and its people. It is my hope that Japan and America will be able to combine their strengths and, by working together, help to achieve their common goal of happiness and prosperity.

Nakama's speech, while it is not earth-shaking in its content, reflects a simple, common-sensical view of life that meshes well with his speaking style and personality. The speech is also general enough to be appealing to many different kinds of business groups, making it possible for Long to develop a speaking tour for Nakama which covers the geographical target areas that are most important to Ino's operation in the U.S. In addition, Long is able to use the topic of the speech as a *hook* for booking interviews for Nakama with various local TV and radio talk show hosts. To prepare Nakama for the talk shows, Long merely extracts the major points from the speech concerning American and Japanese business styles and compiles them into a list for easy reference. He also rehearses the interviews by asking Nakama typical interview questions and helping him devise suitable answers. He videotapes their exchanges so his client can critique his own responses. As a result of these efforts, Long is able to orchestrate an effective speaking tour that promises to help generate goodwill for Ino, Inc. among American businesspeople.

EXERCISES

Test Your Judgment

Suggest the best depth tool or combination of tools (fact sheet/backgrounder, op-ed/by-line article/advertorial, letter to the editor, speech) for each of the following situations:

1 A parent association is lobbying for stricter laws regarding drunk driving.

2 A neighborhood youth organization wants to explain to local high school students the factors leading to suicide among young people.

3 The president of a communication satellite corporation wants to explain the extraordinary innovations which communications technology promises to bring us in the next 50 years.

4 A restaurant chain that believes its food is of excellent quality wants to respond to a magazine article which refers to its food in passing as "junk food."

5 An independent research firm wants to explain the impact of the information revolution on American business.

PR Workshop

Read the following excerpt from a speech delivered by President Ronald Reagan in October 1981. Discuss whether this is an effective speech by evaluating the elements of organization and style as well as the use of example and anecdote.

> My fellow Americans, in recent days all of us have been swamped by a sea of economic statistics, some good, some bad, and some just plain confusing. There are times when I think that the paper traffic that crosses my desk in a week could fill a big city phone book, and then some.
> The value of the dollar is up around the world. Interest rates are down by 40 percent. The stock and bond markets surge upward. Inflation is down 59 percent. Buying power is going up. Some economic indicators are down. Others are up. But the dark cloud of unemployment hangs over the lives of 11 million of our friends, neighbors and family.

At times, the sheer weight of all these facts and figures makes them hard for anyone to understand. What do they really mean, and what can we do to make them better?

Well, the first step is to understand what they mean in human terms, how they're affecting the everyday lives of our people. Because behind every one of those numbers are millions of individual lives: young couples struggling to make ends meet, teen-agers looking for work, older Americans threatened by inflation, small-business men fighting for survival, and parents working for a better future for their children.

'Want to Make It a Better Place'

All of them have one thing in common. They're Americans who love this country of ours and want to make it a better place. They're brave, hard-working people who know that America today faces serious problems that were long years in the making . And they're desperately trying to make sense out of all the statistics, slogans and political jargon filling the airwaves in this election year. Above all, they're concerned citizens who are looking for guideposts on the road to recovery, for ways to help see our country through to better times.

I know because I hear from hundreds of them every day, in meetings here at the White House, on visits to schools, meeting halls, factories and fairgrounds across the county, and in thousands of phone calls and letters. I only wish I could share with you tonight all that they have to say—their hopes, their fears, their concerns and most of all, their quiet, patient courage.

Letter From Selma, Ala.

But let me just give you one example that speaks for so many of you, a letter from a wife and mother named Judith, who lives in Selma, Ala.

"Dear Mr. President," she writes. "It's 3:45 A.M., and for over an hour I've been unable to sleep . . . this morning I need very much to believe in something . . . I'm not writing so much as an individual, but as a representative of so many. We need to talk with you—to believe that you hear us. . . .

"After years of training and experience, we can't find jobs. National unemployment figures sound almost healthy next to the almost 19 percent we're enduring in Selma.

"The costs for basic survival are nearly beyond belief . . . there may never be a house—home of our own—that dream we've worked for for so many years. . . . We have said 'no' to so many things . . . we're afraid and confused. We've worked hard—we conserved—we planned—we were frugal—careful. We feel so out of control. We don't want a handout—we just want to help make the system well again.

"We must know that in the tons of bureaucracy . . . we've not been lost . . . we want to help. We want a better life, and we're willing to work for it. We believe. We must—it's all we have."

The American Dream

Well, Judith, I hear you. And millions of other men and women like you stand for the values of hard work, thrift, commitment to family and love of God that made this country so great, and will make us great again. And you deserve to know what we're doing in these difficult times to bring your dream—the American dream—back to life again after so many years of mistakes and neglect.

Tonight, in homes across this country, unemployment is the problem uppermost on many people's minds. Getting Americans back to work is an urgent priority for all of us—and especially for this Administration.

But remember, you can't solve unemployment without solving the things that caused it—the out-of-control government spending, the sky-rocketing inflation and interest rates that led to unemployment in the first place. Unless you get at the root causes of the problem—which is exactly what our economic program is doing—you may be able to temporarily relieve the symptoms, but you'll never cure the disease. You may even make it worse.

I have a special reason for wanting to solve this problem in a lasting way. I was 21 and looking for work in 1932, one of the worst years of the Great Depression, and I can remember one bleak night in the Thirties when my father learned on Christmas Eve that he'd lost his job. To be young in my generation was to feel that your future had been mortgaged out from under you—and that's a tragic mistake we must never allow our leaders to make again. Today's young people must never be held hostage to the mistakes of the past.

The only way to avoid making those mistakes again is to learn from them. . . .

'It is Not an Easy Job'

But it isn't an easy job, this challenge to rebuild America and renew the American dream. And I know it can be tempting, listening to some who would go back to the old ways and the quick fix. But consider the choice. A return to the big spending and big taxing that left us with 21½ percent interest rates is no real alternative. A return to double-digit inflation is no alternative. A return to taxing and taxing the American people,—that's no alternative. That's what destroyed millions of American jobs. Together we've chosen a new road for America. It's a far better road. We need only the courage to see it through. I know we can. Throughout our history, we Americans have proven again and again that no challenge is too big for a free, united people.

Together we can do it again. We can do it by slowly but surely working our way back to prosperity that will mean jobs for all who are willing to work, and fulfillment for all who still cherish the American dream.

We can do it, my fellow Americans, by staying the course.

Thank you, good night and God bless you.[14]

PR Case Studies

1   You are the PR director of a computer software company that specializes in word processing programs. One day you open the newspaper and read the article below.

Write a letter to the editor for the by-line of your client (Harvey Smith, president of Soft Words, Inc.) which responds to the article.

BUT IS IT WRITING?

Next to games, the use for home computers most touted is probably word processing. Oh, there are numerous software firms pushing educational packages, which for the most part turn out to be games with an educational twist, and home management programs, those pie-in-the-sky promises of personal money management, or, say, computerized cooking, supervision in the form of electronically stored recipes and automatic portion-controlled formulas that end up being far more trouble to use than they are worth. It is not that these programs do not sell. They do. But so did the citizens band radios and pet rocks that now inhabit the remoter corners of hall closets and the cartons of technological refuse piling up in the basements.

The software that stays in the forefront of the home-computer revolution is the entertainment and word-processing wonders, evidently in that order. A recent survey on the home uses of computers by Family Computing magazine showed word processing second to games in popularity. A similar study by Dial, the magazine for public television, indicated that 76 percent of the home users surveyed were involved in word processing.

So, presumptively, the prospect of a literary renaissance of massive proportions follows hard on the heels of the home computer boom. Does it really? Is word processing truly the wonder it seems or will it turn out to be but a mere exercise in verbose verbiage?

There is no denying that even a limited word-processing program makes the writing life easier than a typewriter ever did. Add a spelling checker and a dictionary program, and word processing potentially becomes a writer's dream.

In fact, the software's popularity can be traced to the writing profession. Anything that promises to ease the labors of wandering the Elysian fields in search of Clio, Thalia, Meslpomene and their sister Muses is greeted there with joy. And if the elders of that vocation looked upon the new technology with scorn and trepidation, its almost instantaneous acceptance by the forward-looking of the tribe and by journalists very soon established it as a standard occupational tool. Being writers, they extolled its virtues to the degree that, initially, at least, one had the impression surely as much was being writ-word processors.

Then a curious thing began to happen. Much of what was being written became unintelligible. One need not look far from the word processor itself to find examples of this lack of clarity. Look at the literature of software and hardware "documentation" for instance. For that matter, even the use of the word "documentation" instead of "instructions" is heavy with obfuscation, however unintended.

So every now and then I begin to worry about the future of word processing. Bracing myself against the coming sackful of condemning letters, I offer forthwith the hypothesis that word processing may not be society's hoped-for vehicle to Parnassus.

Over the last couple of years, I've heard word processing discussed much among writers and editors. My information has not been gleaned in any formal interviewing sense. The topic crops up as naturally over a few years as Rupert Murdock's latest moves do. Interestingly enough, as in the Australian's mushrooming empire, the underlying trends in word processing portend a style of writing different from the styles of the past—less grand, more simplistic, even, perhaps, sloppy.

Until rather recently, writing implied a certain permanence. While the physical act of alteration became easier over the centuries during the transition from quill pens and parchment to typewriters and rag paper, it still entailed some labor. One tended to think before letting the ink flow.

Scribed electronically, letters are ethereal forms. They appear, disappear, reappear like so many apparitions called forth from the Ouija board at the writer's fingertips. In such circumstances, the inscriber's thinking takes a new and different turn. The slow, deliberate, linear progression of structured logic, formerly used even when one was writing emotionally, gives way to a here-now, gone-in-a-second manner of composition. One's sense of continuity gives way to free-form thought. Dots of ideas resembling the dots making up the letters on the video screen drift in and out of one's consciousness, perchance to be captured, perchance to slip away unrecorded.

A lot of writers will rejoin that this is exactly the kind of freedom that makes word processing so useful. One can sit down and virtually pour ideas into the computer via the keyboard. It is then so easy to change them, revise them, restructure the sentences, move paragraphs, organize and reorganize the thoughts that flow so spontaneously.

The very ease with which changes can be made also leads to their never being made at all. One tends to overlook a necessary revision in one's haste to capture a fleeting thought. After all, one can always go back and make the correction. But, in the end, it may be forgotten. A manuscript looks so perfect in an electronic environment, where never a crossed out word or insertion mark roams. Individual sentences, too, look different on screen than they do on paper. They are looser, more fluent, more visually attractive. Overly long Germanlike sentences appear shorter on an 80-character screen line than they do in print. So do paragraphs.

Scrolling is different from flipping through a stack of manuscript paper as well. On most computers one cannot put two completed pages next to each other and read them together when you are working with screen copy. Hopping around in a long manuscript becomes a kind of video jambalaya, where a feel for the actual words is, of necessity, almost totally absent. Connotative meaning gives way to denotative excess.

Add to all these unconventionalities the typographic pyrotechnics made available by such programs as MacWrite, which permits the user to request a printout in any number of font styles and sizes, and well may the words themselves, in McLuhan fashion, become the message. I certainly wouldn't go so far as to say that word processing has no saving graces. For some people, it's an aid to leaping over writing blocks—for most, a reasonable painless way to handle revisions. Still, I have the impression we are heading toward a future filled with the emperor's new words, where word processing cranks out fast-food prose, becoming to writing what Xerography has become to the office memo: A generator of millions of copies of contentless words assembled for appearance's sake—rarely read, much less reflected upon.[15]

2   Pair yourself with one of your classmates, and alternately assign yourselves the roles of client and PR practitioner in a speech writing and delivery exercise. Here are some general suggestions for speech topics:

> nuclear power, abortion, corporate-funded university research, school prayer, all-male or otherwise exclusionary clubs, gun control, mandatory seatbelt laws, foreign trade restrictions

In your role as the PR practitioner, interview your partner in-depth on the topic he or she has selected and try to establish an organizing idea for the speech. During the interview, make note of such details as your partner's sense of humor, vocabulary, mannerisms, and other aspects of verbal and physical style—you will want to take these into account when writing the speech. (If it's convenient, you should tape the interview.)

The final speech should be five to seven minutes long and typed in the appropriate speech format (wide margins, double or triple spaced, phonetic spellings of difficult words). Once the speech is completed, listen to your partner deliver it to the class. Prepare a list of challenging, even hostile questions to test the speaker's Q&A skills. Then critique the presentation as a whole.

3   You are the public affairs officer of a nuclear power company that has just decided to open a new plant in Providence, Ohio, a small town 100 miles outside of Cincinnati. The new plant will substantially cut the cost of energy for the area. In preparation for possible public opposition to the project, you have decided to develop a fact sheet and backgrounder for distribution to the local press and to public representatives at the next town council meeting.

Research the nuclear power issue and compile facts to support the value of this form of energy. Then frame an appropriate issue statement and develop a reasoned argument to support it in a backgrounder.

4   You are PR director of Raritan Hospital, a community hospital in Montgomery County. On February 2, you open the local paper and discover the op-ed article by-lined by Dr. Anthony Carr of the Montgomery County Medical Center (see the Model Case Study about an op-ed article in this chapter). Write a letter to the editor of the *Montgomery Times* for Raritan executive director Sidney Field's signature in which you respond to points made in Carr's article.

NOTES

1. See Alan R. Raucher, *Public Relations and Business, 1900-1929* (Baltimore: The Johns Hopkins University Press, 1968).
2. W. Howard Chase, "Public Issue Management: The New Science," *Public Relations Jour-*

nal, 33 (October 1977), 25–26. Also see Chase, *Issue Management: Origins of the Future* (Stamford, Conn.: Issue Actions Publications, 1984).

3. Richard E. Crable and Steven L. Vibbert, "Managing Issues and Influencing Public Policy," *Public Relations Review*, XI (Summer 1985), 3–16.

4. William E. Duke, "Demystifying the Issues," *Public Relations Journal*, 39 (August 1983), 17.

5. Crable and Vibbert, p. 5.

6. Thomas W. Campbell, "Identifying the Issues," *Public Relations Journal*, 39 (August 1983), 20.

7. John F. Akers, "IBM, on South Africa," *New York Times*, March 27, 1985, sec. A, p. 27.

8. See Richard Alan Nelson and Robert L. Heath, "Corporate Public Relations and the New Media Technology," *Public Relations Review*, X (Fall 1984), 27–38.

9. George Watson, "Playing Canute with the News," *New York Times*, November 14, 1984, sec. A, p. 34.

10. Paul N. Bloom, "Six Ways to Sell Ideas," *Public Relations Journal*, 40 (February 1984), 22.

11. Don Hill, "84 Campaign Lesson: Part Two," *Public Relations Journal*, 40 (February 1985), 18–21.

12. *Wall Street Journal*, February 19, 1985, p. 1.

13. See Dana Raphael, ed., *Breastfeeding and Food Policy in a Hungry World* (New York: Academic Press, 1979).

14. *New York Times*, October 14, 1982, sec. B, p. 14 (Copyright © 1982 by the New York Times Company. Reprinted by permission.)

15. *New York Times*, June 26, 1984, sec. C, p. 5 (Copyright © 1984 by the New York Times Company. Reprinted by permission.)

9

Developing New Business

The ability to *sell* is intrinsic to almost all fields of endeavor. Professors seek to sell ideas to students; politicians seek to sell platforms to voters; even poets seek to sell their interpretations of experience to readers. In public relations you are "selling" in effect, when you write a press release to the media about your client or a speech to be delivered by your client to a target audience. In each case you are trying to persuade a person or group to embrace your client's message. But before public relations practitioners can engage in selling on behalf of a client, they must first sell their services *to* the client. The starting point of this process resides in new business development.

Developing new business is an essential part of the ongoing activity of a public relations agency. No matter how small or how large the agency, the infusion of new business is necessary for two reasons: (1) the need to replace old clients who leave or whose projects are completed; and (2) the need to grow—the goal of any healthy business.* As for in-house PR practitioners, they may want to expand their departments or their own responsibilities, obtain budget increases, or protect themselves against retrenchment during a recession. In such cases, they must promote themselves and their services in much the same way that an agency does when it approaches a new business

---

*While agencies generally welcome new business, there are occasions when potential *conflicts of interest* make it necessary to turn down clients. A conflict of interest occurs when a new account overlaps with an existing account, so that promoting the new client's interest means, in effect, thwarting the interests of the existing client. It's always advisable to check your agency's client list and talk over any new business prospects with your supervisor to be sure that potential conflicts are not lurking in the wings. (Fortunately, many large organizations retain several PR agencies to handle different divisions or product lines. This way, it is often possible for an agency to be assigned only that area of a new client's business that does not conflict with an existing client.)

prospect. Obviously, in-house PR people don't need to hunt for clients (though they may have to research whom in the company hierarchy it would be best to approach in getting approval for a new project). Remember, however, that if an agency practitioner fails to win a client, he or she can always move on to pitch another. An in-house practitioner must continue banging on the same door.

While this chapter will concern itself primarily with new business development in an agency context, many of the principles outlined here can be translated for use in in-house PR.

The best and most effective kind of new business prospecting happens indirectly when you do good work for your existing clients. When clients are satisfied, they tell others about your abilities or offer you new or expanded projects. Similarly, agencies which win *Silver Anvil Awards* (offered by PRSA in recognition of the best annual PR programs) or are otherwise honored for professional excellence reap the benefits not only in personal satisfaction but also in the new business opportunities which accompany an enhanced reputation.

But while a good track record obviously encourages new business, many agencies also feel the need to engage in more direct forms of prospecting. A few large agencies even consider new business development important enough to have a department devoted exclusively to this activity. The rationale for creating a specialized new business division, according to management experts, is that developing new business draws on more psychological and creative skills than does servicing existing clients.[1] However, this distinction is probably less true in public relations where psychological and creative skills are as necessary in keeping existing clients satisfied as they are in developing new clients. Perhaps for this reason, the pursuit of new business is often viewed as part of the ongoing responsibility of all agency executives—as a by-product of their social and business lives. More experienced and highly placed staff members obviously have a wider network of contacts from which these prospects are likely to emerge. But this doesn't mean that younger staff—even those relatively new to the field—can't also drum up new business by being alert and conscientious. Learning early how to recognize new business possibilities and how to pursue them can be a boon to your agency and your career. It can also be financially remunerative since many agencies pay *finder's fees* to staff members who bring in new accounts. The fee is often as much as 10% of the first-year fee (excluding out-of-pocket expenses) that the client pays to the agency.

Young account executives who have a flair for new business may also be asked by their agencies to run student internship programs. Directing an internship program usually involves making formal presentations at universities and interviewing interested candidates to fill part-time or summer positions. These activities help hone new business skills because they involve selling the agency in a variety of contexts. They also provide an opportunity for young executives to learn more about the nature and needs of their agencies.

METHODS OF DEVELOPING NEW BUSINESS

To explain the two major methods of client prospecting let's use the analogy of the big-game hunter who carries a rifle and a shotgun. He uses the rifle at close range when he discovers an animal outside his tent eating from his mess kit. He uses the shotgun when the animal is at a distance, perhaps grazing with the herd.

In new business development, the *rifle shot* prospect is often one whom you gain access to through "close range" social or professional activities. Such prospects can be discovered through the mediation of relatives, friends, and acquaintances, fellow members of clubs, or professional associates. These prospects yield the highest rate of return because you either know someone on the inside of the organization or have a reference that will facilitate your contact with someone inside. Moreover, in rifle shot prospecting you can usually learn a great deal about the target organization in advance and are therefore in a better position to make an effective first pitch. Keep in mind, however, that relying upon friends and associates to help find new business prospects requires diplomacy. Let your contacts know that you're using them, request their advice along the way, and ask them whether or not they feel you should use their names in making the pitch.

The rifle shot approach to new business can also involve a targeted prospect whom you do not know personally. Company profile articles in the business sections of newspapers or in specialized trade publications are the source of many such prospects. These articles may provide enough background information to serve as the basis for a new business pitch tailored to the organization's needs.

Another kind of rifle shot prospect is an organization with which you may have had dealings as a customer or patron. Let's say your bank has recently introduced automated teller machines without adequately explaining their use to the public. As a consumer who has experienced some confusion about how to use the machines, you are in a good position to approach the bank's management with a PR plan for educating the public more effectively.

Shotgun prospecting addresses a less clear-cut target audience. It usually involves mass mailings to organizations about which you have no first-hand knowledge but which fall within a predetermined category that you feel could benefit from your agency's services. If, for example, your firm has expertise in a specific industry area, this provides a justification for targeting companies that fall within that industry. A shotgun mailing list can also be compiled according to geographical location, company size, or other limiting factors compatible with your agency's operations. Keep in mind that the size of shotgun mailings should be determined by your capacity to do the required follow-up, since all prospects will eventually need to be individually telephoned.

PRE-PROPOSAL RESEARCH

The more preliminary research you do on a potential client, the more likely you are to frame a pitch that will address the prospect's real needs. Check business directories like *Standard and Poor's* and *Thomas' Register* for general background on profit-making organizations (names of principals, net income, names of subsidiaries and divisions, listing of products and services, and so on). For information on nonprofit organizations consult the specialized directories which exist for hospitals, schools, and trade and professional associations. If you have the time, do a newspaper and magazine search for articles written on the company and on the industry within which it falls (see the discussion on additional research in Chapter 3). In addition, you may want to investigate the financial status of the company before pursuing a new business pitch. Dun and Bradstreet publishes a semi-annual credit rating book where you can check on an organization's financial status. You can also ask that a Business Information Report be prepared detailing a prospect's credit situation. This kind of check is sensible since you don't want to pursue a client who is not financially able or willing to pay for your agency's services.

Develop a file on each new business prospect in which you keep research notes, copies of letters and other materials sent and received, as well as brief summaries of phone conversations. On individual contacts, note relevant personal information, such as spouse's and children's names, principal interests, favorite restaurants, and so forth.

THE PROPOSAL LETTER

The proposal letter is your first written pitch to a prospective client and is crucial to setting the tone for a future relationship. The letter represents an opportunity to convince the prospect of the value of public relations and provide a hint of what you are capable of delivering. The standard proposal letter should therefore include the following information:

An introduction of yourself and your agency.
An explanation of how you heard about the organization (if relevant).
A brief outline of what you perceive to be the prospect's public relations needs.

A few general implementation ideas.

An explanation of why your agency is well equipped to develop a full-scale PR program for the prospective client.

The letter should be brief (rarely more than two pages), with no more than three or four sentences devoted to each of the above topics. Even if you've done thorough research, you will not yet have first-hand knowledge of the organization and should be cautious about what you suggest. Your objective is not to provide a detailed blueprint for a program but to offer a sketch of the possibilities and create a desire for more information.

Remember that proposal writing is an art. It requires that you walk a fine line between assurance and modesty—that you assert a need without sounding presumptuous or bossy, and that you be flexible without appearing wishy-washy. Other aspects of tone are a matter of judgment. A dry, overly serious letter to a friend or an acquaintance is as inappropriate as writing a casual, breezy letter to a prospect you've never met. Whether you use *I* or *we* (the more common pronoun, since it implies that you are speaking for the agency as a whole) also depends on whether you know the prospect personally. Sometimes a calculated mixture of *I* and *we* is the best choice.

A proposal letter should always end with a clear follow-up statement. Generally, you should promise to call in about a week to see whether a meeting can be arranged so that the proposal can be discussed in more detail. Five to seven working days represents adequate time for the prospective client to read the letter and discuss it with colleagues and superiors.

In some cases of shotgun prospecting, the initial pitch is made over the phone to save the time and trouble of typing and mailing proposal letters. The goal in pitching over the phone (as in writing a letter) is to arrange a meeting where a presentation can be made in person. However, whether it's an initial pitch or a follow-up on a letter, sales experts caution you to avoid the temptation of saying too much.[2] Giving too much information over the phone can make a personal meeting seem superfluous, and it is the personal meeting that you depend upon to close the deal.

FOLLOW-UP

A follow-up call should ideally result in an appointment for a meeting. But for many reasons, this isn't always what happens. The prospect may not be persuaded by your proposal, may be too busy to pursue your ideas at the moment, may feel the budget isn't available for a PR program, or may distrust or misunderstand the whole notion of public relations. If a meeting is not immediately forthcoming, you need to make a judgment as to whether there is still hope for developing the prospect in the future or whether this represents a dead-end.

If you feel that time and persuasive tactics may change the prospect's mind, keep the name on your "active" list and continue to follow-up regularly. Follow-up in this case means periodic mailings which keep you in the consciousness of the potential client. These mailings should be spaced so as not to seem obtrusive or pushy (every two months is a good interval). You might, for example, send a copy of a newspaper or magazine article which relates to the prospect's industry with a brief note highlighting specific points in the article that you think might especially apply to the prospect's case. After six to eight months, another proposal letter and follow-up call may be in order.

THE PROPOSAL MEETING

When a new business prospect responds favorably to a written proposal and agrees to schedule a meeting, you are finally in a position to make a more direct pitch. In preparing for this meeting, you can now draw directly on the prospect's own resources by asking to be sent product literature, brochures, annual reports, and other standard materials put out by the organization. You may also want to do more in-depth library research on the company and the industry. Finally, to arrive at a clearer understanding of the organization's public relations situation, you may want to call a number of editors in the prospect's trade area, asking whether they've heard of the organization and, if they have, what is the kind and quality of communication they have received from it. Knowing the prospect's strengths and weaknesses in dealing with the media can help you focus your pitch, and being able to refer to key editors by name and quote them directly can be especially effective. Remember, however, that while you want to convince the prospect of the need for public relations, you don't want to intimidate or place the organization on the defensive. Be diplomatic in presenting criticism, and try to balance weaknesses with strengths wherever possible.

Agencies vary in the way in which they prepare their materials for a proposal meeting. Most proceed informally, discussing their ideas in an unstructured, seminar fashion. A more formal presentation is usually the result of a "bidding" situation, when more than one agency is being considered for an account. In these cases, each competing agency may be asked to develop a full-length program for presentation. This is not the general rule, and when it is done, each agency chosen to compete usually receives a predetermined fee for preparing the program.

Whatever the presentation format, an agency will want to have those members of its staff present who are likely to work on the new account. This might include a vice president of the agency, an account supervisor, and an account executive. It is impossible to overestimate the importance of a good account team in selling a client. Personal rapport as well as expertise are important. An organization is often unconsciously sold by what it perceives to be a winning team whose style meshes well with its own.

Follow-up begins again after a presentation. Thank-you letters should be sent to all the organizational representatives present at the meeting. If the prospect does not contact the agency first, the highest level agency executive involved in the pitch will usually want to call and attempt to work out an agreement. Once an agreement is reached, work on the formal program can begin.

Model Case Studies

DEVELOPING A RIFLE SHOT PROSPECT

To be successful at rifle shot new business is to be continually alert to potential prospects. This means that even when engaged in social activities, you're still selling your agency and yourself. At the same time, even the most aggressive practitioner knows that, beyond a certain point, it is necessary to proceed with caution. Although it's fine to develop an initial contact on your own, a formal pitch should never be made without consultation with your superiors and the explicit backing of your agency. A supervisor can tell you whether a prospect is worth pursuing, whether it represents a potential conflict of interest, or whether it has already been pursued by the agency. If the prospect seems important enough, it may even be taken out of your hands and pitched by a more senior executive.

Martin Grosbeck, a young account executive with a Cleveland public relations agency, is what his colleagues call a "PR natural." He is always singing the praises of his agency and extolling the value of public relations. He is also always on the look-out for new business.

When Grosbeck's fifth college reunion rolls around, he is eager not only to see old acquaintances, but also to sniff out potential clients for the agency. Knowing his inclinations, Grosbeck's date makes him promise not to embarrass her with a hard sell to his former classmates. He assures her that this is not his style.

During the reunion, Grosbeck mixes casually, talking about his work and asking questions about what others are doing. He enters into a long conversation with Robert Shecker, whom he had known casually during his sophomore year (they had once crammed for a history exam together). Shecker is assistant manager of Mills Motors in Maddon Township, a wealthy suburb about ten miles outside of Cleveland. Mills is a dealership devoted exclusively to the Ali, a new high-performance automobile made in Italy with a sticker price of $18,000. Unfortunately, Shecker explains, despite the car's many unique features, business is not what it should be owing to stiff competition from the Audi and Volvo dealerships in the area.

After suggesting that the dealership may have a public relations problem, Grosbeck moves on to discuss other subjects with Shecker. But the new business potential implicit in Shecker's dilemma has not been lost on him.

When Grosbeck returns to the office the next week, he drafts the following short note to Shecker:

Dear Bob,

It was great seeing you at the reunion last week and getting the chance to reminisce about old Perlmutter's history seminar. Did we really eat three pepperoni pizzas the night we crammed for his midterm? Ah, to be young again!

I've been thinking over our conversation about the problems your dealership is having. As I mentioned, it sounds to me as though you have a public relations problem, one which Grissat and Company might be able to help you with. We've done a lot of work for small businesses suffering from stiff competition, and our track record is excellent. Public relations has numerous advantages over advertising, and it can also be a valuable supplement *to* advertising. In the case of the Ali, it definitely sounds as though you need something more than a conventional advertising campaign.

I'd like to give you a call next week to discuss some public relations activities the dealership might want to pursue. Perhaps you could suggest whom I should speak to at Mills about developing a possible program.

Again, great seeing you, and regards to Karen.

Yours,

Marty

When Grosbeck calls Shecker the next week, his friend is enthusiastic. He suggests that Grosbeck write the owner of the dealership, Kevin Small, and propose a meeting. Before proceeding to write the proposal letter to Small, however, Grosbeck first writes an internal memo to his supervisor:

Developing New Business 257

> To: Joel Snyder
> From: Martin Grosbeck *MG*
> Subject: New Business Prospect
> Date: May 25, 198_
>
> At my recent college reunion, I met an old college acquaintance who is now employed as assistant manager of Mills Motors, a foreign car dealership in Maddon Township. (They sell the new Italian sportscar—the Ali; retail: $18,000.) He told me that the dealership hasn't been able to attract its target public of young professionals, who seem to be buying Volvos and Audis instead.
>
> I suggested that he might need PR assistance, and he has encouraged me to write the owner of the dealership, Kevin Small. With your go-ahead, I'd like to draft a proposal letter to Small.
>
> I'll stop by your office this afternoon to discuss this before proceeding further.

Grosbeck is judicious in informing his supervisor before formally pitching a new client. In this case Snyder tells Grosbeck to go ahead and write a proposal letter, which he will review before mailing.

Grosbeck prepares to write the letter by doing some research on the Ali. He finds a number of profile articles on the car and its typical owner which appeared in the business sections of newspapers and magazines over the past few years. He copies the most recent article, which appeared in *Business Week* two months ago, for possible inclusion with his proposal letter. The letter he presents to his supervisor reads as follows:

> Dear Mr. Small,
>
> Robert Shecker suggested I write you about our agency and what it might be able to do for your dealership. Grissat and Company has been practicing public relations in the Cleveland area for over 25 years and has an excellent track record promoting small businesses.
> The Ali is one of the best cars on the market and it should appeal to an "upscale" audience (see attached *Business Week* article). Yet many of the young professionals in your community who should be buying Alis seem to be driving Volvos and Audis instead.
> We can help you remedy this situation by improving your visibility within the local community—and we can do so with more credibility and less expense than it takes to launch an advertising campaign. We can, for example,

do a direct mailing to targeted professionals in the area and prepare a checklist of reasons why the Ali would best serve their professional and personal needs. We can also develop feature ideas on the car and on your dealership which would be of interest to the local media.

I've enclosed an agency brochure and a staff profile to give you an idea of the kind of work we do and the talent we have available.

It would be our pleasure to meet with you to discuss our ideas and the possibility of tailoring a full-scale program to your business. I'll give you a call in a few days to see whether we can arrange a meeting at your convenience. Please feel free to get in touch with me at 555-7000 if you'd like to discuss this proposal sooner.

Sincerely,

Martin Grosbeck

Martin Grosbeck
Account Executive

A few days after mailing the letter, Grosbeck receives an apologetic call from Small explaining his situation. "I'm already in hock to the bank for the renovation I did on the dealership last year," Small says. "Sales have been so bad this year that I've barely been able to pay the interest on the loan. I know I could use some good public relations right now, but I simply can't pay for it. Sorry."

Never one to give up easily, Grosbeck sits in his office pondering what to do next. Finally, he approaches his supervisor with an idea. Why not pitch Ali's U.S. headquarters in New York City and propose a program which could be adapted by individual dealerships like Small's throughout the U.S.? The public relations would help the individual dealers, but it would also increase visibility for Ali in general and help overall sales. Snyder likes the idea and takes it to his superior, Michael Flynn, an agency vice president. Flynn suggests that Grosbeck write a proposal letter to Ali headquarters for Flynn's signature.

Grosbeck drafts the following letter to Ali/USA's president George Flavio:

Dear Mr. Flavio,

We're contacting you as the result of a recent discussion with Kevin Small, owner of Mills Motors, an Ali dealership in our area which has been having problems holding up against the area competition (Volvos and Audis). We sense that this dealership's problems are not unique and may be shared by others. The young professionals who would be most attracted to your cars simply aren't aware of their advantages.

We feel that what's needed is a public relations program for Ali that would develop visibility and credibility for the car's image. This program could be adapted by Ali dealerships like Mr. Small's to help them publicize the car's high performance and dependability as well as the service quality of their individual dealership. Such a program would allow you to localize your promotional efforts for the car and build a solid reputation in targeted professional communities throughout the United States.

Grissat and Company has been doing public relations for large and small organizations for 25 years. We would be able to develop a generic public relations program which could be tailored by individual dealerships to suit their needs. We could help develop promotional materials, mailing lists for direct mailings, and feature ideas which could be the basis for local feature stories. We could also develop a series of special event options which dealerships could either implement themselves or which we could help them implement.

We've enclosed an agency brochure and a staff profile to give you an idea of the kind of work we do and the talent we have available.

It would be our pleasure to meet with you to discuss these ideas in more detail. I'll give you a call in a week or so to see whether we can arrange a meeting at your convenience.

                        Sincerely,

                        Michael Flynn

                        Michael Flynn
                        Vice President

The letter receives a favorable response from Ali/USA, and the account team of Flynn, Snyder, and Grosbeck are invited to meet with some of Ali's top officials in New York City. After discussing their ideas in more detail, the company agrees to a one-year fee of $50,000 (excluding out-of-pocket expenses) and asks the agency to draw up a generic program which can be adapted by individual dealerships like Small's. Once the client has signed the contract, Grosbeck collects his finder's fee from the agency of $5,000.

DEVELOPING A SHOTGUN PROSPECT

Word processing capabilities have done wonders for the shotgun approach to new business prospecting since this technique makes it possible to personalize what would otherwise be form letters. Not only can the address and salutation be tailored to the individual prospect, but also whole sentences and paragraphs can be added or subtracted to further personalize letters.

Jay Heller, an account executive at a small public relations agency in Providence, Rhode Island, also happens to have an advanced degree in engineering. He is convinced that this would make him a valuable resource to a client in the engineering field. Unfortunately, his agency has no engineering clients. Moreover, since Heller has only recently moved from Chicago to join the agency, he has no personal contacts with engineering firms in Rhode Island. Sitting down with his supervisor, Susan Caulkins (an agency vice president), he discusses the possibility of doing a mass mailing to engineering firms in the state. Caulkins likes the idea. She assigns a junior account executive the task of compiling a list of small engineering firms in Rhode Island, and asks Heller to compose a standardized pitch letter (for her signature) to send to the 50 firms on the list.

Heller prepares the following form letter for Caulkins. (Note that he indicates where information tailored to individual prospects should be inserted.)

Wiley Agency
Morris Avenue
Providence, RI 02906
September 3, 198_

(1)
_____
_____
_____

Dear ___(2)___ :

As a growing engineering firm, you probably need to start thinking, if you haven't already, about public relations assistance. There is considerable competition among engineering firms in the ___(3)___ area, and there are a number of publics which you need to reach which you may not be reaching. You can communicate with these audiences through direct mail and through such publications as ___(4)___ .

Wiley Agency has had extensive experience with industrial clients. It also has a trained engineer on staff who is an experienced PR specialist. He will be able to help translate technical concepts into readable, interesting press and consumer material. He will also get the facts right!

> We'd like to give you a call in a week or so to discuss some specific promotional ideas and introduce you to our account team.
>
> Sincerely,
>
> *Susan Caulkins*
>
> Susan Caulkins
> Vice President

Heller also prepares a list that contains the pieces of information that need to be inserted by the word processor for each letter. These include the following: (1) the prospect's name, title, and address; (2) Mr. or Ms. and the last name of the prospect for the salutation; (3) the city in which the prospect is located; and (4) the names of two or three publications geared to the particular engineering specialty of the prospect firm.

Caulkins signs the letter, but she asks Heller to do the follow-up. A week later Heller proceeds to call all 50 companies, introducing himself and requesting a date for a meeting. Of the 50 firms, ten of them agree to meet with him.

Heller and his supervisor study the promotional materials and annual reports of these companies, meet with them to discuss program ideas, and vigorously follow-up on three firms which look most promising. When two of the firms express genuine interest, Heller and Caulkins evaluate the budget commitment that each is willing to make, as well as their respective public relations needs. (Conflict of interest would prevent the agency from accepting both accounts.) They finally agree to handle one of the two firms.

Heller is congratulated for a job well done. (It's rare that an agency gets more than one bite from shotgun prospecting.) Unfortunately, he can only collect the finder's fee for the one client that the agency decides to handle.

EXERCISES

Test Your Judgment

If you heard about the following events and were interested in new business prospects for your agency, what approach (rifle shot, shotgun, or both) would you probably use in each case?

1 A party given by a former college roommate.
2 A trade fair for the computer industry.

3   A charity benefit for high society.

4   A convention for small business owners.

5   A career day at a neighborhood high school.

PR Workshop

Make a list of qualities that you think make a good salesperson, and check off those qualities which you think you possess. As a class, create a composite list of qualities, then go down the list discussing how (or if) a given trait can be cultivated.

PR Case Studies

1   You are an account executive at a public relations agency located in a prosperous suburban town. At least once a week, you eat lunch at a small Italian restaurant several miles from the agency, which your aunt, an aficionada of Italian food, introduced you to. The food is excellent but you notice that the dining room is always practically empty. The owner tells you that this is because the restaurant is out of the way of the main road. He says that his dinner business is good but that the lunchtime crowd from the nearby office park either don't know the restaurant exists or don't think they will be served quickly enough (you find the service to be speedy and efficient).

Write a memo to your supervisor, Ruth Carlyle, about this prospective client. Then write a proposal letter to the restaurant owner, Mario Stella, concerning the need for public relations. Although your agency has never done PR work for a restaurant, it has promoted a supermarket, a clothing store, and a number of other small, consumer-oriented businesses.

2   You were hired to do public relations for a department store, and your present budget limits you to preparing press releases on promotions and special sales. You now feel it's time to develop a special events program for the store and you want to solicit a larger budget for this purpose.

Write a proposal memo to the store manager in which you ask for a $30,000 budget increase in order to develop a special events program. Include the same components in your memo as you would in an agency proposal letter for new business.

3   You are a public relations executive at a large agency (100 executives) which wants to develop a new-business department and asks you to head it. Write a memo to your supervisor in which you enumerate the resources (equipment and personnel) needed and describe how you would organize the department.

4   You have been asked by your agency to help run a student internship program. As your first activity, you will be making a tour of universities to

introduce your agency to undergraduate college students. Write a checklist of the points you would want to include in your presentation.

NOTES

1. George N. Kahn and Abraham Shuchman, "Specialize Your Salesmen!" *Salesmanship and Sales Force Management*, ed. Edward C. Bursk and G. Scott Hutchinson (Cambridge, Mass.: Harvard University Press, 1971), pp. 26–34.

2. Jay Diamond and Gerald Pintel, *Successful Selling* (Reston, Va.: Reston Publishing Co., a Prentice-Hall Co., 1982), p. 130.

10
Entering the Public Relations Field

In Chapter 9 we explained that new business prospecting is a form of selling and that the ability to be persuasive about your agency and its services is the key to success in this area. In this chapter we will focus on the art of selling again; here, however, we are concerned not with the selling of agency services, but with the selling of your own services to a prospective employer. Doing this well is important for obvious practical reasons—you want to land a good job. But it also provides you with an opportunity to plan and implement a public relations program on your own behalf. This means that you will be drawing upon many of the same skills that will be valuable to you once you begin working in the PR field.

COURSEWORK

Ten years ago most practitioners entered the public relations field with a humanities or journalism background and with little or no specialized training in public relations. But as the field of public relations has matured, so has public relations education. A solid liberal education remains a prerequisite, but more rigorous professional standards and stiffer competition for entry-level positions have made specialized training on the college level increasingly helpful to those seeking to break into the field.[1]

In 1975 the Commission on Public Relations Education issued its report, *A Design for Public Relations Education*.[2] This was the first major study to evaluate the theoretical and practical skills needed to effectively engage in public relations practice. The report stipulates that PR education on the undergraduate level should take the form of three concentric circles:

The smallest, central circle would enclose those subjects specifically concerned with public relations practice. The second circle, somewhat larger, would encompass related subjects in the general field of communications. The third and largest circle would represent the general liberal arts and humanities background expected of all students.

The report then goes on to list the specific courses which should be included within each of the concentric circles of study. The largest circle of general education should include courses in English (writing and literature), the social sciences, the humanities, the natural sciences, foreign language or area studies, statistics, and organizational structure and behavior. Within the circle of communications studies, coursework should include core courses in the theory and process of communication, writing for the mass media, copy editing, and graphics of communication. Finally, the public relations core curriculum should include a general introduction to public relations, a course in publicity media and campaigns, public relations case problems, and an internship in which students engage in actual work in the field.

As defined by the Commission, this curriculum, supplemented by electives in an area of concentration, would fulfill the requirements of an undergraduate degree in public relations. Admittedly, this is not an option available to everyone; many schools do not offer the range of specified courses. Yet, more and more schools are increasing their offerings in communications and are including among these at least one introductory course in public relations.

If you are interested in a public relations career and your university does not offer a formal public relations major, explore the course offerings which are available and try to approximate the requirements set forth in the Commission report. Don't assume that communications and public relations courses aren't offered simply because they don't fall neatly within a communications department. Many of these courses may be scattered in departments of business, journalism, social sciences, and humanities. To supplement your coursework, read periodicals devoted to the public relations field (*Public Relations Journal, Public Relations Review,* and *Public Relations Quarterly*), consult the newsletters in the field (*Jack O'Dwyer's PR Newsletter, PR Reporter* and *PR News*), and explore the possibility of joining the nearest university chapter of the Public Relations Student Society of America (PRSSA).

THE JOB HUNT

Focusing a Search

Before embarking on a job search, it's wise to do a thorough evaluation of the kind of public relations work you would be happiest doing and would do best. Public relations is such a diversified field that this kind of evaluation is often difficult. But since a rifle shot approach is preferable to a shotgun approach when it comes to job-hunting, the extra effort involved in focusing your search is certainly worthwhile. You can begin by making some general discriminations—deciding whether you'd prefer agency or in-house PR, and whether you'd rather be involved with a profit or nonprofit organization.

Work in a public relations agency offers the advantages of variety and, some say, a more exciting atmosphere. Yet critics of agency PR complain that the pace can be too brisk—you are often split among multiple clients and given little opportunity to get to know an individual client well. In an agency, moreover, you may be assigned to a client whom you don't especially like or find worth promoting.

In-house public relations, on the other hand, allows you to focus your energy on a single client whom you can get to know well. But in-house PR practitioners will sometimes complain that they fall into a rut and find it difficult to cut through organizational bureaucracy to get new ideas implemented.

The distinction between profit and nonprofit public relations is also worth considering. Some people are clearly nonprofit types: They are drawn to organizations which are involved in making educational, artistic, and other kinds of social contributions. Such people enjoy PR only when it means promoting a cause or service which they personally believe in strongly.

Nonprofit public relations generally pays less than profit-making PR and can be frustrating in that budget allotments may be limited (depending, for example, upon the success of the year's fund-raising efforts). In addition, you may have to rely on volunteers for the majority of support staff. A switch from the nonprofit area into agency or corporate public relations also tends to be more difficult than a switch in the other direction. However, nonprofit experience can sometimes provide practitioners with more responsibility sooner and can help hone specialized knowledge and skills which may eventually prove valuable in the private sector.

If you're interested in nonprofit PR, you may want to zero in on a special interest area, such as health care or the arts, as the focus for your job search. Public relations for educational institutions is also a growing specialization. Volunteering to work several hours a week in your university's public relations or development (fund-raising) office is a good way to pick up some useful nonprofit PR experience while you're still in school.

Research

Once you have established your area of interest and determined a focus for your job search, you will need to research specific organizations. The major source of information on public relations agencies and in-house departments are the O'Dwyer directories. They consist of three volumes: *O'Dwyer Directory of Public Relations Executives*, *O'Dwyer Directory of Public Relations*

Firms, and *O'Dwyer Directory of Corporate Communications* (supplying the names of in-house departments and personnel). The *O'Dwyer Directory of Public Relations Firms* is an especially useful resource. For each agency listed (and there are listings for approximately 1,400 firms throughout the U.S.), the directory gives addresses, number of employees, net income, client lists, areas of specialization, and principal officers. Listings are in alphabetical order with indexes for locating firms according to specialty, geographic location, and client. Being familiar with an agency's client list and/or specialization makes it possible to be more precise in a cover letter or interview about how you could make a contribution to the firm.

In addition to O'Dwyer's, you might also want to consult these standard business directories: *Standard and Poor's Register of Corporations, Directors, and Executives; Thomas' Register of American Manufacturers;* and the *Fortune Double 500 Directory*, as well as these standard nonprofit directories: the *Encyclopedia of Associations;* the *Foundation Directory;* and the *National Trade and Professional Associations Directory.*

Another helpful source of information on individuals in the public relations field is the *Public Relations Journal/Register* issue put out annually by the Public Relations Society of America, which lists all PRSA members alphabetically, as well as by geographical location and organizational affiliation.

Don't forget to check newspapers for "help wanted" advertisements, but don't be discouraged if many of your responses to ads go unanswered (some of these ads aren't authentic and may have been placed after the job was filled in order to appear to comply with equal opportunity employment guidelines). Also, before responding to an ad, be sure it has been placed by the organization itself rather than by a placement agency. Placement agencies tend to use promising job descriptions as bait to get you to consult them, but can rarely do much to help you get your first job unless you're looking for secretarial or low-level administrative work. However, when you're ready for a second or third job, PR-oriented placement agencies or executive recruiters (called *headhunters*) are worth consulting. If you turn out to be a superstar, they may even call you and suggest new job possibilities.

In the course of your job search, talk to your friends and acquaintances about whom they know. If you can, join organizations and clubs where you would be likely to meet people with contacts in the PR field. This is *networking*—cultivating a network of contacts who can assist you (and whom you can assist in turn, not only during an initial job hunt but throughout your career). The Public Relations Student Society of America, which operates on over 100 college campuses, is a good place to start developing contacts. You may also want to inquire about local chapters of the International Association of Business Communicators (IABC) and Women in Communications—two organizations with a PR orientation which often sponsor workshops and special programs. Finally, check with the local chapter of PRSA about whether they provide any student-oriented services or activities.

Don't neglect to consult your college placement office in the course of your job search. Many colleges and universities have files on organizations in your field and may help arrange interviews for you with recruiters from these organizations. Some schools also post job openings on bulletin boards. A sympathetic placement officer can be a valuable asset if he or she comes to believe in your abilities and is willing to give you a tip on a job or offer a character reference to a recruiter.

Remember that the entry-level position is the hardest position to land in public relations, and it requires patience and perserverance to get the job you want. Sometimes, in order to break into the field, it may be necessary to lower your expectations. Many organizations, for example, hire entry-level people as secretaries or administrative assistants, then promote quickly when an individual exhibits talent and industry. But be sure to inquire about the promotional policy of an organization before accepting such a position, and find out how long it generally takes to be considered for promotion. Six months of typing may be endurable, but two years may not be worth the investment.

Letters and Résumés

In seeking a job, it's usually a good idea to send your inquiries directly to the top. For an agency position, address your letter to a senior or executive vice president, unless the agency is small enough to make an approach to the president seem feasible. In the case of a nonprofit organization, write to the director/president or assistant director. In a corporation, write to a president, executive vice president, or senior vice president, again according to the corporation's size. Always try to bypass the personnel department if you can, but remember that there's always a good chance your letter will be passed routinely on to that department.

Your personal résumé and cover letter function like a pitch letter on your own behalf. They create the crucial first impression which determines whether or not you are seriously considered for the position, and they set the tone for all subsequent dealings with your potential employer. Here are some guidelines for the effective preparation of this initial pitch:

1 Know the nature of the organization you are writing to (what it does, its size, its general reputation within its field).
2 Know at least one specific thing you can do (talent, skill, interest) which meshes well with the organization's overall goals or the nature of its business.
3 Have a clear sense of the kind of job you could do in the organization.
4 Have a clear sense of your qualifications to perform that job.

Your cover letter should be short—no more than one page in length—and should be written in a style which is neither stilted nor overly casual in tone. Begin by explaining how you heard about the position (if you know there is one) or about the organization (if you are applying for a job without knowing whether a position is available). Then briefly give one or two reasons why you think you could fill the position or make a contribution to the organization. Finally, describe the kind of job you could perform. End the letter by stating your intention to phone in a week to see whether a meeting might be arranged.

The accompanying résumé should serve as back-up for the claims made in the letter. Unless you have real reason to take up two pages, a one-page résumé is easier for the reader to take in and shows that you know the art of selection and condensation. Résumé form may vary, but a standard, easy-to-read presentation which tends to work well for novice job-hunters is the following:

Name　　　　　　　　　　**Optional Data**
Address　　　　　　　　　(Height, Weight,
Phone　　　　　　　　　　Marital Status)

Objective: a position as . . .
(This one-sentence career objective should be as specific as possible and may have to be altered slightly for each position to which you apply. For example, in applying for a job at a large PR agency with a broadcast department, you might compose the following objective: *a position as an account executive with a large PR agency where I could contribute through my writing and verbal skills and my technical knowledge of video and film production*)

Education: College or University, City, State—Degree (with honors, if any)
　　　　　　　Area of Concentration (include minor if relevant)

　　　　　　　High School, City, State

Work Experience: (Usually start with your most recent job; however, if you've held a position that has special relevance to the job you want, you may want to highlight this by presenting it first. Give a one- or two-sentence description of each job which relates to the position you are applying for, devoting more space to those jobs which are most relevant.)

Honors and Awards: (Briefly explain the nature of an honor or award if this is not self-explanatory. Any offices held at school or in clubs and organizations can also be included here.)

Memberships: (list)

> **References:** (It adds little and takes up too much room to list the names and addresses of references on the résumé. Simply note that "References are available upon request," or give the address of the college placement office at which they are filed. If one of your references is a notable PR practitioner, you may want to mention his or her name and affiliation in your cover letter.)

In order to assess the PR value of your past work experience, analyze each job you've held in terms of the tasks you were required to perform and the kinds of skills these tasks helped you cultivate. The general skills most important in public relations include the ability to *write, edit, research, plan, exercise critical judgment, interact well with people,* and *organize and manage resources.* Specific skills in such areas as computers, broadcast journalism and production, graphics, foreign languages and cultures, financial affairs, the arts, and fashion can also be valuable if you are applying for a position with a firm which is geared to a particular industry or which has a specialized division in one of these areas.

If you are serious about your job search, you should be willing to prepare a résumé tailored to each position you apply for by altering the "objective" and perhaps changing the order or emphasis of your job descriptions under "work experience."

The Interview

"Why are you interested in public relations?"

"Why are you interested in our organization?"

"What PR experience have you had?"

"Why do you think you would be successful in this job?"

These are probably the most popular questions asked of job-hunters in the public relations field. Be prepared for them, but don't be surprised if you're asked more unusual questions as well, such as "What was the last book you read?" "What newspapers and magazines do you like to read?" "Which local newscaster do you like best and why?" Also be prepared to ask questions of your own.

The personal interview, so important in any job search, is especially crucial in public relations where the ability to express oneself well and interact well with others is highly valued. The best way to approach an interview is to treat it as a conversation in which you take an active role. The passive interviewee who answers all questions but asks none is not likely to land many PR jobs.

To prepare for the interview, review your notes on the organization and the particular job. Then draw up a list of questions relating to both. The best questions build on a knowledge base: the more you know about the job you are applying for, the more sophisticated your questions will be. Thus, asking what clients an agency handles is less impressive to an interviewer than asking what kind of work the agency does for its Japanese clients.

You can also prepare for the interview by writing down a list of points you'd like to make about your own experience, goals, and interests. Having these points in mind before the interview will help you remember to work them into the course of discussion. Don't forget that in answering one question it's possible to lead into another point. Graceful transitions of your own making give you control over the direction of the interview. This is the same skill that practitioners try to teach when preparing their clients for Q&A sessions.

Finally, be conscious of the style and personality of the interviewer and adjust yourself to him or her. This doesn't mean that you should distort your own personality or lie about your interests and abilities. Just be sensitive to the other person and try to establish a rapport. Direct eye contact, a confident handshake, and a good sense of humor will almost always get you off on the right foot. At some point in the interview it's perfectly appropriate, and can help break the ice, to ask the interviewer to tell you about his or her job or to describe an average working day.

INTERNSHIPS

Public relations internships are short-term (usually lasting the summer or a semester) employment which offer minimal or no pay but are invaluable in providing on-the-job training and a first-hand look at how a particular organization operates. At many schools, particularly those with PR majors, internships are built into the program—students receive college credit and advisors make it their business to place students in internships which fit in well with their coursework and interests. At other schools, students who want to do internships must find their own and must work during the summer or take a semester without credit in order to do so. Yet even when the internship carries no credit and no salary, more and more students are realizing the advantages to having one or more such experiences during their college career. Given the stiff competition for jobs after college, they know that the "real world" experience which internships provide can place them at an advantage. They also know that internships offer a chance to get references from working PR practitioners for their subsequent job search. Many students hope that they will perform so impressively at their internships that these will become full-time jobs following graduation.

Although the aspiring intern has the advantage over the typical job-hunter of being willing to work for no pay, organizations rarely want to take on new bodies—even at no salary—unless these bodies can make a solid contribution. In seeking an internship, therefore, you need to engage in much of the same kind of background research and selling that you do in seeking a regular job. Some organizations have formal internship programs with application procedures which are extremely rigorous and competitive. Others may never have considered using interns and need to be persuaded. In seeking a position from an organization that has never hired an intern before, it helps to convince potential employers that they will be making a contribution to your education. Implicit in making this contribution, of course, are the PR possibilities attached to being a good corporate citizen.

Some organizations with formal internship programs will allow students to take on a limited amount of responsibility in order to get a sense of what working in the organization is really like. In small or short-staffed organizations, interns may actually find themselves taking on an abundance of challenging work very quickly. More commonly, however, internships do not provide much in the way of responsibility. As an intern, you are an unproven quantity and most employers won't want to run the risk of giving you important assignments. You may have to reconcile yourself to low-level "gofer" tasks and consider photocopying, running errands, or staffing a reception desk as an opportunity for simply observing the life of the organization. By keeping your eyes and ears open, you can learn about the quality of work being done, the workload, the rapport among employees, the organizational structure, and the opportunities for advancement—salient information which can help you evaluate other organizations when it comes time for you to look for a full-time job.

ON THE JOB

Once you land the job you've been searching for, you should know what to expect. Since one of the great advantages of public relations work is the variety of tasks it encompasses, you are not likely to be stuck in a boring routine. Nonetheless, like any career, PR has its own initiation rites. Those who have spent their college years learning how to analyze and deal with all aspects of a public relations problem may be disappointed to discover that they are not immediately asked to handle an account, write a program, meet with a client, or even pitch a story.

Although the level of responsibility generally assigned to a novice can vary depending upon the size and nature of the organization, most first jobs involve a variety of tasks but a limited level of responsibility. The level of responsibility usually increases with each year of practice as follows:

First Year—Logistical and Organizational

Compiling and checking press lists.

Helping to set up and confirm arrangements for PR events.

Researching background facts and figures for a supervisor.

Second Year—Routine Implementation

Continuation of above responsibilities.
Telephone call-backs.
Press releases.

Third Year—Creative Implementation

Continuation of above responsibilities.
Telephone pitches.
Some client contact (at an agency).
Creative sessions with supervisor in the development of programs and new implementation ideas.
Fact sheets/backgrounders, speeches, annual reports, other writing.

Fourth-Fifth Year and up—Supervisory

Continuation of above responsibilities.
Supervisory responsibilities—management of resources and staff.
Client counseling.

Note that even among more senior practitioners, the basic logistical and organizational responsibilities remain an ongoing part of their jobs. This is especially true at small agencies where one person may be assigned to an account and expected to do everything for that client, from compiling a press list to composing a speech for the chief executive. In larger organizations and agencies, senior practitioners will be more likely to have junior practitioners performing the basic tasks for them. But even here, it is not uncommon to find a senior executive making last-minute media calls or typing the final copy of a press release in order to meet a deadline.

EXERCISES

Test Your Judgment

1 List the PR-related skills which are probably utilized in each of the following jobs. Draw from the list of general skills given in this chapter (writing, editing, researching, planning, exercising critical judgment, interacting well with people, and organizing and managing resources). Also, evaluate the jobs for other, more specialized skills that you feel might have value in PR practice. In each case give specific examples of the tasks involved which illustrate the use of these skills.
a   Camp counselor
b   Editor of school newspaper

c   Waitress
d   Campus activities director
e   President of student body
f   Manager of rock band
g   Administrative assistant in journalism department

2   Bill Cantor, a management consultant and executive recruiter for the public relations field, lists ten "winning" personality traits which he feels are especially valued in PR.[3] These are (1) good response to tension; (2) individual initiative; (3) curiosity and learning; (4) energy drive, and ambition; (5) objective thinking; (6) flexible attitude; (7) service to others; (8) friendliness; (9) versatility; and (10) lack of self-consciousness. Evaluate yourself in relation to each of these traits, giving yourself a score from 1 to 10 (with 10 being the highest). After you've finished the evaluation, see if you can discern a pattern to your scores. Write a brief assessment (one to two paragraphs) in which you summarize your strengths (scores above 7) and weaknesses (scores below 6); correlate them with the general skills (listed in the first exercise above) in which you feel you are strongest; and describe the kind of PR job that you think would draw on your personality and skills (think in terms of agency vs. in-house, profit vs. nonprofit, as well as size, pace, specialization, working hours, and so on).

PR Workshop

Critique the following cover letter and résumé for problems of presentation, style, organization, and content. Discuss what could be omitted and what could be added to make this a more effective pitch:

---

18 Scrabble Road
Willington, NJ 08033
April 8, 198-

John Winston
The Fulton Agency
Philadelphia, PA 19104

Dear Mr. Winston:

I am a college senior with a strong interest in going into the public relations field. Your firm came to my attention through a friend who worked as an intern for you several years ago.

I have taken coursework in mass communication and communications theory, as well as an introductory course in PR. My work as promotional director for the college play (for two years in a row) has given me first-hand experience in the field.

I think I could be an asset to your firm and hope it may be possible to meet with you to discuss my qualifications further.

Sincerely,

Sara Feld

Sara Feld

Sarah Feld
18 Scrabble Road
Willington, NJ 08033
tel: (609)555-0090

Objective: a challenging position in the public relations field.

Education:
    B.A. Springfield College,198- –198-
    Willington High School, 198- –19-

Work Experience:
198- part-time waitress and receptionist—The Village Inn, Philadelphia, Pa.

198- (summer) administrative assistant—Sawyers Company (accounting firm) read and filed correspondence, answered phones, helped write company newsletter.

198- and 8-- promotion director—*As You Like It* and *The Little Foxes* (Springfield College productions).

198- (summer) Stoneybrook Camp counselor, Stoneybrook, N.Y.

Honors and Awards:
    National English Honor Society, 198- –8-.
    Counselor of the Summer, Stoneybrook Camp,198-.

Interests: jogging, skiing, travel.

> References:
> Susan Jeffries, 4 Oak Drive, Moorestown, N.J.
> Professor Richard Stern, Dept. of Journalism, Springfield College, Philadephia, Pa.

PR Case Studies

1   Research three organizations for which you might be interested in working. Write a summary of the operations and orientation of each organization and, following each summary, attach a list of questions that you would want to ask if you were interviewing for a job with the organization.

2   Interview three people working in the PR area which interests you most (agency, in-house corporate, or in-house nonprofit) and who have started working in the field within the past two years. (To find suitable prospects, you might contact your university placement office or get the names of recent members of the nearest PRSSA chapter.) Ask each person to describe an average working day; then, compare the responses and write a composite narrative describing the average working day of a beginning PR practitioner within your area of interest.

3   Rewrite your résumé and compose a sample cover letter geared to your ideal public relations position. (This can be a real or a hypothetical position.) Have a member of the class play the role of the organization's representative and interview you for the job. After the interview, sit down with your classmate and critique the résumé, cover letter, and interview for strengths and weaknesses.

NOTES

1. See Celia Kuperszmid Lehrman, "Educational Pulse Taking," *Public Relations Journal*, 41 (April 1985), 16–17. Also in this issue, see E.W. Brody, Melvin L. Sharpe, James E. Grunig, and Raymond Simon, "Hard Thinking on Education," pp. 27–32.

2. *A Design for Public Relations Education: The Report of the Commission on Public Relations Education* (New York: Foundation for Public Relations Research and Education, Inc., 1975; reprinted 1981), p. 8.

3. Bill Cantor, "Winning Personality Traits," *Public Relations Journal*, 39 (June 1983), 30–31. Also in this issue, see Jo Procter, "The Path to the Top, pp. 25–29 and Cynthia Schwartzberg, "What Makes a Practitioner Tick?" pp. 32–33.

JOB SEARCH BIBLIOGRAPHY

GUIDES TO THE GENERAL JOB SEARCH

Bolles, Richard Nelson. *What Color Is Your Parachute?: A Practical Manual for Job-Hunters and Career Changers.* Berkeley, Calif.: Ten Speed Press, 1985. (The classic job-hunter's guide.)

Figler, Howard. *The Complete Job-Search Handbook.* New York: Holt, Rinehart and Winston, 1979. (Good on the mental process behind successful job-hunting: clarifying your values and skills, conceptualizing the right job.)

Stansfield, Richard. *The Best Ever How-to-Get-a-Job Book.* Radnor, Pa. Chilton Book Company, 1980. (Good on goal-oriented techniques for job-hunting: résumé-writing, getting-in-the-door strategies.)

GUIDES TO THE PR JOB SEARCH

Dow Chemical Company. *Finding That First Job in Public Relations*, 1985. (Order from: Recruiting Coordinator, Communications Dept., Dow Chemical USA, 2020 Willard H. Dow Center, Midland, MI 48674.)

Hellweg, Susan A., and Raymond L. Falcione. *Internships in the Communication Arts and Sciences.* Scottsdale, Ariz.: Gorsuch Scarisbrick, 1985.

Mainstream Access, Inc. *The Public Relations Job Finder.* Englewood Cliffs, N.J.: Prentice-Hall, 1981.

Monaghan, Patrick. *Public Relations Careers in Business and the Community.* New York: Fairchild Books and Visuals, 1972.

Public Relations Society of America. *Careers in Public Relations.* New York: Public Relations Society of America, 1983. (Free from PRSA.)

Rotman, Morris. *Opportunities in Public Relations.* Lincolnwood, Ill.; VGM Career Horizons, 1983.

PR Glossary

account team The group of public relations practitioners assigned to handle an account in a PR agency.

accreditation (APR) Involves passing a written and oral examination administered through PRSA; practitioners who have worked full-time in the field for five years are eligible.

ad hoc **committees** Groups which meet to resolve specific issues or complete projects.

advertorials Opinion essays which are "placed" like advertisements by purchasing space in print or broadcast media.

agenda A brief outline of major points to be covered at a meeting; usually distributed before the meeting to alert participants.

annual report The presentation and interpretation by an organization of its yearly financial data; must conform to Security and Exchange Commission (SEC) guidelines.

assignment editor The editor on a TV news program who is responsible for assigning a crew to cover a story.

backgrounder (position paper) Supplies a reasoned argument for a client's position on a particular issue; intended as a reference tool for the media and target publics.

brainstorming sessions Group meetings for the development of creative ideas.

brochure A short pamphlet containing information on an event, issue, product or personality, or providing general background on an organization.

by-line article A signed article; generally placed in a technical, business, or other special-interest publication.

caption The identifying material for a photo.

chief executive officer (CEO) Usually the top-ranking decision-maker in a corporation.

Code of Professional Standards The PRSA code which governs the ethical behavior of public relations practitioners; new PRSA members must sign a statement agreeing to abide by the Code.

communications audit (public relations opinion audit) A scientific study for internal planning purposes done with the concepts of PR in mind. The *identity audit* and the *social responsibility audit* are specialized versions of the communications audit.
contact The individual who can be reached for more information.
content analysis The evaluation of the kinds of messages being relayed in a given communications context.
controlled messages Messages which are relayed to a target audience without being subject to interpretation and change by the media.
crisis management An attempt to deal systematically with an unexpected or controversial situation.
dateline The city and date which directly precedes the first paragraph of a press release.
depth tools Communications tools which are especially well suited to dealing with issues.
fact sheet A compilation of facts relating to a given issue; intended as a reference tool for the media and target publics.
finder's fee The fee paid to an agency executive for bringing in new business (often 10 percent of the retainer fee paid by the client to the agency).
flip charts Oversized pads used in presentations to small audiences.
focus groups Groups assembled by researchers to discuss and evaluate ideas or products.
galleys Typeset printed copy.
headhunters Executive recruiters.
hook An idea or angle which draws the reader into a story.
house organs Internal newsletters.
identity An organization's essential personality; sometimes referred to as *image*.
in-house public relations A public relations function within an organization.
internships Part-time or summer jobs, often at low or no pay; available to students or recent graduates to provide experience in a given field.
issues management A systematic method of dealing with issues likely to have impact on a client.
issues statement The organizing idea of a backgrounder.
layout The specific ordering of pictures and text.
media directories Directories which give relevant information about newspapers, magazines, radio and TV stations, and which help the PR practitioner determine where and to whom to pitch a story.
media kit A folder of materials (press release, fact sheet, speech, photos, and so on) prepared for the media to provide appropriate background on a topic or an event.
media training Practice sessions provided to a client representative to help him or her become more adept at dealing with the media.
mini-docs (video news releases [VNRs] or news clips) One- to three-and-a-half-minute documentary-style film or audio clips produced on behalf of a client for placement on TV or radio.
mock-up (dummy) A preliminary version of a document which indicates where photos and printed material will go in the finished version.
news What's objectively new and important; the content of news releases and news conferences. See also *newsworthy*.
news conference A formal, "live" announcement of important information to the media.

newsroom A site designed to accommodate the media in the gathering of information and writing of stories.
newsworthy What's subjectively interesting; generally the content of feature releases, feature stories, and pitch letters. See also *news*.
omnibus questions (caravan questions) Questions added on to national surveys.
on-line data retrieval Computerized method of collecting information.
op-ed article An opinion essay named for its placement opposite the editorial page in a newspaper.
PERT diagram A diagram for determining how tasks relate to each other and can be performed most efficiently to arrive at a desired end within a specified time frame.
pitch The act of persuasively presenting a story idea to the media.
pitch letter A letter to the media suggesting an idea for a story.
press party A social, less news-oriented variation on a news conference.
press proof A sample of a document as it comes off the press.
public affairs Title often given to the public relations function in a corporation or government agency.
public information Title often given to the public relations function in a nonprofit organization.
publicity Coverage in the media which, when positive, assists a client in accomplishing its public relations objectives.
publicity outlets Media channels by which an organization can reach its target publics.
publicity tracking method Computerized computation and data retrieval system used to calculate an "index" of the visibility of a client in the media.
public relations message The organizing idea for a program; derived from the *PR objectives* and the *target audience*.
public relations program The rationale and practical map of proposed public relations operations to be performed on behalf of a client.
Public Relations Society of America (PRSA) The professional society for the field; its junior counterpart is the Public Relations Student Society of America (PRSSA).
public service announcements (PSAs) Messages prepared by nonprofit organizations to be aired by broadcasters free of charge.
qualitative information Information arrived at through in-depth analysis rather than statistical measurement.
quantitative information Information supplied by formal surveys and statistical measurement.
readability The clearness and coherence of a message.
release date The date at which a press release can be used by the media.
rifle shot prospect An organization which has been individually targeted as a potential new business prospect. See also *shotgun prospect*.
sample The group calculated to provide a reliable reading of the target audience.
shotgun prospect An organization which is part of an undifferentiated group of potential new business prospects. See also *rifle shot prospect*.
Silver Anvil Awards Presented by PRSA to the best annual public relations programs.
slugline The shortened form of the headline used on subsequent pages of a press release.
speakers bureau An in-house department that oversees the writing of speeches, the

selection of spokespeople, the development of speaking engagements and spokesperson tours, and the handling of publicity before and after presentation.

special event   An event planned by an organization to appeal to its target publics and to the media.

spin-off   An event, an activity, or a material which derives from a special event and prolongs its publicity value over time.

spokesperson   An individual who represents an organization by making speeches and answering questions on topics associated with that organization.

spokesperson tour   An itinerary of speaking engagements, often in different geographic locations, where a spokesperson for an organization addresses targeted publics on appropriate topics.

standing committees   Committees which exist on an ongoing basis to monitor issues or deal with persisting problems.

storyboards   A practical method of drafting slide shows (and other audiovisual presentations) by coordinating script and visuals on pasteboard.

talking heads   TV jargon for footage that contains people talking or making verbal presentations; that is, uninteresting visuals.

target publics   The segmented audience that an organization wishes to reach and whose opinions are crucial to its success.

task timetable   A chart for planning tasks relating to a public relations event or project.

teleconferencing   Satellite transmission of an event to different geographical locations.

tie-in   The linking of another, secondary activity to a main event.

two-way communication   Involves both outgoing (*active*) communication from the client organization and feedback (*receptive*) communication from the target publics.

uncontrolled messages   Messages which are subject to interpretation and change by the media.

visibility   Being in the public and the media eye; having a high "profile."

visibility study (public issues study)   Research sponsored by an organization in order to generate significant newsworthy information on a predetermined topic.

voice-over   When the individual narrating the film or tape is not seen on screen.

white paper   A report resulting from formal research on a controversial or socially significant topic.

Index

Account executives, 10
Accounts, 10
Account supervisors, 10
Active phases of public relations, 2
Ad hoc committees, 30
Adolph Coors Company, 86
Advertising:
    advocacy, 220–21
    vs. public relations, 4–5
    in public relations program:
        implementation with, 83
        model case study, 105
Advertising agencies, mergers with, 15–16
Advertorials, 220–21
Advocacy advertising, 220–21
Agencies, public relations, 10–12, 15–16
    -client communication, 43–45
    ethics and, 22–23
    new business prospecting by (*see* New business prospecting)
    work in, 266
Agenda, 31
American Express, 114
American Lawyer, The, 187
Annual reports, 188–90
    preparation of, 189–90, 197–203
    standard contents of, 189
Appendix section of public relations program, 85
Area sample, 56
Assignment editor, TV news, 126
Associated Press (AP), 120
Associated Press Stylebook and Libel Manual, 125
Asymmetric communications models, 5
Audience (*see* Target audience)
Automotive industry, 81

Backgrounders:
    defined, 217–18
    model case studies:

        identity campaign, 91
        issue presentation, 227–31
Background information for client use, 39–41
Bacon's Publicity Checkers, 57n, 115n
Barnum, P. T., 7
Bernays, Edward, 1, 6, 8–9, 19, 141, 163
Bias, interviews and, 53
Bidding situations, 254
Brainstorming, 29, 41–43
Broadcast releases, 125–26
    (*See also* Press releases)
Brochures, 185–88
    format of, 185, 187–88
    organizing idea for, 185
    model case studies:
        identity campaign, 91
        public information program, 97–98
    preparation of, 186–88
    types of, 185
BRS, 58n
Budget of public relations event, 155–56
Budget section of public relations program, 84
    model case studies:
        identity campaign, 94
        public information program, 100–101
By-line articles, 221

Captions, photograph, 124–25
Caravan questions, 59
Case histories, 99
Case studies (*see* Model case studies)
Charity events, 92
Chemical industry, 214
Chevron, U.S.A., 36–37
Clients, 10
    in active and receptive phases of public relations, 2

283

284 Index

Clients (*cont.*)
 background information for, 39–41
 communicating with, 43–45
Coca-Cola Company, 51
Code of Professional Standards for the Practice of Public Relations, 19–21, 24
Colleagues, creative input from, 41–43
College placement office, 268
Color brochures, 187
Commission on Public Relations Education, 264–65
Committee on Public Information, 8
Communication:
 models of, 5
 role of, in public relations program:
  defined, 82
  model case study, 103–4
 skills (*see* Internal communication)
Communications audits (*see* Opinion audits)
Computerized publicity tracking, 61–62
Computerized statistical evaluations, 17
Conclusion section of public relations program, 84
Confirmations, news conference, 167, 168, 172
Conflict of interest, 249*n*
Connecticut General Life Insurance Company, 53
Contact, of press release, 121
Content analysis, 61
Content of publicity, 113–14
Controlled message, 182–209
 advertising vs. public relations, 4–5
 in electronic media, 83, 190–97
  films, 93, 191–94
  overhead projection, 196, 197
  public service announcements (*see* Public service announcements)
  slide presentations, 195–96
 model case studies, 197–209
  annual report preparation, 197–203
  mini-doc preparation, 206–9
  public service announcement preparation, 203–4
 in print, 183–90
  annual reports, 188–90
  brochures (*see* Brochures)
  flip charts, 196, 197
  flyers, 183–84
  posters, 183–85
 reasons for, 182–83

Corporate social responsibility, 8, 213
Coursework, 264–65
Cover-up campaign, 81
Creative input from colleagues, 41–43
Credibility, news conferences and, 158–59
Crisis, dealing with the media in, 135–40
Crisis management, 136
Crystallizing Public Opinion (Bernays), 6
Cumulative time notation, 192–94
Data bases, 57–58
Data retrieval systems, on-line, 16
Dateline, of press release, 121
Depth tools, 215–42
 impersonal:
  backgrounders, 217–18
  fact sheets, 217
  model case studies, 227–42
   backgrounder, 227–31
   fact sheet, 227–30
   op-ed article, 231–35
   speech, 235–42
 personal, 218–27
  advocacy advertising, 220–21
  by-line articles, 221
  letters to the editor, 221–22
  op-ed articles, 218–20
  speeches (*see* Speeches)
Design for Public Relations Education, 264–65
DIALOG, 58*n*
Dichotomous questions, 52
Directories, 266–67
Documentaries, 192–94, 205–9
Dummy, 188
Dun and Bradstreet, 252
Education, 17–18, 264–65
Electronic mail, satellite transmission of, 17
Electronic media presentations, 83, 190–97
 defined, 83
 films 93, 191–94, 205–9
 overhead projection, 196, 197
 public service announcements (*see* Public service announcements)
 slide presentations, 195–96
 tapes, 191–94
Elite interviews, 52
Employee relations (*see* Internal communication)

Index **285**

Encyclopedia of Associations, 267
Ethics, 19–23
Evaluation, 59–62
  functions of, 59–60
  level of exposure measurement, 61–62
  level of reaction to exposure measurement, 62
  model case study, 72–75
  in public relations program formulation, 84
  research and, 59–60
Events (*see* Public relations events)
Executive summary, 82
Exposure, level of, 61–62
  level of reaction to, 62

Fact sheets:
  construction of, 217
  model case study, 227–30
Feature releases, 123–24
Federal Trade Commission (FTC), 23
Figgie Report, The, 70
Films, 93, 191–94, 205–8
Finder's fees, 250
Flesch Readability Formula, 61*n*
Flip charts, 196, 197
Flyers, 183–84
Focus groups, interviewing of, 53
Follow-up:
  in new business prospecting, 253–54
  news conference, 167, 170, 174
Fortune Double 500 Directory, 267
Foundation Directory, 267
Fund-raising events (*see* Charity events)

General background brochures, 185
Group interviews, 53
Group meetings, 30–31

"Hard" news vs. "soft" news, 114
Headhunters, 267
Headline, of press release, 121
"Help wanted" ads, 267
Hertz Rent A Car, 162
Historical overview of public relations, 6–10

Idea memos, 32–34
Identity audits, 54
Identity (image) campaign, 54, 85–94
Identity system, 183, 185
Implementation (*see* Public relations program implementation)
In-depth interviews, 51–53

Industrialization, 7–8
Informal surveys:
  method of, 51–52
  model case study, 62–67
Information, public relations as, 1–2
Informational memos, 32–33
In-house public relations, 12–14, 16
  internal communication and, 35–36
  work in, 266
Internal audience, public relations program for, 101–6
Internal communication, 28–45
  model case studies, 35–45
    agency-client communication, 43–45
    background information for client use, 39–41
    creative input from colleagues, 41–43
    in-house public relations function definition, 35–36
  program development, 36–39
  oral:
    group meetings, 30–31
    one-on-one meetings, 29–30
    telephone, 31
  written (*see* Inter-office memos)
Internal relations (*see* Internal communication)
International Association of Business Communicators (IABC), 267
International Business Machines (IBM), 86
Internships, 250–51, 271–76
Inter-office memos, 32–35
  model case studies, 35–45
  tips on writing, 34–35
  types of, 32–34
Interviews:
  in-depth, 51–53
  job, 270–71
  media, 90–91
Introduction (rationale) of public relations program:
  defined, 82
  model case studies:
    identity campaign, 89
    program for internal and external audience, 103
    public information program, 96–97
Invitations, news conference, 167, 168, 171
Issues, dealing with, 213–42
  identification of issues, 215–16

286 Index

Issues, dealing with (*cont.*)
  impersonal depth tools for, 217–18
    backgrounders, 217–18
    fact sheets, 217
  model case studies, 227–42
    backgrounders, 227–31
    fact sheets, 227–30
    op-ed articles, 231–35
    speeches, 235–42
  personal depth tools for, 218–27
    advocacy advertising, 220–21
    by-line articles, 221
    letters to the editor, 221–22
    op-ed articles, 218–20
    speeches (*see* Speeches)
Issues management 214–15

Jack O'Dwyer's Newsletter, 265
Job hunt, 265–71
Jockey International, Inc., 164
Junior account executive, 10

Lawyers, 23
Lee, Ivy Ledbetter, 8, 17
Legal council, role of, 23
Letters to the editor, 7, 221–22
Library searches, 57–58
Lobbying, 227–31

Macy's Department Store, 162
Mailings, news conference, 167, 168, 172
Mead Data Central, 58*n*
Media directories, 115–16
Media interest, engaging (*see* Publicity component of public relations)
Media interview campaign, 90–91
Media kits, news conference, 167, 170, 174
Media lists, news conference, 167, 168, 171
Mediating function of public relations, 2, 4
Megatrends, 57
Megatrends Newsletter, 57
Mergers with advertising agencies, 15–16
Message, 49–50, 79–82
  controlled (*see* Controlled message)
  evaluation of, 61–62
  in public relations program formulation, 88, 96, 97, 102
  revised, 59–60
  uncontrolled, 4
Methodology section of public relations program:
  defined, 82
  model case studies:
    identity campaign, 90
    program for internal and external audience, 104
Mini-docs, 192–94, 205–9
Mini-timetables, 152–54, 167–70
Mobil Corporation, 220–21
Mock-ups, 188
Modernization, 7–8
Multiple-choice questions, 52

National publicity, 91–92
National Trade and Professional Associations Directory, 267
Networking, 267
New business prospecting, 249–61
  follow-up, 253–54
  importance of, 249–50
  model case studies, 255–61
    rifle shot method, 255–59
    shotgun method, 259–61
  pre-proposal research, 252
  proposal letter, 252–53
  proposal meeting, 254–55
  rifle shot method, 251
  shotgun method, 251–52
News, defined, 114
News conferences, 157–61
  advantages of, 157
  decision to hold, 158–59
  model case studies:
    format development, 165–70
    tasks, 171–74
  pitching of, 158–59
  press parties, 160–61
  question and answer sessions, 160
Newsletters, 265
Newspapers, 57
News releases, 123, 124
  model case studies:
    crisis handling, 136–40
    routine development, 127–30
Newsworthiness, defined, 114
Newsworthy angle, finding, 130–35
Non-event handling, 141–44
Nonprofit organizations:
  public information program for, 95–101

Index **287**

public service announcements of (*see* Public service announcements)
special events sponsored by, 162–64
Nonprofit public relations, 266
Nonscientific vs. scientific research, 53–54
N. W. Ayer's Directories, 57n

Objectives, public relations, 49–51, 79–82
  in public relations program:
    defined, 82
    model case studies, 88–90, 95, 97, 102, 103
    revised, 59–60
O'Dwyer Directory of Corporate Communications, 267
O'Dwyer Directory of Public Relations Executives, 266
O'Dwyer Directory of Public Relations Firms, 15, 266–67
Office design, 29
Office of War Information (OWI), 9
Omnibus questions, 59
One-on-one meetings, 29–30
One-way asymmetric communication model, 5
One-way symmetric communication model, 5
On-line data retrieval systems, 16, 57–58
On-the-job levels of responsibility, 272–73
Op-ed articles, 218–20
  model case study, 231–35
  writing, 219–20
Open-ended questions, 52
Open office plan, 29
Opinion audits:
  method of, 53–56
  model case study, 67–69
Oral communication:
  group meetings, 30–31
  one-on-one meetings, 29–30
  telephone, 31
Organizational structure, 10–14
Overall exposure index, 61–62
Overall value index, 62
Overhead projection, 196–97

Periodicals, 265
Personal interviews, 52–53
Personal meetings, 29–30

Personnel section of public relations program, 84
PERT (Program Evaluation and Review Technique) diagrams, 152, 154, 166
Photographs, 187–88
Physical set-up, news conference, 167, 169, 172–73
Pitch:
  news conference, 159–60
  press release (*see* Press releases)
  special event, 163–64
  telephone, 116–19
Pitch letters, 126–27
  model case studies:
    newsworthy angle, 134–35
    non-event handling, 141–44
Political use of public relations, 6–7, 9
Position papers, 217
Posters, 183–85
PR Reporter, 265
Presentation, news conference, 167, 169, 173–74
President, 10–14
Press activity:
  defined, 83
  (*see also* News conferences; Press releases)
Press agentry vs. public relations, 4
Press agents, 7, 112–13
Press parties, 160–61
Press proof, 188
Press releases, 119–27
  form and style of, 120–23
  model case studies:
    crisis handling, 136–40
    identity campaign, 91
    newsworthy angle, 130–34
    routine development, 127–30
  types of, 123–24
  (*See also* Broadcast releases)
Print clipping services, 61
Print media presentations, 183–90
  annual reports (*see* Annual reports)
  brochures (*see* Brochures)
  flip charts, 196, 197
  flyers, 183–84
  posters, 183–85
Procter & Gamble Company, 157, 164–65
Product promotions, 164–65
Professional ethics, 19–23
Program (*see* Public relations program)
Promises to clients, 18–19

Promotions, 83
Proposal letters, 252–53
Proposal meetings, 254–55
Prospecting (*see* New business prospecting)
Publications, 57
　as sources of publicity outlets, 115–16
　types of, 83
Public information program, 95–101
Public issues studies (*see* Visibility studies)
Publicity by press agents, 4, 112–13
Publicity component of public relations, 112–44
　content of, 113–14
　context of, 115–16
　historical overview of, 6–7
　implementation methods, 116–27
　　broadcast release, 125–26
　　photographs and captions, 124–25
　　pitch letter, 126–27
　　press releases (*see* Press releases)
　　telephone pitch, 116–19
　model case studies, 127–44
　　crisis management, 135–40
　　newsworthy angle, finding, 130–35
　　non-event handling, 141–44
　　routine development handling, 127–30
　roots of, 112
Publicity outlets, 113, 115–16
Publicity tracking method, 17
Public opinion (*see* Issues, dealing with; Opinion audits)
Public relations:
　active and receptive phases of, 2
　vs. advertising, 4–5
　agency (*see* Agencies, public relations)
　communication models of, 5
　defined, 1–6
　education, 17–18, 264–65
　historical overview of, 6–10
　in-house (*see* In-house public relations)
　issues in practice of, 18–24
　legal counsel, role in, 23
　mergers with advertising agencies, 15–16
　new technology, application of, 16–17
　professional ethics and, 19–23
　promises to clients, 18–19
　vs. publicity by press agents, 4, 5

Public Relations Society of America
　Official Statement on, 2, 3
　research (*see* Research)
　specialization within the field, 14–15
　trends in, 14–15
　turning down assignments, 23–24
Public relations events, 151–79
　budgets for, 155–56
　location of, 151
　model case studies, 165–79
　　news conference development tasks, 171–74
　　news conference format, 165–70
　　special event selection, 175–77
　　special event tie-ins and spin-offs, 177–79
　PERT diagrams and, 152, 155
　reserving space for, 156
　risks in, 151
　steps in organizing, 156–57
　task timetable for, 152–54
　timing of, 151
　types of (*see* News conferences; Special events)
Public relations field, 264–73
　coursework, 264–65
　internships, 271–72
　job hunt, 265–71
　on-the-job levels of responsibility, 272–73
Public Relations Journal, 18, 265, 267
Public relations message (*see* Message)
Public Relations News, 265
Public relations objectives (*see* Objectives, public relations)
Public relations opinion audits (*see* Opinion audits)
Public relations practitioners, 2
Public relations program, 79–106
　defined, 79
　format of, 82–85
　groundwork for (*see* Research)
　implementation of (*see* Public relations program implementation)
　model case studies, 85–106
　　identity campaign, 85–94
　　for internal and external audience, 101–6
　　for nonprofit organizations, 95–101
Public relations program implementation:
　defined, 82–83
　model case studies:
　　identity campaign, 90–93

program for internal and external audience, 104–6
public information program, 97–99
Public relations program research and evaluation (*see* Evaluation; Research)
Public Relations Quarterly, 18, 265
Public Relations Review, 18, 265
Public Relations Society of America (PRSA):
  Board of Directors of, 21
  Code of Professional Standards for the Practice of Public Relations of, 19–21, 24
  formation of, 9
  Grievance Board of, 21
  Information Center of, 116n
  Official Statement on Public Relations of, 2, 3
  Silver Anvil Awards of, 250
Public Relations Student Society of America (PRSSA), 265, 267
Public service announcements, 98
  defined, 192
  preparation of, 192, 195, 203–4
Public Relations World Congress (1978), 4

Qualitative information, 52
Quantitative information, 52
Question and answer sessions, 160
Questionnaires:
  informal survey, 52, 62–65
  opinion audit, 56
Questions:
  omnibus, 59
  open-ended, 52
  responding to, following speeches, 225–26
Quota sample, 56
Quotations, press release, 122

Radio and TV Reports, 115n
Readability, evaluation of, 61n
Receptive phases of public relations, 2
References, press release, 122
Release date, 121
Research, 49–59
  evaluation and, 59–60
  as groundwork for public relations program, 49–59
  in-depth interviews, 51–53

informal surveys, 51–52
library searches, 57–58
message, 49–50, 79–82
objectives, 49–51
opinion audits, 53–56
publications, 53
target audience, 49–50, 79–82
visibility studies, 58–59
during job hunt, 266–68
model case studies, 62–72
  informal survey, 62–67
  opinion audits, 67–69
  visibility study, 69–72
on potential clients, 252
Resumes, 268–70
Rifle shot prospecting:
  defined, 251
  model case study, 255–59
Routine developments, publicizing, 127–30

Satellite transmission of electronic mail, 17
Scientific vs. nonscientific research, 53–54
Scoops, 157
Securities and Exchange Commission (SEC), 23, 188–89
Senior vice president, 10
Shotgun prospecting:
  defined, 251–52
  model case study, 259–61
Silver Anvil Awards, 250
Slide presentations, 195–96
Social reform, 6–7
Social responsibility, corporate, 8, 213
Social responsibility audits, 54
"Soft" news vs. "hard" news, 114
Speakers bureau, 99, 227
Speakers programs, 83
Special events, 83, 161–65
  forms of, 161–62
  model case studies:
    event selection, 175–77
    identity campaign, 92–93
    tie-in and spin-off development, 177–79
  pitching of, 163–64
  setting up newsrooms for, 164
  variations on, 164–65
Specialization, 14–15
Special-purpose brochures, 185
Speeches, 222–27
  delivery of, 225

Speeches (cont.)
  model case study, 235-42
  preparation of, 223-25
  responding to questions after, 225-26
  speakers bureaus, 227
  spokespersons, 226
Spin-offs from special events, 177, 179
Spokespersons, 226
Standard and Poor's Register of Corporations, Directories, and Executives, 267
Standing committees, 30
Statistical evaluations, computerized, 17
Storyboards, 195
Strategy (*see* Methodology section of public relations program)
Symmetric communication models, 5

Table-of-contents section of public relations program, 82-85
Tapes (*see* Films)
Target audience, 79-82
  in active and receptive phases of public relations, 2
  brochures and, 185
  communication models and, 5
  controlled and uncontrolled messages and, 4
  flyers and, 183
  internal and external, public relations program for, 101-6
  for opinion audits, 55-56
  in public relations program formulation, 88, 95, 102
  research and, 49-50
  revised, 59-60
  speeches and, 223
  telephone pitch and, 119
Task timetables (*see* Timetables)
Technology, application of, 16-17
Teleconferencing, 16, 165n
Telephone calls, news conference and, 167, 168, 172
Telephone communication, 31
Telephone pitch, 116-19
Thomas' Register of American Manufacturers, 267

Tie-ins to special events, 177-79
Timetables:
  annual report, 198-200
  public relations event, 152-54, 167
Timetable section of public relations program, 86, 100
Trade publications, 57
Transparencies, 197
Turning down assignments, 23-24
Twinings Tea Company, 161-62
Two-way asymmetric communication model, 5
Two-way symmetric communication model, 5

Uncontrolled messages, 4
Underwriting projects, 92-93
United Press International (UPI), 120
U.S. Publicity Directory, 115n
Universe, 55

Vice president, 10-13
Video annual reports, 190
Video news releases (*see* Mini-docs)
Video releases, satellite transmission of, 17
Videotape (*see* Films)
Virginia Slims American Women's Opinion Poll, 69-70
Visibility development (*see* Controlled messages; Publicity component of public relations; Public relations events)
Visibility studies:
  method of, 58-59
  model case studies, 69-72, 93
Voice-overs, 191

Welfare capitalism, 9
White papers, 59
Women in communications, 267
Word processing, 16
Working Press of the Nation, 115n
Written communication (*see* Interoffice memos)